Communications
in Computer and Information Science　1843

Rationale

The CCIS series is devoted to the publication of proceedings of computer science conferences. Its aim is to efficiently disseminate original research results in informatics in printed and electronic form. While the focus is on publication of peer-reviewed full papers presenting mature work, inclusion of reviewed short papers reporting on work in progress is welcome, too. Besides globally relevant meetings with internationally representative program committees guaranteeing a strict peer-reviewing and paper selection process, conferences run by societies or of high regional or national relevance are also considered for publication.

Topics

The topical scope of CCIS spans the entire spectrum of informatics ranging from foundational topics in the theory of computing to information and communications science and technology and a broad variety of interdisciplinary application fields.

Information for Volume Editors and Authors

Publication in CCIS is free of charge. No royalties are paid, however, we offer registered conference participants temporary free access to the online version of the conference proceedings on SpringerLink (http://link.springer.com) by means of an http referrer from the conference website and/or a number of complimentary printed copies, as specified in the official acceptance email of the event.

CCIS proceedings can be published in time for distribution at conferences or as post-proceedings, and delivered in the form of printed books and/or electronically as USBs and/or e-content licenses for accessing proceedings at SpringerLink. Furthermore, CCIS proceedings are included in the CCIS electronic book series hosted in the SpringerLink digital library at http://link.springer.com/bookseries/7899. Conferences publishing in CCIS are allowed to use Online Conference Service (OCS) for managing the whole proceedings lifecycle (from submission and reviewing to preparing for publication) free of charge.

Publication process

The language of publication is exclusively English. Authors publishing in CCIS have to sign the Springer CCIS copyright transfer form, however, they are free to use their material published in CCIS for substantially changed, more elaborate subsequent publications elsewhere. For the preparation of the camera-ready papers/files, authors have to strictly adhere to the Springer CCIS Authors' Instructions and are strongly encouraged to use the CCIS LaTeX style files or templates.

Abstracting/Indexing

CCIS is abstracted/indexed in DBLP, Google Scholar, EI-Compendex, Mathematical Reviews, SCImago, Scopus. CCIS volumes are also submitted for the inclusion in ISI Proceedings.

How to start

To start the evaluation of your proposal for inclusion in the CCIS series, please send an e-mail to ccis@springer.com.

Cornel Klein · Matthias Jarke · Jeroen Ploeg ·
Markus Helfert · Karsten Berns · Oleg Gusikhin
Editors

Smart Cities, Green Technologies, and Intelligent Transport Systems

11th International Conference, SMARTGREENS 2022
and 8th International Conference, VEHITS 2022
Virtual Event, April 27–29, 2022
Revised Selected Papers

Springer

Editors
Cornel Klein
Siemens AG
Munich, Germany

Matthias Jarke
RWTH Aachen
Aachen, Germany

Jeroen Ploeg
Siemens Industry Software Netherlands B.V.
Eindhoven, The Netherlands

Markus Helfert
Maynooth University
Maynooth, Kildare, Ireland

Karsten Berns
University of Kaiserslautern
Kaiserslautern, Germany

Oleg Gusikhin
Ford Motor Company
Commerce Township, MI, USA

ISSN 1865-0929   ISSN 1865-0937 (electronic)
Communications in Computer and Information Science
ISBN 978-3-031-37469-2   ISBN 978-3-031-37470-8 (eBook)
https://doi.org/10.1007/978-3-031-37470-8

This Springer imprint is published by the registered company Springer Nature Switzerland AG
The registered company address is: Gewerbestrasse 11, 6330 Cham, Switzerland

Preface

The present book includes extended and revised versions of a set of selected papers from the 11th International Conference on Smart Cities and Green ICT Systems (SMART-GREENS 2022) and the 8th International Conference on Vehicle Technology and Intelligent Transport Systems (VEHITS 2022), which were exceptionally held as online events, due to COVID-19, from 27–29 April, 2022.

SMARTGREENS 2022 received 21 paper submissions from 16 countries, of which 19% were included in this book. VEHITS 2022 received 64 paper submissions from 26 countries, of which 5% were included in this book.

The papers were selected by the event chairs and their selection is based on a number of criteria that include the classifications and comments provided by the program committee members, the session chairs' assessment and also the program chairs' global view of all papers included in the technical program. The authors of selected papers were then invited to submit a revised and extended version of their papers having at least 30% innovative material.

The purpose of the 11th International Conference on Smart Cities and Green ICT Systems (SMARTGREENS 2022) was to bring together researchers, designers, developers and practitioners interested in advances and applications in the field of Smart Cities, Green Information and Communication Technologies, Sustainability, and Energy-Aware Systems and Technologies. The papers selected to be included in this book contribute to the understanding of relevant trends of current research on Smart Cities and Green ICT Systems, including: novel Frameworks and Models for Smart City Initiatives, Smart Technologies for Green Electric Load Analytics, new approaches to Network Mode Simulation, and Green ICT approaches to More Sustainable AI Applications.

The purpose of the 8th International Conference on Vehicle Technology and Intelligent Transport Systems (VEHITS 2022) was to bring together engineers, researchers and practitioners interested in advances and applications in the field of Vehicle Technology and Intelligent Transport Systems. VEHITS focuses on innovative applications, tools and platforms in all technology areas such as signal processing, wireless communications, informatics and electronics, related to different kinds of vehicles, including cars, off-road vehicles, trains, ships, underwater vehicles or flying machines, and the intelligent transportation systems that connect and manage large numbers of vehicles, not only in the context of smart cities but in many other application domains. The papers selected to be included in this book contribute to the understanding of relevant trends of current research, including Intelligent Roadside Infrastructure, Vision and Image Processing, Vehicle Information Systems and Mobility Services.

We would like to thank all the authors for their contributions and also the reviewers who have helped to ensure the quality of this publication.

Cornel Klein
Matthias Jarke
Jeroen Ploeg
Markus Helfert
Karsten Berns
Oleg Gusikhin

Organization

SMARTGREENS Conference Chair

Matthias Jarke   RWTH Aachen, Germany

VEHITS Conference Chair

Oleg Gusikhin   Ford Motor Company, USA

SMARTGREENS Program Chair

Cornel Klein   Siemens AG, Germany

VEHITS Program Co-chairs

Jeroen Ploeg   Siemens Industry Software Netherlands B.V.,
                                         The Netherlands
Markus Helfert   Maynooth University, Ireland
Karsten Berns   University of Kaiserslautern-Landau, Germany

SMARTGREENS Program Committee

Javier M. Aguiar   Universidad de Valladolid, Spain
Nuri Azbar   Ege University, Turkey
Blanca Caminero   Universidad de Castilla-La Mancha, Spain
Chia-Chi Chu   National Tsing Hua University, Taiwan, Republic
                                         of China
Wanyang Dai   Nanjing University, China
Cléver Ricardo de Farias   University of São Paulo, Brazil
Venizelos Efthymiou   University of Cyprus, Cyprus
Adrian Florea   University "Lucian Blaga" of Sibiu, Romania
Andre Gradvohl   State University of Campinas, Brazil
Kerry Hinton   University of Melbourne, Australia
Dryver Huston   University of Vermont, USA
Jai Kang   Rochester Institute of Technology, USA

Mani Krishna	University of Massachusetts Amherst, USA
Annapaola Marconi	Fondazione Bruno Kessler, Italy
Hazlie Mokhlis	Universiti Malaya, Malaysia
Antonio Moreno-Munoz	Universidad de Cordoba, Spain
Elsa Negre	Paris-Dauphine University, France
Vitor Pires	Instituto Politécnico de Setúbal, Portugal
Ana Carolina Riekstin	Kaloom, Canada
Eva González Romera	University of Extremadura, Spain
Hussain Shareef	United Arab Emirates University, UAE
Gerard Smit	University of Twente, The Netherlands
Nirmal Srivastava	Dr. B. R. Ambedkar National Institute of Technology Jalandhar, India
Norvald Stol	Norwegian University of Science and Technology (NTNU), Norway
Afshin Tafazzoli	Siemens Gamesa Renewable Energy, Spain
Alexandr Vasenev	ESI (TNO), The Netherlands
Ramin Yahyapour	GWDG - University of Göttingen, Germany
Sotirios Ziavras	New Jersey Institute of Technology, USA

SMARTGREENS Additional Reviewers

| Darine Ameyed | Sherbrooke University/Baune/Synchromedia Lab-ETS, Canada |
| Enrique Arias Antunez | University of Castilla-La Mancha, Spain |

VEHITS Program Committee

Paolo Barsocchi	National Research Council (CNR), Italy
Luis Miguel Bergasa	University of Alcala, Spain
Roberto Caldelli	National Inter-University Consortium for Telecommunications (CNIT), Italy
Pedro Cardoso	Universidade do Algarve, Portugal
Rodrigo Carlson	Federal University of Santa Catarina, Brazil
Gihwan Cho	Jeonbuk National University, South Korea
Baldomero Coll-Perales	Universidad Miguel Hernandez de Elche, Spain
Gonçalo Correia	TU Delft, The Netherlands
Noelia Correia	University of the Algarve, Portugal
Sabeur Elkosantini	University of Carthage, Tunisia
Oscar Esparza	Universitat Politècnica de Catalunya, Spain
Peppino Fazio	University of Calabria, Italy
Dieter Fiems	Ghent University, Belgium

Lino Figueiredo	Instituto Superior de Engenharia do Porto, Portugal
Paul Green	University of Michigan, USA
Sonia Heemstra de Groot	Eindhoven Technical University, The Netherlands
Sin C. Ho	Chinese University of Hong Kong, China
Hocine Imine	Gustave Eiffel University, France
Govand Kadir	University of Kurdistan Hewlêr, Iraq
Athanasios Kanatas	University of Piraeus, Greece
Tetsuya Kawanishi	Waseda University, Japan
Lisimachos Kondi	University of Ioannina, Greece
Anastasios Kouvelas	ETH Zurich, Switzerland
Zdzislaw Kowalczuk	Gdansk University of Technology, Poland
Francine Krief	University of Bordeaux, France
Yong-Hong Kuo	University of Hong Kong, China
Reza Langari	Texas A&M University, USA
Michael Mackay	Liverpool John Moores University, UK
Barbara Masini	Italian National Research Council (CNR), Italy
José Manuel Menéndez	Universidad Politécnica de Madrid, Spain
Lyudmila Mihaylova	University of Sheffield, UK
Wrya Monnet	University of Kurdistan Hewlêr, Iraq
Jânio Monteiro	Universidade do Algarve, Portugal
Antonio Montieri	University of Napoli Federico II, Italy
Pedro Moura	University of Coimbra, Portugal
Fawzi Nashashibi	Inria, France
Daniela Nechoska	St. Kliment Ohridski University, North Macedonia
Marialisa Nigro	Universita degli Studi Roma Tre, Italy
Dario Pacciarelli	Roma Tre University, Italy
Brian Park	University of Virginia, USA
Cecilia Pasquale	Università degli studi di Genova, Italy
Paulo Pereirinha	Polytechnic of Coimbra, Portugal
Fernando Pereñiguez	University Centre of Defence, Spanish Air Force Academy, Spain
Joshue Pérez Rastelli	Tecnalia, Spain
Valerio Persico	University of Naples "Federico II", Italy
Hesham Rakha	Virginia Tech, USA
Gianfranco Rizzo	University of Salerno, Italy
Enrique Romero-Cadaval	University of Extremadura, Spain
Jose Santa	Technical University of Cartagena, Spain
Oleg Saprykin	Samara State Aerospace University, Russian Federation
Milica Selmic	University of Belgrade, Serbia

Todor Stoilov	Bulgarian Academy of Sciences, Bulgaria
Wai Yuen Szeto	University of Hong Kong, China
Jean-Claude Thill	University of North Carolina at Charlotte, USA
Junfang Tian	Tianjin University, China
Costin Untaroiu	Virginia Tech, USA
Ottorino Veneri	Institute of Sciences and Technologies for Sustainable Energy and Mobility (STEMS), Italy
Alexey Vinel	Karlsruhe Institute of Technology (KIT), Germany
Francesco Viti	University of Luxembourg, Luxembourg
Elias Xidias	University of the Aegean, Greece
Yuanchang Xie	University of Massachusetts Lowell, USA
Chung-Hsing Yeh	Monash University, Australia

VEHITS Additional Reviewers

Michail Makridis	ETH Zurich, Switzerland
Jeroen Ploeg	Siemens Digital Industries Software and Eindhoven University of Technology, The Netherlands

Invited Speakers

SMARTGREENS

Rob Kitchin	Maynooth University, Ireland
Mark Deakin	Edinburgh Napier University, UK

VEHITS

Henk Nijmeijer	Eindhoven University of Technology, The Netherlands
Jonas Sjoberg	Chalmers University of Technology, Sweden
Luis M. Bergasa	University of Alcalá, Spain

SMARTGREENS and VEHITS

Alexey Vinel	Karlsruhe Institute of Technology (KIT), Germany

Contents

Smart Cities and Green ICT Systems

Simulation of Modes of Electric Networks with Electric Transmission Lines Using Earth as Current-Live Part

Yuri Bulatov[1] , Andrey Kryukov[2,3] , Le Van Thao[2], Konstantin Suslov[2,4](✉) ,
and Tran Duy Hung[5]

[1] Bratsk State University, Bratsk, Russia
[2] Irkutsk National Research Technical University, Irkutsk, Russia
dr.souslov@yandex.ru
[3] Irkutsk State Transport University, Irkutsk, Russia
[4] National Research University "Moscow Power, Engineering Institute", Moscow, Russia
[5] Military Industrial College, Hanoi, Vietnam

Abstract. In power supply systems (PSS) of facilities located in areas remote from power system grids, one can employ power transmission lines that use earthing as a current-carrying part. To address electrical safety issues related to the flow of ground currents, double "two wires - earth" (TWE) lines can be constructed, in which special transformers are used to ensure phase opposition of vectors of voltages of the terminals being grounded. This ensures that there are no currents in the ground during symmetric operation. In today's context, the task of creating computer models of such PSSs, which give the opportunity to adequately simulate the steady state operating conditions, becomes particularly relevant. The paper presents the findings of research aimed at the implementation of computer models of electric networks, which include double TWE lines as their part. In addition, the structural designs of TWE transmission lines of the cable type are proposed. The simulation results allowed us to draw the following conclusions: in comparison with the double-circuit power line, the double "two wires - earth" line allows one to significantly reduce the cost of base metal; however, the asymmetric design of this power transmission line causes a decrease in the values of power quality metrics at its receiving end; in addition, higher power losses are observed; the double TWE line can be implemented based on two or four single-phase shielded cables with crosslinked polyethylene insulation.

Keywords: Power supply systems · Double two wires and earth Lines · Modeling

1 Introduction

In agricultural areas, distribution electrical networks are of considerable importance. In order to save base metals, their implementation sometimes implies construction of power lines that use ground as a conducting part. Such solutions can also be used to provide electrical energy to facilities located in areas remote from the networks of electric power systems.

© The Author(s), under exclusive license to Springer Nature Switzerland AG 2023
C. Klein et al. (Eds.): SMARTGREENS 2022/VEHITS 2022, CCIS 1843, pp. 3–21, 2023.
https://doi.org/10.1007/978-3-031-37470-8_1

A number of works are devoted to solving the problems of researching power supply systems equipped with single-wire power lines with earth as a return wire (Single Wire Earth Return, SWER).

The article [1] discusses the issues of increasing the capacity of these lines. A solution to a similar problem for rural SWER networks is presented in [2, 3]. The paper [4] describes methods for detecting faults in single-wire distribution networks. The paper [5] is devoted to the problems of upgrading SWER networks. Models for selecting wires in networks with SWER lines are proposed in [6]. The results of studies of the influence of distributed generation on operating conditions of electrical networks with SWER lines are given in [7, 8]. The article [9] discusses the challenges of using SWER lines in rural Africa. The article [10] provides a solution to the problem of narrow-band modeling of single-wire power lines.

When currents flow in the ground, electrical safety becomes an issue. To address it, double "two wires - earth" lines (TWE) can be built, which were first considered in the papers [11, 12]. The development of this idea is given in [13]. These lines use special transformers in which the voltage vectors of the grounded terminals have an angular shift of 180°. Due to this, there are no currents in the ground in the case of symmetrical operation.

In the context of the electric power industry digitalization [14], the problems of creating digital models of PSSs with double TWE lines to ensure adequate simulation of steady state operation become particularly relevant. Such models can be formed on the basis of developments [15] implemented in the Fazonord software package. These developments are based on the ideas of building models of elements of electric power systems (EPS) based on phase coordinates; at the same time, the main power elements of the EPS, which include an electric power transmission line and transformers, are considered as multi-wire or multi-winding facilities and are presented in the form of equivalent lattice circuits with a fully connected topology. Based on this approach, methods and computer technologies have been implemented, the distinctive features of which are as follows:

- *multi-phase,* which implies the possibility of modeling multi-phase systems (single-phase, three-phase, four-phase, six-phase and their various combinations within a single network);
- *multiple operating conditions,* which allows modeling a wide range of EPS operating conditions: normal and emergency, asymmetric, non-sinusoidal, limiting in terms of static aperiodic stability;
- *multiple tasks,* which provides the possibility of solving additional problems relevant for practical work: determination of induced voltages on adjacent transmission lines; calculation of the intensity of electromagnetic fields created by traction networks; parametric identification of transmission lines and transformers according to measurement data; taking into account active elements of the EPS; modeling of thermal processes during de-icing.

2 Double TWE Line

To justify the use of double TWE lines and to determine their effectiveness, it is necessary to develop adequate computer models. Since the double TWE lines are characterized by an asymmetric structure, it appears reasonable to build their models on the basis of phase coordinates. Below are the results of simulating the power flows and electromagnetic fields [16] of a double TWE line with a voltage of 35 kV with respect to the ground, Fig. 1.

Simulation was performed in the Fazonord software package [15]. The software package is designed to solve the following problems of simulating AC an DC electric power systems and power supply systems of railroads using the phase frame of reference,

1. Calculations of power flows with the determination of voltage deviations, asymmetry and anharmonicity metrics values, including moving traction loads, calculations of power flows with short circuits.
2. Calculations of electromagnetic fields (EMF) of substation lines corresponding to the power flow.
3. Identification of parameters of overhead lines, three-phase two-winding and three-winding transformers based on measurements of currents and voltages on the terminals of the above facilities.
4. Determination of power flows for de-icing.

Simulation is performed using visual components selected from a set of elements. The system being calculated can include overhead lines and overhead contact systems of any configuration, bus ducts, single-phase and three-phase transformers with any winding connection, sources of current and EMF, loads at individual nodes and between them.

In its general form, the problem of simulating power flows of an electric network can be represented in the form of the following relation:

$$\mathbf{A} : \mathbf{D} \Rightarrow \mathbf{X}, \tag{1}$$

where $\mathbf{A}$ – nonlinear operator; $\mathbf{D} = \mathbf{S} \cup \mathbf{Y}$ – vector of input data; $\mathbf{X}$ – vector of power flow parameters; $\mathbf{S}$ – set of data describing the structure and parameters of power supply system (traction power system) elements; $\mathbf{Y}$ – parameters characterizing generators and loads.

The transform (1) forms a system of steady-state equations, which, in the general case, is nonlinear:

$$\mathbf{F}(\mathbf{X}, \mathbf{Y}) = \mathbf{0}, \tag{2}$$

where $\mathbf{X}$ – vector formed from the components of node voltages in Cartesian $\left(U_k^{'}, U_k^{''} \right)$ or polar (U_k, δ_k) coordinates; $\mathbf{Y}$ – vector including active and reactive powers of generators and loads.

The models and methods considered in this paper are based on the technique of simulating power flows of electric power systems using the phase frame of reference [15]. The methods for simulating electric power plants are based on the application of equivalent lattice circuits (ELC), which have a fully-connected topology. The following formal definition can be written for ELCs:

$$TEC : hub \cup con, \forall i, j \subset hub \rightarrow con_{i,j} \subset con, \qquad (3)$$

where *TEC* - ELC designation; *hub* - set of ELC hubs; *con* - set of ELC connections.

The main elements forming a power system can be divided into two groups:

- elements for transporting electricity: overhead and cable power lines, current-carrying wires, traction power systems;
- transducer elements which are transformers of various designs.

These devices can be generalized as static multi-wire elements, which can be represented as a set of wires or windings with electromagnetic couplings.

After determining the power flow of the instantaneous circuit as a result of solving the system of Eqs. (2), we can calculate the strengths of the electromagnetic field created by any of the multi-wire systems that are part of the simulated system. The components of the electric field strength of the system of N wires at the point with coordinates (x, y) are determined as per the following equations [16]:

$$\dot{E}_Y = -\frac{1}{\pi \, \varepsilon_0} \sum_{i=1}^{N} \dot{t}_i \frac{y_i[(x-x_i)^2 - y^2 + y_i^2]}{\xi_i}, \quad \dot{E}_X = \frac{2}{\pi \, \varepsilon_0} \sum_{i=1}^{N} \dot{t}_i \frac{(x-x_i)yy_i}{\xi_i}, \qquad (4)$$

where $\xi_i = [(x-x_i)^2 + (y+y_i)^2][(x-x_i)^2 + (y-y_i)^2]$; $\dot{t}_i$ is the charge of the wire i per unit length, determined from the first group of Maxwell's equations

$$\dot{\mathbf{T}} = \mathbf{A}^{-1} \cdot \dot{\mathbf{U}}. \qquad (5)$$

Here $\dot{\mathbf{U}} = \begin{bmatrix} \dot{U}_1 \ldots \dot{U}_N \end{bmatrix}^T$ – column vector of wire voltages with respect to ground; $\dot{\mathbf{T}} = \begin{bmatrix} \dot{t}_1 \ldots \dot{t}_N \end{bmatrix}^T$ – column vector of wire charges, $\mathbf{A}$ is a symmetric matrix of potential coefficients, where

$$\alpha_{ii} = \frac{1}{2\pi \, \varepsilon_0} \ln \frac{2y_i}{r_i}, \quad \alpha_{ij} = \frac{1}{2\pi \, \varepsilon_0} \ln \frac{\sqrt{(x_i - x_j)^2 + (y_i + y_j)^2}}{\sqrt{(x_i - x_j)^2 + (y_i - y_j)^2}}, \qquad (6)$$

where x_i, y_i – coordinates of the location of the wire i with the radius of r_i above the ground ($y = 0$ corresponds to the surface of a flat ground), ε_0 – vacuum permittivity.

Extreme values of electric field strength are calculated as per the following equation:

$$E_{\Psi E} = \left[\frac{(E_X^2 + E_Y^2)^2}{2} \pm \lambda \right]^{\frac{1}{2}}, \quad \lambda = \frac{\sqrt{(E_X^2 + E_Y^2)^2 - 4E_X^2 E_Y^2 \sin^2(\varphi_X - \varphi_Y)}}{2} \qquad (7)$$

Here the plus sign corresponds to the maximum, and the minus sign - to the minimum.

The horizontal and vertical components of the magnetic field strength created by all wires are calculated as per the following equations:

$$\dot{H}_X = \frac{1}{2\pi} \sum_{i=1}^{N} \dot{i}_i \frac{y - y_i}{(x_i - x)^2 + (y_i - y)^2}, \quad \dot{H}_Y = -\frac{1}{2\pi} \sum_{i=1}^{N} \dot{i}_i \frac{x - x_i}{(x_i - x)^2 + (y_i - y)^2}.$$

(8)

Extreme values of magnetic field strength are calculated as per the following equation:

$$H_{\psi E} = \left[\frac{\left(H_X^2 + H_Y^2\right)^2}{2} \pm \nu \right]^{\frac{1}{2}}, \quad \nu = \frac{\sqrt{\left(H_X^2 + H_Y^2\right)^2 - 4H_X^2 H_Y^2 \sin^2(\varphi_X - \varphi_Y)}}{2}.$$

(9)

To determine the electric and magnetic field strengths, the network power flow is calculated, the charges and currents of the wires, included grounded ones, are determined, and the components of the $\dot{E}_X, \dot{E}_Y, \dot{H}_X, \dot{H}_Y$ are found. The described methodology is implemented in the software package Fazonord so that the electromagnetic field strengths can be determined both for a single power flow and for their entire array that determines the dynamics of EMF strengths change over time.

The described problem statement allows one to significantly simplify the calculation of EMF strengths. Indeed, in the traditional statement, this problem requires solving partial differential equations. Its solution achieved by traditional methods is significantly more complicated in the presence of non-uniformities of the underlying surface, as well as the need to take into account the extended conductive facilities (e.g., underground pipelines, etc.). The use of sets of grounded wires as part of the corresponding multi-wire element to model non-uniformities of the terrain and conductive facilities allows us to apply (without added complexity and modifications) the proposed methodology to determine the EMF values, while taking into account the conditions of the environment.

Below are the results of simulating the power flows and electromagnetic fields of a double TWE line with a voltage of 35 kV relative to ground, Fig. 1.

The coordinates of the wires of this line with a length of 5 km with 95 mm^2 aluminium conductor steel reinforced cables are shown in Fig. 2. To assess energy efficiency, power quality and electromagnetic safety conditions, the corresponding indicators were compared with the results of simulating the modes and electromagnetic fields (EMF) of a three-phase power trans-mission line with 95 mm^2 aluminium conductor steel reinforced cables, non-standard voltage of 35 kV with respect to the ground and a line voltage of 60 kV.

A detail of the computational model circuit is shown in Fig. 3. The lack of current in the ground can be illustrated using vector diagrams of voltages on the secondary windings of transformers (Fig. 4). These diagrams were obtained as a result of determining the mode of the double TWE line without the grounding of phase C. The mode calculation was carried out with loads of $4 + j3$ MV·A per phase at the receiving end.

Figure 4 shows that for the groups of transformers 5 and 11, the voltage vectors of the grounded terminals are in antiphase. This ensures that there are no ground currents in symmetrical modes.

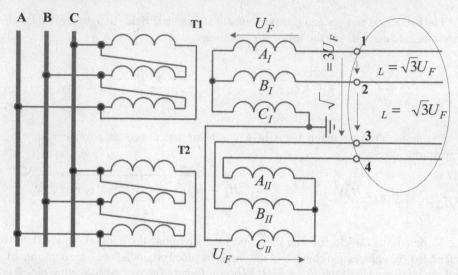

Fig. 1. Schematic diagram of the overhead TWE lines [17].

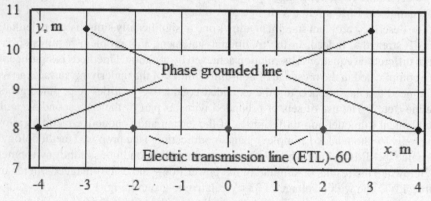

Fig. 2. Wires location coordinates [17].

The vector diagrams of voltages at the sending end of the double TWE line are shown in Fig. 5.

The results of determining the PSS power flows by the double TWE line show that on the 10 kV side of the consumer substation, connected at its receiving end and at the loads indicated above, the voltage asymmetry factor in the return sequence is 0.8%, and the total current flowing into the ground is 0.16 A. Dependences of losses and asymmetry in the electric transmission line (ETL)-60 and a double TWE line on the transmitted active power are shown in Figs. 6 and 7. They were obtained given a power factor of 0.89. The analysis of these dependences implies that the double TWE line is characterized by higher losses in comparison with the ETL-60 (Fig. 6). At the receiving end of this ETL, a significantly greater asymmetry is observed. Figures 8 and 9 show the dependences of

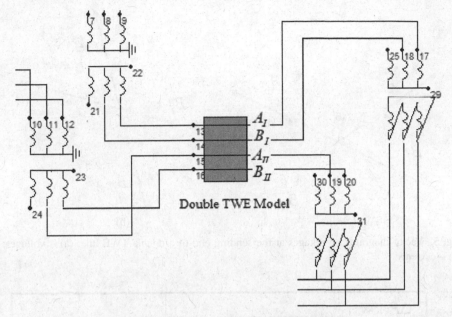

Fig. 3. Detail of the computational model circuit.

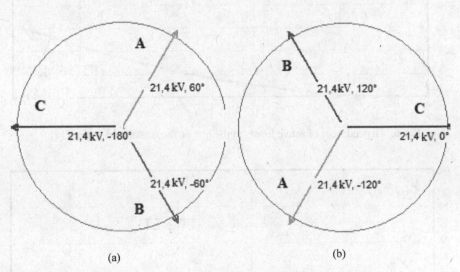

(a)   (b)

Fig. 4. Vector voltage diagrams of the phases of the secondary winding of transformers [17]:
(a) – T1, the fifth group of connections; (b) – T2, the eleventh group of connections.

the EMF strengths of the double TWE line on the x coordinate, which is measured from the center of the line.

Figure 10 shows three-dimensional diagrams of the strengths of the electric (a) and magnetic (b) fields created by the double TWE line.

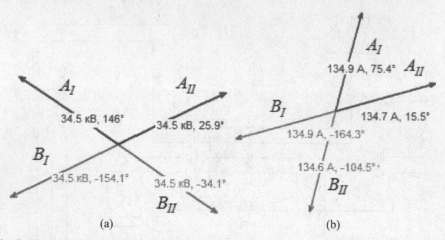

(a)   (b)

Fig. 5. Vector diagrams of voltages at the sending end of a double TWE line: (a) – voltages; (b) – currents.

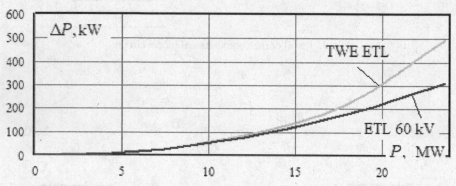

Fig. 6. Dependences of active losses in the line on the transmitted power [17].

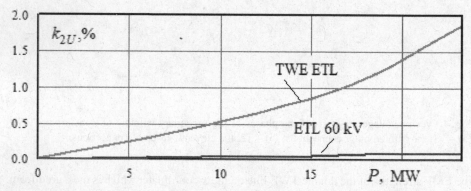

Fig. 7. Dependencies of the asymmetry coefficient on the transmitted power [17].

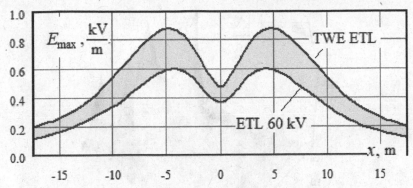

Fig. 8. Dependences of the amplitudes of the electric field strengths at the height of 1.8 mon the x coordinate [17].

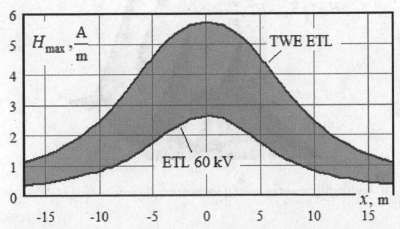

Fig. 9. Dependences of the amplitudes of the magnetic field strengths at the height of 1.8 mon the x coordinate [17].

The simulation results draw us to the following conclusions:

1. In comparison with the ETL of traditional design, the TWE line has higher losses and voltage asymmetry at the receiving end;
2. The strengths of the electric field directly under the wires of the TWE ETL is 33% higher than the value of the same metric for the 60 kV ETL;
3. The maximum amplitude of the magnetic field of the TWE ETL is twice as high as that one of the 60 kV ETL.

In addition, the following emergency conditions were simulated: single-phase short circuit at the point A_I; two-phase short circuit between points A_I and B_I; phase loss at the point A_I.

The results of the simulation are summarized in Table 1. The data presented in Table 1 attest to a significant difference between the emergency operating conditions in the double TWE line and similar operating conditions of power transmission lines of

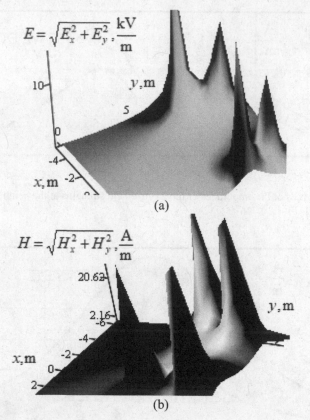

$$E = \sqrt{E_x^2 + E_y^2}, \frac{kV}{m}$$

(a)

$$H = \sqrt{H_x^2 + H_y^2}, \frac{A}{m}$$

(b)

Fig. 10. Volumetric diagrams of electric (a) and magnetic (b) field strengths of the double TWE line [17].

traditional design where the neutrals of transformers are isolated from the ground. Due to the presence of grounding of phases C_I, C_{II} single-phase short circuits are accompanied by a large current reaching up to 1077 A in the faulted phase. In addition, there is a significant current observed in the wire B_{II} connected to the transformer T.

In the event of two-phase short circuits, the currents of the wires connected to the transformer T1 exceed one kiloampere, moreover, the wires connected to T2 carry currents of up to 450 A. When a wire breaks at the point A_I, the wire A_{II} currents increase to 207 A and those of the wire B_{II} – to 308 A. The results of calculating the electromagnetic fields of the double TWE line are shown in Figs. 11 and 12. The results presented in Figs. 11, 12 allow us to draw the following conclusions:

1. In the case of a single-phase short-circuit there is a slight increase in the electric field strengths and a significant increase in the magnetic field strengths as compared to normal load operating conditions (Fig. 8 and Fig. 9). The symmetry of the relationship $E_{max} = E_{max}(x)$ with respect to the ordinate axis is broken.
2. In the case of two-phase short circuits, if compared to normal operating conditions, the maximum levels of electric field strengths practically do not change. The symmetry

Table 1. Results of calculation for emergency conditions.

Measurement point	Single-phase short circuit at the point A_I		Two-phase short circuit between points A_I and B_I		Phase loss at the point A_I	
	U, kV	I, A	U, kV	I, A	U, kV	I, A
A_I	1.56	1076.93	32.11	1027.37	37.60	0.00
B_I	30.83	6.38	32.13	1027.45	33.71	134.01
A_{II}	33.74	7.44	33.47	452.84	33.61	207.43
B_{II}	21.78	482.23	33.85	452.72	29.32	308.72

of the relationship $E_{max} = E_{max}(x)$ with respect to the ordinate axis is also broken. The maximum magnetic field strength increases to 31 A/m.

3. In the case of a phase loss fault, the maximum levels of electric field strength are close to the data characterizing normal operating conditions with a similar breaking of the symmetry of the relationship $E_{max} = E_{max}(x)$ as in the previous cases. The maximum magnetic field strength increases by a factor of two compared to operating load conditions.

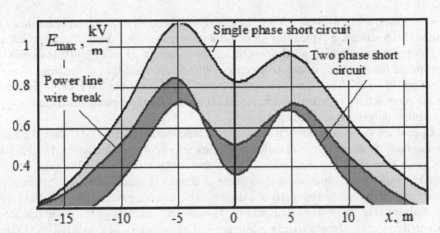

Fig. 11. Dependences of the amplitudes of electric field strengths at a height of 1.8 m on the coordinate x, as derived from the calculation results for emergency operating conditions.

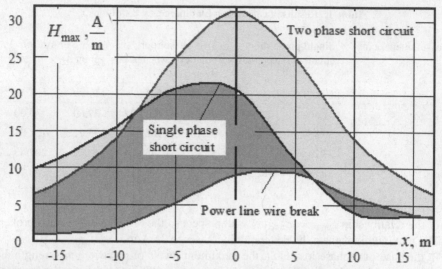

Fig. 12. Dependences of magnetic field strength amplitudes at a height of 1.8 m on the coordinate x, as derived from the calculation results for emergency operating conditions.

3 The TWE Line Build with Two Special Design Cables

In some cases, when forming a PSS, the use of overhead electric transmission lines is limited. Such cases are typical for some settlements, sites of industrial enterprises, as well as for areas with high wind loads. In addition, the use of cable TWE lines can be appropriate for the transmission of electricity by submarine cables to facilities located on islands of rivers, lakes, and seas. Implementation of a double TWE cable line may use the proposed in constructive scheme based on two single-core shielded cables with crosslinked polyethylene insulation.

In contrast to the commonly used designs, cable shields for this ETL should ensure that the flow of currents are proportionate to the currents of the conductors. In addition, they must have the same insulation class as the conductors. Such cable lines can be placed in galleries, overpasses, and on other structures of a similar type. The location coordinates of the conducting parts of a double cable line are given in Fig. 13. The cable line diagram (Fig. 14) corresponds to Fig. 1; operating currents of the cable line flow through the shields. The electrical parameters of the conductors and shields are the same as in the overhead TWE power transmission line discussed above.

The diagram showing the currents distribution through the wires of overhead and cable lines is given in Fig. 15. We can observe some differences in the currents of conductors and shields of the cable TWE ETL which is associated with its asymmetric design.

Vector diagrams characterizing currents and voltages at the receiving and sending ends of the cable TWE line are shown in Figs. 16 and 17. The input voltages and currents of cable lines are far from a symmetrical four-phase system, but the voltages and load currents on busbars of the 10 kV transformers are symmetrical with a return sequence voltage asymmetry coefficient equal to 0.5%.

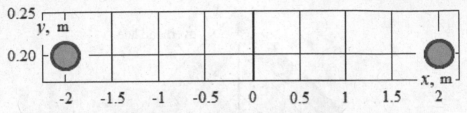

Fig. 13. Coordinates of conducting parts [17].

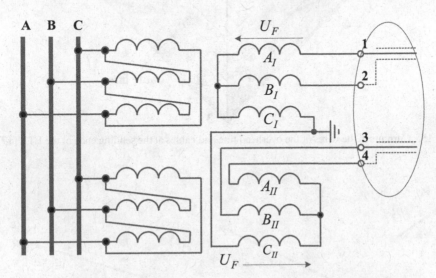

Fig. 14. Schematic diagram of the two-cable TWE line connection [17].

Figures 18, 19 and 20 show comparative graphs characterizing energy efficiency, power quality metrics for asymmetry and electromagnetic safety of the considered cable line design in comparison with a four-wire overhead line.

Compared with the overhead line, the TWE cable line is characterized by a significantly lower level of asymmetry. However, higher magnetic field strengths are created near the cables. Given the same cross-section of the conducting parts, the active power losses for overhead lines and TWE cable lines differ insignificantly.

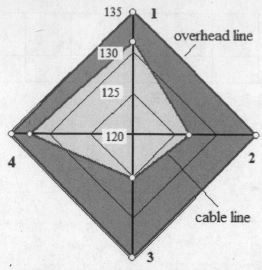

Fig. 15. Currents in the wires of the overhead line and cables at the sending ends of the ETL [17].

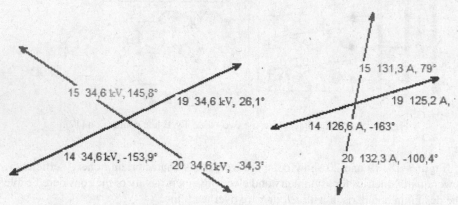

Fig. 16. Vector diagrams of at the sending end of the cable TWE line [17].

4   The TWE Structure Based on Four Cables of a Standard Structure

It is possible to consider a scheme of the TWE line which implementation requires four standard cross-linked polyethylene cables, Fig. 21. Its cross-section is shown in Fig. 22.

In simulation, it was assumed that the cable shields are grounded on one side. At shield currents of 8.2 A, the total current did not flow through the ground electrode. Dependences of losses on the transmitted active power at are shown in Fig. 23 for the following types of TWE lines: overhead, two-cable, and four-cable lines. For all types of TWE lines, the losses are almost the same (Fig. 24). Asymmetry at high transmitted powers is the greatest in the double overhead TWE line. However, at low powers, asymmetry is greater in the four-cable line, although the asymmetry coefficient does not

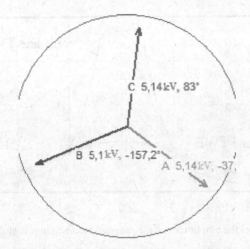

Fig. 17. Vector diagrams of voltages on 10 kV busbars [17].

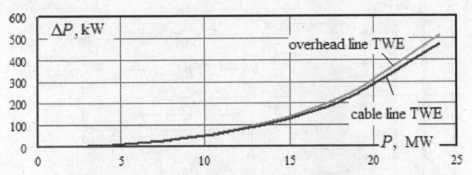

Fig. 18. Dependences of losses on the transmitted active power [17].

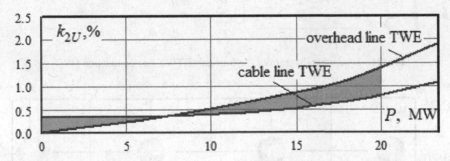

Fig. 19. Dependences of the return sequence asymmetry coefficient on transmitted power [17].

exceed 0.5%. The dependences of the amplitudes of the magnetic field strengths on the x coordinate are shown in Fig. 25.

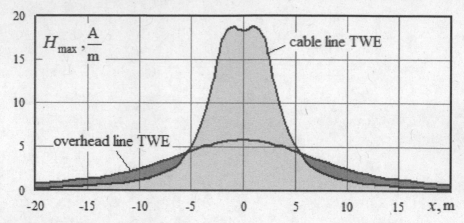

Fig. 20. Dependences of the amplitudes of the magnetic field strengths at the height of 1.8 m on the x coordinate [17].

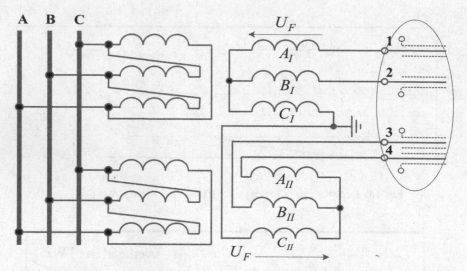

Fig. 21. Schematic diagram of the four-cable TWE line connection [17].

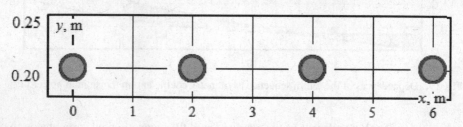

Fig. 22. Coordinates of cable locations [17].

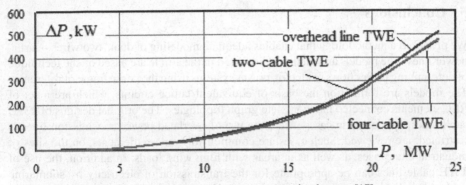

Fig. 23. Dependences of losses on transmitted power [17].

Analysis of the simulation results allows us to conclude that the four-cable TWE line, when compared to the two-cable one, is characterized by a higher level of asymmetry and creates a magnetic field of the same order.

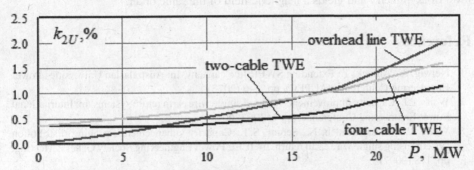

Fig. 24. Dependences of the asymmetry coefficient on transmitted power [17].

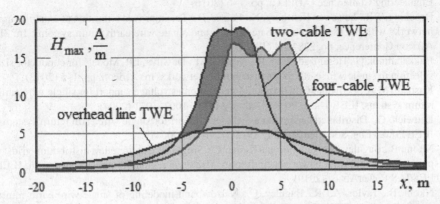

Fig. 25. Dependence of the amplitude of the magnetic field strength on the x coordinate [17].

5 Conclusions

We proposed a methodology that enables adequate modeling of dual "two wires - earth" power lines. The models and methods discussed in the article are based on the technique of determining power flows of electric power systems using the phase frame of reference. The models are formed on the basis of equivalent lattice circuits, which are a set of RLC elements connected into complete graph topologies. The original designs of TWE cable lines, applicable in cases where the use of overhead power transmission lines is restricted, are reviewed. Such cases are common for some settlements, on the sites of industrial enterprises, as well as in areas with high wind loads. In addition, the use of TWE cable lines can be appropriate for the transmission of electricity by submarine cables to facilities located on islands of rivers, lakes, and seas.

The first design of a "two wires - earthing" cable line is based on the use of two shielded cables, whose shields must ensure the flow of currents commensurate with the currents of the cores. The second design uses four standard cables with crosslinked polyethylene insulation. Analysis of the simulation results allowed us to conclude that the four-cable TWE line, compared to the two-cable one, is characterized by a higher level of asymmetry and yields a magnetic field of the same order.

References

1. Helwig, A., Ahfock, T.: Extending SWER line capacity. In: Australasian Universities Power Engineering Conference (AUPEC), pp. 1–6 (2013)
2. Wolfs, P.J.: Capacity improvements for rural single wire earth return systems. In: International Power Engineering Conference, pp. 1–306 (2005)
3. Wolfs, P.J., Hosseinzadeh, N., Senini, S.T.: Capacity enhancement for aging distribution systems using single wire earth return. In: IEEE Power Engineering Society General Meeting, pp. 1–8 (2007)
4. Kavi, M., Mishra, Y., Vilathgamuwa, D.M.: Detection and identification of high impedance faults in single wire earth return distribution networks. In: Australasian Universities Power Engineering Conference (AUPEC), pp. 1–6 (2016)
5. Brooking, T.R., Janse van Rensburg, N., Fourie, R., The improved utilisation of existing rural networks with the use of intermediate voltage and single wire earth return systems. In: 3D Africon Conference, pp. 228–234 (1992)
6. Bakkabulindi, G., Hesamzadeh, M. R., Amelin, M., Da Silva, I.P., Models for conductor size selection in single wire earth return distribution networks. In: Africon, pp. 1–5 (2013)
7. Kashem, M.A., Ledwich, G.: Distributed generation as voltage support for single wire earth return systems. IEEE Trans. Power Delivery 19(3), 1002–1011 (2004)
8. Ledwich, G.: Distributed generation as voltage support for single wire earth return systems. IEEE Power Eng. Soc. Gen Meeting 19, 1002–1011 (2004)
9. Nkom, B., Baguley, C., Nair, Nirmal-Kumar C.: Single wire earth return distribution grids: a panacea for rapid rural power penetration in Africa via regulatory policy transfer. In: IEEE PES/IAS PowerAfrica (2019)
10. Nkom, B., Taylor, A.P.R., Baguley, C.: Narrowband modeling of single-wire earth return distribution lines. IEEE Trans. Power Delivery 33(4), 1565–1575 (2018)
11. Andreev, V.V.: Four-phase power transmission scheme with three-phase transformers. Electricity 1, 15–17 (1952)

12. Filshtinsky, A.A.: Four-wire power transmission as a means of improving the efficiency and reliability of high-voltage networks. Electricity 1, 17–22 (1952)
13. Buryanina, N.S., Korolyuk, Y.F., Lesnykh, E.V., Maleeva, E.I.: Power lines with a reduced number of wires in mountainous areas. Sustain. Dev. Mountainous Territories 10, 3(37), 404–410 (2018)
14. Vorotnitskiy, V.E.: Digitalization in the economy and electric power industry. Energetik 12, 6–14 (2019)
15. Zakaryukin, V.P., Kryukov, A.V.: Difficult asymmetric modes of electrical systems. Irkutsk (2005)
16. Buyakova, N., Zakarukin, V., Kryukov, A.: Imitative modelling of electromagnetic safety conditions in smart power supply systems. Adv. Intell. Syst. Res. 158, 20–25 (2018)
17. Bulatov, Y., Kryukov, A., Le Van Thao, S., Tran Hung, K.: Modeling of power supply systems equipped with double two wires and earth transmission lines. In: Proceedings of the 11th International Conference on Smart Cities and Green ICT Systems - SMARTGREENS, pp. 23–31 (2022)

On Developing Sustainable Deep Learning Applications Using Pre-calculating Energy Usage

Supadchaya Puangpontip$^{(\boxtimes)}$ (iD) and Rattikorn Hewett (iD)

Texas Tech University, Lubbock, TX 79409, USA
{supadchaya.puangpontip,rattikorn.hewett}@ttu.edu

Abstract. Sustainable computing is essential to our modern digital society. It deals with how computing resources and devices can be developed and used to perform operations as efficiently and eco-friendly as possible. With the explosive use of Deep Learning (DL) application systems whose development is known to be computationally intensive, this paper investigates sustainable development of DL applications to exemplify other software development. While much research on sustainable hardware development has made good progresses to reduce electronic waste and power consumption, sustainable software development is relatively behind. Most aim to find energy-efficient solutions as a result from improving computational efficiency (e.g., via optimization). This is useful but not direct. Before one can develop sustainable software, it is necessary to be able to assess and measure energy usage of the software computation. This paper presents an analytical modeling approach to quantifying energy consumption and illustrates how it can help achieve sustainable software development. In particular, we develop an energy model, for DL application systems, that has been evaluated theoretically and empirically on real systems. Unlike most existing work, our approach provides the ability to pre-determine the required energy consumption of DL applications prior to system implementation. The paper illustrates how the approach can help sustainable development of DL application system for monitoring crop health in smart agriculture in two scenarios: 1) when scaling the DL applications based on energy consumed by various design choices, and 2) when deciding whether to use sensors or drones to expand monitoring coverage.

Keywords: Sustainable computing · Energy consumption · Deep learning · Energy modelling · Application systems · Internet of drones

1 Introduction

In today's digital world, an increasingly large number and continuous use of computing and smart electronic devices to function, communicate and control deplete energy resources even more than ever. While energy consumption drives economies, its production impacts global warming, environments and societal sustainability. *Sustainable computing* (or *green computing*) [1–4] was coined as parts of solutions in pursuit of

C. Klein et al. (Eds.): SMARTGREENS 2022/VEHITS 2022, CCIS 1843, pp. 22–46, 2023.
https://doi.org/10.1007/978-3-031-37470-8_2

a sustainable future. Sustainable computing aims to maximize economic profits (e.g., power efficiency, usage effectiveness) and minimize negative environmental impacts (e.g., waste and pollution reduction) [1]. It involves designing, manufacturing, managing and using electronic/computing artifacts to operate as energy efficient and eco-friendly as possible as well as device disposal to reduce electronic waste and power consumption [2, 3].

Research on developing sustainable computing systems have been studied extensively including using alternative energy sources (e.g., renewable energy and energy harvesting [4–6], improving energy efficiency of infrastructures (e.g., cloud and data centers [1, 3, 7]), communication protocols [1, 8, 9] and hardware devices (e.g., circuit boards and sensors [1, 5, 10, 11]). While sustainable hardware development has made good progresses, sustainable software development is relatively behind. Most aim to find energy-efficient solutions as a result of improving computational efficiency (e.g., optimizing scheduling [1, 6, 10]). While this approach for sustaining energy in software computing is useful, it is not direct. The direct approach naturally requires the ability to measure energy usage of the software computation.

Our research focuses on a direct approach to sustaining software development by estimating energy consumption of software computation prior to its implementation. Deep Learning (DL) [12–14] has been extensively applied in many domains including healthcare, autonomous vehicle and smart systems [12]. With the explosive use of DL application systems whose development (especially training computation) is known to be computationally intensive [7], this paper investigates sustainable development of DL applications to exemplify other software development. In particular, we develop a direct approach to building sustainable DL applications by quantifying energy consumption of DL computation.

Existing approaches to estimating energy consumption mostly employ measurement tools [15–18], simulation [19, 20], or analytical modeling [18, 19, 21, 22]. Using tools is simple but it is system-specific and relies on probing that may not always be accessible. Using simulation requires understanding of computational behavior of the system and can also take a long time to run. Both tools and simulation require implementation, either on the real systems or the simulators. The analytical approach can overcome these drawbacks [19]. We propose an analytical modeling approach that allows pre-calculating of energy usage *prior* to system implementation. In most software systems including DL applications, energy constraints are often addressed after the system has been implemented or deployed as an *afterthought* process [12, 13]. While energy constraints can easily be fixed in many cases, for a large and complex system, this may not be feasible and has to deal with earlier during the system design. Our approach provides the ability to estimate energy usage during the system design.

This paper is an extension from our previous work [23]. It includes two additional components. First is an evaluation of the energy DL model on real systems. Second is an extra scenario on a sustainable design and development of DL application system to expand the coverage area for crop monitoring. The paper describes a fundamental capability to estimate energy consumption of DL applications for developing sustainable application systems prior to system implementation. In particular, we present an analytical modeling approach to quantifying energy consumption of DL, specifically, convolution and artificial neural networks. We illustrate how the approach can help sustainable development of DL application system for monitoring crop health in smart agriculture in two scenarios: 1) when scaling the system based on energy consumed by various design choices including network structure, bandwidth and number of sensors designated to a distributed server, and 2) when deciding whether to use sensors or drones to expand monitoring coverage.

The rest of the paper is organized as follows. Section 2 discusses the proposed approach and Sect. 3 gives details of the approach on specific computing units, i.e., the execution of the trained deep learning model. Section 4 presents our illustration of energy modeling approach on two case studies in smart farming, including experimental design and setup. Results of experiments of the first and second case studies are given in Sects. 5 and 6, respectively. Section 7 presents evaluation and discussion, followed by related work in Sect. 8. The paper concludes in Sect. 9.

2   Energy Estimation of Application Systems

In this section, we describe our approach to estimating energy consumption of computing units of the smart systems as presented in [23]. We start with the overview energy consumption of the system in Sect. 2.1. The methodology to estimate such consumption is shown in Sect. 2.2.

2.1   System Energy Estimation

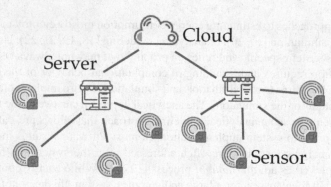

Fig. 1. Sensor-based network [23].

Figure 1 shows an example of a sensor-based distributed system consisting of a network of sensors (or sensing nodes) and distributed servers (or server or edge node) as a computing unit. Generally, the sensors send data to the server at the edge which is capable of computing software tasks (e.g., object detection) and transmitting data to cloud or centralized server. Total energy consumption of the system denoted as $E_{network}$ can be expressed by

$$E_{network} = N_{sense}(E_{sense}) + N_{server}(E) \tag{1}$$

where N_{sense}, N_{server} is the number of sensors and servers, respectively. E_{sense} is energy consumed by each sensing node, which includes consumption during all sensor operations e.g., sensing, logging and transmission [11]. Finally, E is energy consumed by each server for software execution and data transmission, obtained by modeling approach which will be discussed in the next section.

2.2 Energy Estimation of a Computing Unit

Energy consumption of a computing unit consists of: (1) energy consumed from computation (E_{comp}), (2) energy consumed from the associated data movement (E_{data}) and (3) energy consumed from transmission to other units (E_{trans}), i.e.,

$$E = E_{comp} + E_{data} + E_{trans} \qquad (2)$$

Figure 2 summarizes an overall concept of how to compute E in (1).

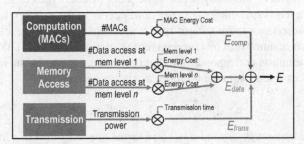

Fig. 2. Energy consumption methodology of a computing unit [23].

Details on the modeling the energy from computation, data access, and transmission are presented below.

Computation Energy

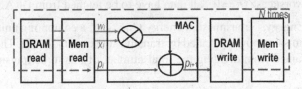

Fig. 3. A MAC operation [23].

The fundamental element of the computation is a multiply-and-accumulate (MAC) operation (Yang et al., 2018). Suppose we want to compute $\sum_{i=0}^{n} w_i x_i$. Figure 3 depicts a MAC operation, where for each iteration i, two inputs w_i and x_i are multiplied and the result is added to the (accumulated) partial sum p_i, producing an updated partial sum

p_{i+1} for the next iteration (or the accumulated sum of the multiplication pairs so far). This accounts for one MAC operation in one iteration. Since the final summation is a result of n iterations of MACs, we say it takes n MACs. As a result, computation energy depends on the number of MACs, giving

$$E_{comp} = \alpha c \qquad (3)$$

where c is the number of MACs and α is hardware energy cost per 1 MAC operation.

Data Access Energy. For each computation, data of different types (e.g., input and output) need to be stored in the memory. In particular, as shown in Fig. 3, each MAC performs four data accesses, three reads (i.e., two inputs w_i and x_i and one previous accumulated partial result p_i) and one write (i.e., new partial result p_{i+1}). Since energy spent accessing different levels of memory hierarchy are significantly different, data movement energy depends on how data moves in the memory hierarchy (Yang et al., 2018).

Let M be a memory hierarchy level, V be a set of data types (e.g., input, output, weight), β_m be a *hardware energy cost per data access* in the memory level m, $a_{v,m}$ be the *number of data accesses* for data of type v accessed at memory level m, and p be a precision in terms of number of bits for data representation (e.g., 8, 16). We can estimate the energy consumption corresponding to data movement based on the number of data accesses and access location in the memory as shown below.

$$E_{data} = \sum_{v \in V} \sum_{m=1}^{M} \beta_m a_{v,m} p \qquad (4)$$

Note that we express β_{cache} and β_{DRAM} in terms of energy cost of a MAC operation α, resulting in $\beta_{cache} = 6\alpha$ and $\beta_{DRAM} = 200\alpha$, used in (Yang et al., 2018).

In this study, without loss of generality, we consider data moves between two memory levels: cache ($m = 1$) and DRAM ($m = 2$) with a cache hit rate h. Data are looked up in the cache first. If they are not found (cache miss), they will be fetched from DRAM and stored in cache. As a result, we can simplify data movement energy to be as follows.

$$E_{data} = \sum_{v \in V} (\beta_{cache} a_v + \beta_{DRAM} (1 - h) a_v) p \qquad (5)$$

As seen in (5), in the best-case scenario ($h = 1$), all data are fetched from cache, whereas in the worst case ($h = 0$), all data have to be fetched from DRAM as expected.

Transmission Energy. Transmission energy (E_{trans}) of a computing unit can be calculated from transmission power p scaled by transmission time t [21, 22]. The transmission time can be obtained from dividing the total number of bits to be transmitted s by the achievable rate r.

$$E_{trans} = pt = p(s/r) \qquad (6)$$

Depending on communication protocols, the achievable rate r can be calculated differently. For example, in Frequency Division Multiple Access protocol (FDMA) [22], r can be achieved by:

$$r = b \log\left(1 + \frac{ph}{N_0 b}\right) \qquad (7)$$

where b is bandwidth, p is transmission power of the edge node, h is channel power gain and N_0 is power spectral density of the Gaussian noise. Similarly, in non-orthogonal multiple access (NOMA) protocol [21], r can be found by:

$$r = B \log \left(\frac{\sigma^2 + \sum_{i=1}^{n} p_i h_i}{\sigma^2 + \sum_{i=1}^{n-1} p_i h_i} \right) \tag{8}$$

where B is bandwidth, p is transmission power, h is channel power gain, n is the number of edge nodes and σ^2 is a variance for the additive white Gaussian noise (AWGN).

3 Energy Modeling of Deep Learning

As discussed in [23], to further explain energy modeling of computing units in more detail (i.e., to show how one can count the number of MACs and data access in the memory), we need to work on specific software units. Here we choose a relatively difficult computing unit of a popular Deep learning or deep neural network (DNN). DNN has been widely used for various tasks such as control, automation, detection, and monitoring. This section further describes the methodology in Sect. 3.1 to estimate energy of DNN computation. Specifically, we focus on energy consumption of computation and data access during the execution of the trained DNN model on one data instance. That is, we do not deal with energy usage for training DNN.

Background of DNN and how to assess the number of MACs and the number of data access from the DNN model are described in Subsects. 3.1, 3.2, 3.3, respectively.

3.1 Background on DNN

Artificial neural networks (ANN) are a computational model consisting of layers of neurons. Each output is obtained by computing a weighted sum of all inputs, adding a bias, and (optionally) applying an activation function as shown in (9). Examples of activation functions are sigmoid function and Rectified Linear United (ReLU).

$$y = f \left(\sum_{i=0}^{n} w_i x_i + b \right) \tag{9}$$

where y, x_i, w_i, b and n are the output, inputs, weights, bias and number of inputs, and $f(.)$ is an activation function [24].

A convolution neural network (CNN) is a type of DNN that has been successfully applied to image analysis and computer vision (e.g., face recognition, object classification). Figure 4 shows a typical CNN architecture where multiple convolution (CONV) layers are used for feature extraction and fully connected (FC) layers are used for classification. Since CNN usually deals with images with high dimensions, pooling (POOL) layers are used to reduce the dimensionality using pooling operations (e.g., max, average). As shown in Fig. 4, the POOL layer selects the maximum element of an input region and reduces the dimension of a 4×4 input to a 2×2 output.

The CONV layer, a building block of CNN, consists of high-dimensional convolutions. Equation (10) defines the computation of each CONV layer. For each layer,

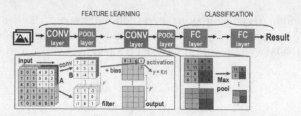

Fig. 4. A Convolutional Neural Network (CNN) [23].

an input (also called input feature map) is a set of 2-dimensional matrices, each of which is called a channel. Each channel is convolved with a distinct filter channel (i.e., 2-dimensional weights). As seen at the bottom of Fig. 4, a convolution starts with the 2-dim filter slides over a region of the 2-dim input of the same size, performing pointwise multiplication and summing the results into a single value. The convolution results are summed across all channels (3rd dimension of input block). The bias b can be added to the result, yielding the single output value z (as shown in (10)).

$$z_{s,f,m,n} = \left(\sum_c \sum_i \sum_j w_{f,c,i,j} x_{s,c,m+i,n+j} \right) + b_f \qquad (10)$$

where $z_{s,f,m,n}$ is the output feature map of layer l, batch s, channel f and location (m, n), w is the weight of filter f, channel c and location (i, j), x is the input and b is bias. The filter repeats this process as it slides over all the input regions, yielding a filled output matrix. The process then repeats for all F filters. Each of the output values (LHS of (10)) then goes through an activation function and becomes an input to the next layer.

Since a DNN model consists of multiple layers of different types (e.g., convolution, pooling and fully connected), the total consumption of the DNN is the summation of computation and data access energy from all layers. Next, we estimate number of MACs (for computation energy) and data access (for data access energy) per layer.

3.2 Estimation of Number of MACs

Since different types of layers require different computation, we provide estimation of number of MACs for each layer as follows.

Fully Connected (FC) Layer
Consider Fig. 5 representing a FC layer l of n neurons, each of which is connected with every neuron of an FC's input layer (or previous layer) of m neurons. (Note that if the FC's previous layer is a convolution or pooling layer whose output is represented in a stack of h 2-dimensional square planes, say $k \times k$ then the input layer of FC has $m = h \times k \times k$ neurons).

As shown in Fig. 5, for each of n neurons in the FC layer, we compute m weighted sums (as in f's argument) and one activation (by function f). Thus, c, the total number of MACs in the FC layer is shown below in (11).

$$c = mn + c_{act} n \qquad (11)$$

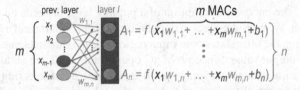

Fig. 5. Computation and associated data in FC layer [23].

where c_{act} is the number of MACs used in the activation function which is determined in our previous work [23].

Convolutional (CONV) Layer

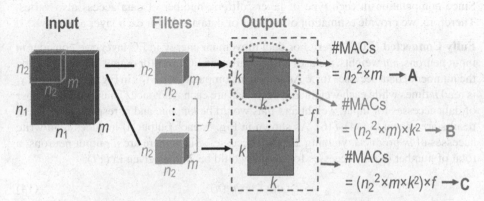

Fig. 6. Computation and associated data in CONV layer [23].

The convolution layer aims to extract features by means of weights in filters. It results in a large number of computations and corresponding data movements. An input of n_1 width and height and m channels is convoluted with f filters, each of dimension $n_2 \times n_2 \times m$, and results in an output of size $k \times k \times f$.

As shown in Fig. 6, the convolution process starts with a pointwise multiplication of a filter and an input region where the results are summed across all channels. To obtain this one output value (e.g., the top leftmost cell of the output), it takes $n_2^2 m$ MACs (A in Fig. 6). The convolution process continues for the rest of the input region, yielding the output of size k by k yielding the number of MACs (B in Fig. 6). The process then repeats for the rest of the f filters, ultimately producing f outputs and taking $n_2^2 m k^2 f$ MACs, shown as C. Note that the output value can go through to an activation function which takes another c_{act} MACs. In other words, to obtain each output value, it takes $n_2^2 m$ and c_{act} MACs. The operation repeats $k^2 f$ time for all output values giving the total number of MACs in the CONV layer as:

$$c = (n_2^2 m)(k^2 f) + c_{act}(k^2 f) \tag{12}$$

Pooling Layer. The energy consumption of a pooling layer depends on the type of the pooling operation. We consider the two popular types: max pooling and average pooling.

In max pooling, the filter slides over input region, the maximum element in the region is selected as an output value. Since no MAC operation is used, we obtain $c = 0$.

Similar operation is done in average pooling, but instead of selecting the maximum value of the input region, the operation averages the values in the region. Each operation is estimated to use one MAC. Since the number of pooling operations in a layer is equal to the size of the output, number of MACs operation is as follows:

$$c = n_2^2 m \tag{13}$$

3.3 Estimation of Number of Data Access

Since computation in each type of layers differs, number of data access also varies. Therefore, we provide estimation of number of data access for each layer as follows.

Fully Connected (FC) Layer. For data movement energy in FC layer, we consider m input neurons, mn weights, n biases and n neurons in FC layer (or output layer). Let a_x be the number of data accesses for x. As shown in computation of A_i's in Fig. 5, each input x_i is read n times while each weight and each bias are each read once. Thus, a total number of data accesses for input, weight and bias would be mn, mn, and n, respectively. These results are shown in (14)–(16). As shown in Fig. 5, each output A_i includes read/write accesses of m products, yielding $2m$ data accesses. Since there are n output neurons, a total of number of data accesses for output would be $2mn$ as given in (17).

$$a_{input} = m(n) \tag{14}$$

$$a_{weight} = m(n) \tag{15}$$

$$a_{bias} = n \tag{16}$$

$$a_{output} = n(2m) \tag{17}$$

Next section shows how to compute MACs and data movement energy in convolution (CONV) layers.

Convolutional (CONV) Layer. Data movement energy in this layer involves input, filters (i.e., weights), biases and output. As shown in Fig. 6, each input data is accessed at least once for each filter requiring $n_1^2 m$ MACs. As the filter slides over the input, some of the input data are being accessed again (i.e., being reused). Let t be the maximum bound of the number of reuses and r_i be the number of data that are reused i times. Thus, for f filters, number of input data accesses is shown in (18).

Similarly, each weight in the filter and each bias is accessed once to calculate one output value. To complete the output for one filter of size k^2, as circled in blue in Fig. 6, the weights and bias hence are accessed k^2 times. Since there are $n_2^2 m$ weights and 1 bias for one filter, with f filters, total number of weight and bias data access can be expressed in (19) and (20), respectively. As labeled as A in the Fig. 6, each of the output value takes $n_2^2 m$ iterations of MAC. This means the output value is being accessed $2n_2^2 m$ times accounting for data read and write. Since there are $k^2 f$ output values, number of output data access can be expressed as shown in (21).

$$a_{input} = (n_1^2 m + \sum_{i=2}^{t} r_i i) \cdot f \qquad (18)$$

$$a_{weight} = n_2^2 mfk^2 \qquad (19)$$

$$a_{bias} = fk2 \qquad (20)$$

$$a_{output} = k^2 f (2n_2^2 m) \qquad (21)$$

Pooling Layer. Data movement energy for max pooling and average pooling involves only input and output. The input data access depends on the size of the filter (i.e., pooling size) and stride. Similar to how (18) is obtained, number of input data access can be determined by (22). In addition, stride is sometimes set to be equal to the size of the filter. As a result, the input region is not overlapped, causing each the input value to be accessed only once. In this case, the second term of (23) is zero. In this layer, each output data is accessed once, which accounts for data write.

$$a_{input} = (n_1^2 m + \sum_{i=2}^{t} r_i i) \qquad (22)$$

$$a_{output} = n_2^2 m \qquad (23)$$

where n_1 is the width and height of the input, m is number of channels, n_2 is the width and height of the output. Note that, n_2 is derived from the input, pooling size k and stride s (i.e., $n_2 = (n_1 - k/s) + 1$).

4   Case Studies of Smart Agriculture Systems

This section illustrates how the model can be applied in practice to help the design and management of applied deep learning system, particularly a crop health monitoring in a smart agriculture. Section 4.1 describes the system and the unit under Case Study 1, as presented in [23]. Section 4.2 describes the system and design problems for Case Study 2. Section 4.3 gives experiments and initial setup for both case studies.

4.1   Case Study 1: Sensors

Smart agriculture systems include smart farming and smart CPS for controlled environments for precision agriculture and food security supply [25]. These systems typically employ sensors to collect data from the field and use them for various tasks (e.g., crop

health monitoring, and management of soil nutrients, pesticides, fertilizer, and irriga-
tion) to increase the crop yields. To sustain such a system, one needs to manage cost
derived from energy consumption from computation in these units.

Consider a crop health monitoring subsystem of the smart agriculture CPS. The
subsystem includes a disease detection unit that deploys a trained DNN model to analyze
plant images sent from neighboring cameras (sensing nodes) in the field. The server in
the disease detection unit executes the DNN model to detect if the plant has a disease or
to classify the disease type. It then transmits those images with corresponding results to
the cloud for backup and further analysis or to be alerted by another unit.

Suppose a farm owner wants to expand the farm to grow more plants, cover larger
areas with more sensors and disease detection computing units. This will lead to higher
energy consumption. The farm owner or the smart agriculture system engineer needs
to manage energy resource constraint as well as appropriate structures to maximize the
overall net gain to the farm. Planning for resource management to make such a smart
agriculture system sustainable can be challenging. In this paper, we limit the scope of our
investigation to energy consumptions of computing units to identify appropriate scale
and structure for a design of a sustainable future system.

4.2 Case 2: Drones

Drones or Unmanned Aerial Vehicles (UAV) become more affordable and thus popular in
numerous applications from surveillance and monitoring to package delivery and disaster
mitigation. They are widely used in various systems including Smart Agriculture systems
to manage or improve operations and tasks. Unlike sensors that are deployed at fixed
locations, drones are mobile with enhanced capabilities. They can be more advantageous
as they can perform tasks sensors cannot.

Consider the same crop health monitoring subsystem which requires sensing and
disease detection units. Instead of using sensors, two options of drone with different
capabilities and costs are offered. The first option is a typical drone equipped with a
camera. The drone is to fly to each location as scheduled, capture an image of the plant
and transmit it to the server. The server performs the same tasks as in Case 1. In other
words, we can replace sensors in Case 1 with drones but still need the servers.

The more expensive but sophisticated option is a modern drone which is equipped
with both camera with intelligent software on board to execute disease detection. The
modern drone is also to fly to each location as scheduled and capture the plant. However,
it can perform the classification task without the need for servers. It is also able to
transmit the images and corresponding results to the cloud for further actions. Hence,
this type of drone can replace both sensing and edge nodes. This type of drone can cost
more than the typical one.

Suppose the farm owner or the system engineer considers whether to use sensors
or drones. The decision needs to be made prior to and will consequently affect system
design and implementation, yet it is not trivial. Sensors are cheaper and consume little
energy, they are needed in a large amount to cover a large area. On the other hand, a
drone is more expensive and consumes more energy, but is more capable and required
in a smaller quantity. The modern drone is more sophisticated yet more costly. In this
study, we limit the investigation to the three options and not a combination of them. We

aim to identify appropriate choices in terms of energy consumption in order to design a sustainable system.

4.3 Experiments and Initial Setup

We consider two CPS network structures: *star* and *mesh*. The left of Fig. 7 shows two stars, each of which has four sensing nodes, where each directly connects to its assigned distributed server. The right of Fig. 7 shows two meshes, each of which also has four sensing nodes, all of which are directly connected to one another. Sensing nodes sense and transmit their own data but also serve as repeaters that relay data from other nodes. For example, sensing nodes that are not connected to the distributed server will send their data to their neighbors which will forward the data to the distributed server. Distributed servers in both structures connect to the cloud to store their data.

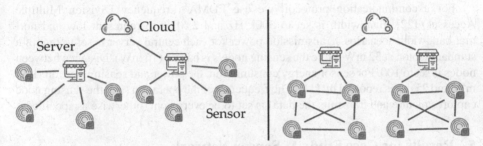

Fig. 7. Star and Mesh Topology [23].

Since in each star or mesh 80% of nodes are sensing nodes and 20% of nodes are distributed server, we use the same ratio between sensing nodes and distributed servers when we scale total number of nodes from 100 to 10,000 nodes in our experiments. Note that each star or mesh maintains 4 sensing nodes and one distributed server unless specified differently. From this point on, we use *server* to mean *distributed server*.

For drone network, two types of drones are focused: typical and modern. The difference between the two is that the latter is equipped with software onboard for deep learning execution and can perform the servers' tasks. Both types are programmed to fly automatically and autonomously to a set of locations as scheduled. In other words, if the typical drone is selected, the network consists of servers and typical drones. On the other hand, if the modern drone is selected, the network only consists of modern drones since they are capable of performing tasks of both sensors and servers.

Drones consume more energy than sensors, since they perform multiple functions. We consider energy consumption of the drone to be from hovering (while taking pictures), transitioning (i.e., flying) and data transmission. The energy consumption of such functions can be obtained through the formulae in [26]. Additionally for a modern drone, since it can execute a deep learning model, software energy is included.

The setup for the drones are as follows. The drone's mass and battery capacity are 0.5 kg and 20,000 mAh, respectively. Each drone has 4 propellers of 0.2-m radius. The drone's full speed is 15 m/s and the hardware power of the drone at full speed is 5

W. Height of flight is 50 m. Gravitational acceleration is 9.8 m/s^2 and air density is 1.225 kg/m^3. Coefficient of transmission power is 4.8 W, power of the drone during no transmission is 8 W and power spectral density is 4.004×10^{-21} W/Hz. Distance from locations are distance between sensors, which is set to be 50 m. Number of locations are the same as number of sensors and locations are where the sensors would have been.

For a deep learning model deployed at the server and the modern drone of each structure, we choose Alexnet [27], a CNN model to be deployed at the server due to its popularity and successful use in many smart agriculture applications [28]. Alexnet's architecture contains 5 convolution layers with ReLu activation, 3 pooling layers and 3 fully connected layer with Softmax for classification.

In our illustration, data are fetched from cache and DRAM at 50% cache hit rate. Data precision is 16 bits. The energy consumption is expressed in terms of the number of MAC operations as it directly translates to energy usage. We also assume that each MAC operation consumes about 10 pJ.

For a communication protocol, we use FDMA (Frequency Division Multiple Accesses) [22]. Bandwidth is set to 500k Hz and 2 MHz to represent low and normal bandwidth scenarios. Transmission power for each central server is set to that of a standard laptop at 32 mW while the sensing node's is halved (16 mW). Distance between nodes is set to 100. For sensor energy consumption, the power and sensing time are 10.5 mW and 25 ms as reported by [11]. The frequency of the operation (i.e., the sensing node captures picture and transmits the data) is set to be every hour, otherwise as specified.

5   Results for Case Study 1: Sensor Network

Three sets of experiments are performed to help gain understanding of sources of energy consumption of the computing units of the smart agriculture system, as presented in [23]. The designer of the crop health monitoring units might ask the following: (1) Does different structure matter to energy consumption? (2) How does the number of sensors in each structure affect energy consumption? (3) Which of the tasks between computation or communication consumes more energy? (4) How much does the bandwidth affect total energy consumption? Our experiments aim to answer these questions with respect to scales (i.e., number of nodes) of the smart agriculture system.

The results of the experiments along with some explanations are discussed in the three sections below. The results should help the farm owner or the smart agriculture system engineer in designing and selecting appropriate structures and scales to sustain energy usage of the new smart disease detection computing units.

5.1   Effects from Network Structures

We use our analytical energy model to estimate energy consumptions of two structures: star and mesh when scaling the number of nodes (i.e., sensors and distributed servers) up to 10,000 nodes.

As shown in Fig. 8 (left), as we increase number of nodes, energy consumption linearly increases for both structures (or topologies) as expected as execution of each unit requires approximately the same energy usage in a normal situation (i.e., no transmission

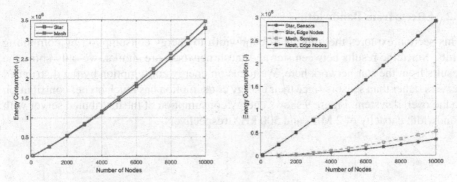

Fig. 8. (left) Energy consumption of star and mesh networks. (right) Energy consumption of sensors vs. distributed servers (edge nodes) [23].

delays). However, the mesh structure consumes slightly higher energy consumption than the star structure. This is due to the differences in energy consumption by data transmissions to be investigated in more details below.

Figure 8 (right) compares energy consumed by sensing nodes and (distributed) servers (or edge node) of both star and mesh structure. In both topologies, shown in Fig. 9, the servers consume significantly higher energy than the sensors. This is mainly due to high energy consumption from deep learning execution. Moreover, as shown in Fig. 9, energy consumption at the servers in both topologies are the same. This is because the servers in both topologies perform approximately the same amount of deep learning computation and transmit the same amount of data.

On the other hand, Fig. 8 (right) shows that the transmission (or communication) energy at sensing nodes of the mesh is higher than that of the star. As the number of nodes increases, the differences in transmission energy grow. This is because, as opposed to direct transmission in the star structure, sensing nodes in the mesh that are not connected to its designated server require multi-hop transmission. Since some nodes need to send not only their data but also data from other nodes, more energy is consumed. Consequently, the mesh structure has higher transmission energy and higher total energy consumption. In our experiments, we consider at most 2-hop data forwarding as depicted in Fig. 7. If more hops are needed to reach the distributed server, even higher energy consumption is expected.

In general, despite being simple and cheaper in terms of energy, the star structure has limitation in the maximum transmission range between the sensing node and the server. Since sensing node and the server must be in transmission coverage of one another, having more sensing nodes may not mean increased coverage area. Using communication technology such as LoRa can overcome this issue as it enables long range transmission with low power consumption, but it has a low bandwidth. Mesh topology does not have the same issue as the sensing nodes can relay data from other nodes and hence can be anywhere as far as they are connected to another node. Moreover, it can provide better reliability since data can be rerouted using different paths in case a node fails. The smart farming designer has to take these tradeoffs into consideration along with energy consumption effects.

5.2 Effects from Bandwidths

This section explores the impacts of bandwidth to energy consumption by computing units. Since the results between star and mesh networks are similar, we only show the results from the star network here. We focus on energy consumption by the distributed servers rather than sensors since their energy consumption has much higher contribution to the overall system. Figure 9 shows energy consumption of the distributed server with bandwidth capacity of 2 MHz and 500 kHz, respectively.

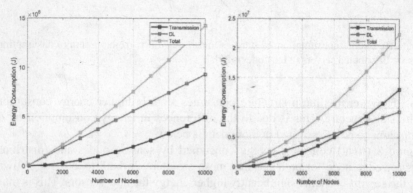

Fig. 9. (left) Energy consumption where bandwidth is 2 MHz. (right) Energy consumption where bandwidth is 500 kHz [23].

As shown in Fig. 9 (left), with a high bandwidth of 2 MHz, deep learning energy consumption dominates that of data transmission. Also, total energy consumption contributed by the DL computation and data transmission of the distributed server is scalable. However, this is not the case with a lower bandwidth.

As shown in Fig. 9 (right), when there are more than 7,000 nodes, transmission energy starts to dominate deep learning computation energy. This is because bandwidth is shared among the nodes. When there are nodes, higher traffic is expected. This results in longer transmission time and thus higher energy consumption. Thus, in the scenario of this experiment with low bandwidth, the system should not grow more than 7000 nodes, otherwise, more energy will be wasted on transmissions instead of actions to gain productivity (i.e., more images being analyzed). For the system designer, the ability to estimate energy consumption per computing units prior to implementation can give insights on the scale of the smart farm system to fit the energy budget constraint or to determine investment on bandwidth capacity.

5.3 Effects from Sensors and Servers Ratios

Results obtained in Sect. 5.1 indicate that structures (i.e., mesh, star) of the computing units do not appear to impact energy consumption that much. In our previous experiments, the number of sensors in each structure is set to be four. We want to investigate further the number of sensors in each structure impacts energy consumption. This section considers only the star structure as it is baseline energy consumption of the two structures.

Table 1. Effect of number of sensors in a star-structured group [23].

Energy Consumption	10 sensors + 1 edge node	100 sensors + 1 edge node	Ratio Difference
Sensing	0.06	0.63	10.00
Sensor Transm.	173.06	2,376.75	13.73
Total at Sensor	173.13	2,377.38	13.73
DL execution	11,624.73	116,247.29	10.00
Edge Transm.	181.67	3,003.42	16.53
Total at Server	11,806.40	119,250.71	10.10

We consider two sets of sensors, 10 and 100. Table 1 shows comparison of energy consumption between having ten and a hundred sensors sending data to one server. The ratio difference in the last column represents the ratio of energy consumption in the 100-sensor case over that in the 10-sensor case. Thus, it gives a multiplying factor of the former to the latter. As shown in the first line of Table 1, since the number of sensors increases 10 times, sensing energy consumption increases 10 times as expected. Similarly, at the distributed server, more number of sensors means more number of images being processed. Thus, the server has to do 10 times more image analysis, thus, the energy consumption of DL execution increases 10 times as it should be.

Nevertheless, transmission cost does not necessarily increase linearly. Transmission energy of the 100-sensor case is about 13.7 times more than that of the 10-sensor case. This is due to higher traffic which in turn increases the latency and energy. Similarly, the transmission cost at the server is over 16 times more expensive. Since the server transmits larger data size than the sensors, this causes heavier transmission traffic and results in much higher energy consumption. With the results shown here we make a conjecture that the number of sensors in each structure can lead to larger difference of energy consumption produced by mesh and star topologies.

Overall, our experiments and results aim to show methodology to help the farm owner or engineer design and scale a sustainable smart farming system based on estimated energy consumption of computing units.

6 Case Study 2: Drone Network

Three sets of experiments are performed to decide the appropriate choice of sensing and computing units for the crop health monitoring system. This study aims to consider 3 options of networks: a) sensors with servers, as seen in Case Study 1, b) typical drones with servers, and c) modern drones. Questions raised to make the decision may include (1) Does the size of the areas or locations to monitor affect the decision? (2) How does the number of servers and number of drones affect time and energy consumption? (3) How many drones are needed to cover the area without recharging? (4) Which type of drones is better in terms of energy and time?

38   S. Puangpontip and R. Hewett

The results of the experiments in Case Study 2 along with some explanations are discussed in three sections below. The results should help the farm owner in designing and selecting appropriate decisions for the sustainable crop monitoring system.

6.1 Effects of the Size of the Area

We use our analytical energy model to estimate energy consumptions of the sensor network and drone network for different area sizes. Figure 10 shows energy consumption and time consumed in different networks of different sizes. As shown om Fig. 10 (left), when the area is 1 km^2, Option a) for 100 sensors and one server gives the best results as it consumes least energy, about 40% of those consumed by the other two options. However, it takes about 1.5 and 6 times longer than typical drone and modern drone networks, respectively. The typical drone network consumes the highest energy, which is slightly higher than the modern drone but takes 4 times longer to complete the task. This is because the modern drone does not need data transmission to the server, saving both energy and time. As a result, when the area size is not large and the application is not time-sensitive (such as our example of the crop health monitoring system), a sensor network is the best option. However, if time is a critical concern such as healthcare or security systems, the modern drone should be selected.

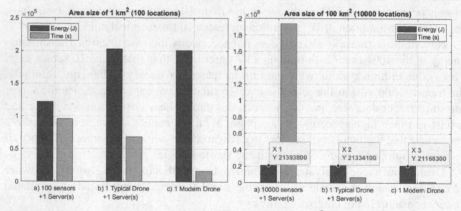

Fig. 10. Energy and time consumed to monitor area size of 1 km^2 (left) and 100 km^2 (right).

On the other hand, Fig. 10 (right) shows that the sensor network is no longer the option for the larger area that requires more sensors. As shown in Fig. 10 (right), the sensor network, i.e., option a), consumes the highest energy and time while the modern drone consumes the least in both aspects. Although the difference in energy consumed by the three options is not much, the modern drone offers the best time consumption. The sensor network would take to finish the daily job. This is due to the bottle neck at the server since there is only one server to perform the classification. The way out is to increase the number of servers, which will be discussed in the following section.

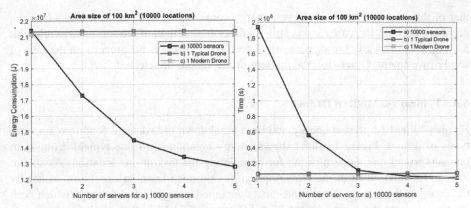

Fig. 11. Energy (left) and time (right) consumed as the number of servers increases.

6.2 Effects of Number of Servers and Number of Drones

A large number of sensors cannot work with only one server. In this section, we experiment to see the effect of number of servers for the sensor network while keeping the settings for the drones to be the same. Figure 11 shows energy and time consumption when increasing the servers up to five. Energy consumption and time of the option a) sensor network reduces significantly as the servers increase. As seen in Fig. 11, energy consumption when the network has five servers reduces 1.6 times and takes about the same time as the drone options. This is because energy and time consumption of the server is significantly higher than that of the sensors. Nevertheless, this also means the system owners need to invest more in servers, resulting in higher cost of implementation and maintenance.

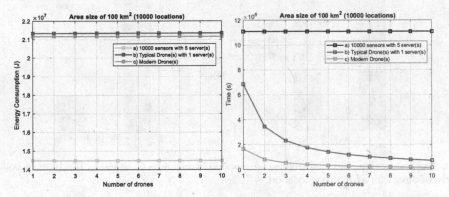

Fig. 12. Energy (left) and time (right) consumed as the number of drones increases.

Figure 12 shows the energy and time consumed as the number of drones increases. As shown in Fig. 12 (right), the time taken to complete the task decreases as the number of drones increases as expected, since each drone has less number of locations to cover. We also see that the time taken for both types of drone networks are much lower than that of the sensor network. However, energy consumption does not differ much as the number of drones increases and is still 4.4 times higher than of the sensor network with 5 servers. In this case, sensor network is preferred if there is no concern on the cost of server investment. Otherwise, the modern drone should be selected.

6.3 Typical vs. Modern Drones

Figures 13 and 14 present energy and time breakdown of tasks and functions for both types of drones. Figure 13 (left) shows energy breakdown of one typical drone with one server and one modern drone for completing the task at one location. As shown in Fig. 13 (left), most of the consumption lies on deep learning execution, either by the drone or the server. The second-most consumed energy is flight energy which both drones consume the same amount. The difference of 21 kJ in the energy consumption comes from typical drone server's transmission energy that the modern one does not have, as shown in Fig. 13 (left).

Figure 13 (right) shows time breakdown for both types of drones. Deep learning execution may take a lot of energy but does not take a long time. The majority of time consumption for the typical drone network and the reason why the modern drone is the fastest to complete the tasks is data transmission to the server, as shown in Fig. 13 (right). Since the modern drone can process deep learning tasks by itself, it does not need to transmit data to the server, whereas the typical drone does. Similar to the sensor network issue, the number of servers can be increased for higher financial cost to improve the time performance.

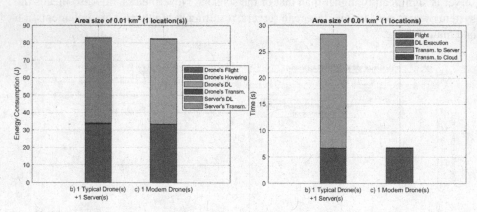

Fig. 13. Energy (left) and time (right) consumption breakdowns of tasks and functions of both types of drones for a trip to one location.

Figure 14 shows energy and time breakdown of one typical drone with five servers and one modern drone for completing the task at all locations. Figure 14 (right) shows that by adding more servers, it improves the time performance of the typical drone. However, the modern drone is still faster to complete the tasks. As a result, the modern drone should be selected over the typical one.

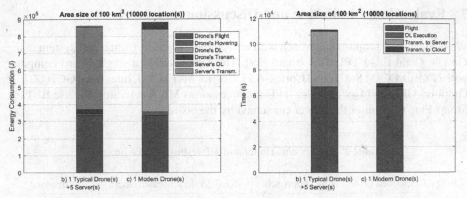

Fig. 14. Energy (left) and time (right) consumption breakdowns of tasks and functions of both types of drones for a trip to all locations.

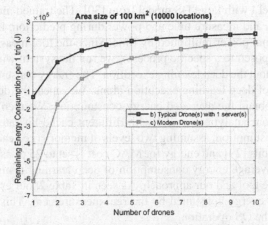

Fig. 15. Remaining energy consumption after completing the task for all locations as the number of drones increases.

Drones have limited battery capacity. Although the battery is rechargeable, flying back to the charging station can disrupt and delay the mission or operation. Hence, recharging in the middle of the task execution is not desirable as the time taken to complete the task would be longer. Figure 15 shows remaining energy consumption after one trip, i.e., finishing the tasks at all locations. For both types, one drone cannot cover all locations (10000 locations) without recharging before the task could be completed, as seen in negative values of Fig. 15. As shown in Fig. 15, only two typical drones would be sufficient to cover all locations without the need for a recharge, whereas four would be required for the modern type. In this case, typical drones should be selected for economic reasons (i.e., using smaller number of drones and less energy consumption).

7   Evaluation, Limitation and Discussion

We evaluate our proposed approach with energy measurement from a real system using Google Coral Edge TPU Dev Board [29]. The Dev board is a single-board computer with NXP i.MX 8M SoC (quad Cortex-A53, Cortex-M4F) CPU, Integrated GC7000 Lite Graphics GPU and Google Edge TPU coprocessor as ML accelerator. We use BNLink Smart Plug to monitor the power consumed by the board.

Table 2. Energy consumption of DL testing per one image.

Energy Consumed (J)	Our Approach	Real System Measurement	Difference
Model I [30]	0.58	0.70	−0.12

We trained model I with large DS model from [30]. The trained model is run to test one hundred images and measure time and power during prediction. Energy consumption is calculated from power multiplied by time. Since the tool measure consumption of a machine (as opposed to a specific process), we run the system with minimum processes with and without the deep learning execution. The energy consumption difference is considered to be of deep learning execution alone. We repeat the deep learning testing five times and obtain the averaged energy consumption. We then compute energy consumption from our analytical model with different cache hit rates and obtain the averaged energy consumption, assuming two levels of memory (i.e., cache and DRAM). Precision is set to 8 bits [29] and energy for MAC cost is set to 25 pJ as reported in [31]. Table 2 shows the average energy consumption of deep learning testing (or inference) of an image from the tool and our approach. As seen in Table 2, our estimation is about 0.12 J less than the energy consumed by the real measurement. This could be due to some overheads in the OS operation.

We also evaluate the proposed model theoretically with published results from [24] and results obtained by an online analytical tool [19]. Due to lack of information on data energy from the two existing works, we compare only the computation energy (in terms of the number of MACs). Our result matches the result reported [24], yielding 724M MACs (i.e., 666M from CONV layers and 58.6M from FC layers). However, the estimates from the tool given by [21] yields about 20% less than ours and that of [24], giving 528M MACs for CONV layers.

8   Related Work

Most research in deep learning focus on improving accuracy [13, 14, 27]. They either propose new architectures that outperforms the state-of-the-arts [13, 27] or adapt states-of-arts for specific tasks (e.g., plant disease classification) [13, 32]. None of these considers energy consumption or consider energy issues as an afterthought after the system was implemented or deployed [7, 33]. Our approach estimates energy consumption to be used in designing the system prior to system development.

Research on developing sustainable computing systems has been studied extensively on alternative energy sources (e.g., renewable energy and energy harvesting [4–6], or improving energy efficiency of infrastructures (e.g., cloud and data centers [1, 3, 7]), communication protocols [1, 8, 9] and hardware devices (e.g., circuit boards and sensors [1, 5, 10, 11]). While making good progress, these studies are specific to physical artifacts or do not address energy modeling of software. Sustainable software development, on the other hand, is relatively behind. Most aim to find energy-efficient solutions as a result of improving computational efficiency (e.g., optimizing scheduling [1, 6, 10]). This is useful but not direct. The direct approach naturally requires the ability to measure energy usage of the software computation, which is our focus.

Research in estimating energy consumption of software components uses various techniques. Most rely on power measurement tools, e.g., hardware sensors [5, 34], WattsUp? Pro [35], Intel's Running Average Power Limit (RAPL) interface and/or nvidia-smi [15, 17, 18], and the Streamline Performance Analyser [16], to measure actual energy consumption. They are used to study power behavior or report energy usage [15, 18], or to build a prediction model [16–18]. Nevertheless, these tool-based approaches can be hardware specific and can only measure energy at the device level. They are unable to measure specific software computation. Moreover, implementation is required in order to obtain the consumed energy.

Another technique uses simulation to estimate energy consumption of software units [19, 20]. Work in [20] estimates energy consumption of ANN training in a distributed computing framework. Unlike our approach, the model uses only MAC operations and not data movement. The work also only deals with ANN model, whereas ours estimates energy consumption of both ANN and CNN. Yang et al. [19] estimates energy consumption of deep learning based on two factors: number of Multiply-and-Accumulate (MAC) operations and data movement in the hierarchy. The number of MACs and data accesses are obtained through simulation. Although the simulation approach is reported to give accurate results, it requires long runtime for large DNNs and requires knowledge of a specific hardware system. Furthermore, implementation is still required on the simulator to obtain energy results.

To overcome the above limitations, few studies employ analytical approach [18, 19, 21, 22]. Most of these [18, 21, 22] presents a mathematical model to estimate software computing units based on numbers of CPU cycles/frequency, floating point operation, and/or multiply-and-accumulate (MAC) operation. None considers energy consumed by data movement within memory hierarchy which is rather significant to the overall consumption. Yang et al. [19] proposes analytical way to estimate energy consumption of DNN based on the network architecture. However, there are no details on the analytical models employed. Our work is most similar to [19] in applying basic elements of MACs and data movement, and present energy modeling of energy consumption during deep learning execution (i.e., testing phase of deep learning model). However, this work differs from ours in that it does not show how the core elements (i.e., the number of MACs and data movement) are obtained, whereas we do. Our model explicitly defines how to calculate number of MAC operations as well as frequencies of data access to quantify energy consumption of deep learning.

9 Conclusions

As a number of electronic devices, applications, computing systems and networks substantially grow and expand, significant and inevitable impacts to the environment are made. Sustainable computing is thus of great importance for future technologies and society. The paper presents a fundamental capability to pre-calculate energy consumption for developing sustainable deep learning application systems prior to system implementation. Specifically, we propose an analytical modeling approach to quantifying energy consumption of deep learning computation. Although our presented model is specific to deep learning applications in distributed networks, the building block concept of our approach is general and applicable to other software in other distributed environments (e.g., IoT, edge computing). The paper also illustrates practical applications of the proposed approach to help with design, decision, and energy resource management and planning for sustainable system development.

Future work includes (1) expanding the proposed approach plan and manage system resources under constraints and in consideration of economy, energy, quality of service, and environment, (2) modeling energy consumption of other software (e.g., other machine learning techniques or algorithms), and (3) applying the approach to other real-world applications such as healthcare and cybersecurity.

References

1. Benhamaid, S., Bouabdallah, A., Lakhlef, H.: Recent advances in energy management for Green-IoT: an up-to-date and comprehensive survey. J. Netw. Comput. Appl. **198**, 103257 (2022)
2. Gomes, C., Dietterich, T., Barrett, C., et al.: Computational sustainability: computing for a better world and a sustainable future. Commun. ACM. **62**, 56–65 (2019)
3. Dhaini, M., Jaber, M., Fakhereldine, A., Hamdan, S., Haraty, R.A.: Green computing approaches-a survey. Informatica **45** (2021)
4. Lu, M., Fu, G., Osman, N.B., Konbr, U.: Green energy harvesting strategies on edge-based urban computing in sustainable Internet of Things. Sustain. Cities Soc. **75**, 103349 (2021)
5. Zhu, S., Ota, K., Dong, M.: Green AI for IIoT: energy efficient intelligent edge computing for industrial Internet of Things. IEEE Trans. Green Commun. Netw. **6**(1), 79–88 (2021)
6. Ma, D., Lan, G., Hassan, M., Hu, W., Das, S.K.: Sensing, computing, and communications for energy harvesting IoTs: a survey. IEEE Commun. Surv. Tutor. **22**, 1222–1250 (2020)
7. Hossain, M.S., Rahman, M.A., Muhammad, G.: Towards energy-aware cloud-oriented cyber-physical therapy system. Future Gen. Comput. Syst. **105**, 800–813 (2020)
8. Haseeb, K., Ud Din, I., Almogren, A., Islam, N.: An Energy efficient and secure IoT-based WSN framework: an application to smart agriculture. Sensors **20**, 2081 (2020)
9. Razooqi, Y.S., Al-Asfoor, M.: Intelligent routing to enhance energy consumption in wireless sensor network: a survey. In: Shakya, S., Bestak, R., Palanisamy, R., Kamel, K.A. (eds.) Mobile Computing and Sustainable Informatics. LNDECT, vol. 68, pp. 283–300. Springer, Singapore (2022). https://doi.org/10.1007/978-981-16-1866-6_21
10. Fu, H., Sharif-Khodaei, Z., Aliabadi, M.H.F.: An energy-efficient cyber-physical system for wireless on-board aircraft structural health monitoring. Mech. Syst. Sig. Process. **128**, 352–368 (2019)

11. Bouguera, T., Diouris, J., Chaillout, J., Andrieux, G.: Energy consumption modeling for communicating sensors using LoRa technology. In: 2018 IEEE Conference on Antenna Measurements & Applications (CAMA), pp. 1–4 (2018)
12. Atitallah, S.B., Driss, M., Boulila, W., Ghézala, H.B.: Leveraging Deep Learning and IoT big data analytics to support the smart cities development: review and future directions. Comput. Sci. Rev. **38**, 100303 (2020)
13. Liu, Y., Sun, P., Wergeles, N., Shang, Y.: A survey and performance evaluation of deep learning methods for small object detection. Expert Syst. Appl. **172**, 114602 (2021)
14. Too, E.C., Yujian, L., Njuki, S., Yingchun, L.: A comparative study of fine-tuning deep learning models for plant disease identification. Comput. Electron. Agric. **161**, 272–279 (2019)
15. Strubell, E., Ganesh, A., McCallum, A.: Energy and policy considerations for deep learning in NLP. In: Proceedings of the Conference on 57th Annual Meeting of the ACL, pp. 3645–3650 (2020)
16. Faviola Rodrigues, C., Riley, G., Luján, M.: SyNERGY: an energy measurement and prediction framework for Convolutional Neural Networks on Jetson TX1. In: Proceedings of the International Conference on Parallel and Distributed Processing Techniques and Applications, pp. 375–382 (2018)
17. Cai, E., Juan, D.-C., Stamoulis, D., Marculescu, D.: NeuralPower: predict and deploy energy-efficient convolutional neural networks. In: Asian Conference on Machine Learning, pp. 622–637 (2017)
18. García-Martín, E., Rodrigues, C.F., Riley, G., Grahn, H.: Estimation of energy consumption in machine learning. J. Parallel Distrib. Comput. **134**, 75–88 (2019)
19. Yang, T.J., Chen, Y.H., Emer, J., Sze, V.: A method to estimate the energy consumption of deep neural networks. In: Conference Record of 51st ACSSC 2017, pp. 1916–1920 (2018)
20. Rouhani, B.D., Mirhoseini, A., Koushanfar, F.: DeLight: adding energy dimension to deep neural networks. In: Proceedings of the International Symposium on Low Power Electronics and Design, pp. 112–117 (2016).
21. Mo, X., Xu, J.: Energy-efficient federated edge learning with joint communication and computation design. J. Commun. Inf. Netw. **6**(2), 110–124 (2020)
22. Yang, Z., Chen, M., Saad, W., Hong, C.S., Shikh-Bahaei, M.: Energy efficient federated learning over wireless communication networks. IEEE Trans. Wireless Commun. **20**, 1935–1949 (2021)
23. Puangpontip, S., Hewett, R.: Energy-aware deep learning for green cyber-physical systems. In: Proceedings of the 11th International Conference on Smart Cities and Green ICT Systems - SMARTGREENS, pp. 32–43. SciTePress (2022)
24. Sze, V., Chen, Y.H., Yang, T.J., Emer, J.S.: Efficient processing of deep neural networks: a tutorial and survey. Proc. IEEE **105**, 2295–2329 (2017)
25. Rajasekaran, T., Anandamurugan, S.: Challenges and applications of wireless sensor networks in smart farming—a survey. In: Dinesh Peter, J., Alavi, A.H., Javadi, B. (eds.) Advances in Big Data and Cloud Computing: Proceedings of ICBDCC 2018, pp. 353–361. Springer, Singapore (2019). https://doi.org/10.1007/978-981-13-1882-5_30
26. Yao, J., Ansari, N.: QoS-aware power control in internet of drones for data collection service. IEEE Trans. Veh. Technol. **68**, 6649–6656 (2019)
27. Krizhevsky, A., Sutskever, I., Hinton, G.E.: ImageNet classification with deep convolutional neural networks. Commun. ACM **60**, 84–90 (2017)
28. Gikunda, P.K., Jouandeau, N.: State-of-the-art convolutional neural networks for smart farms: a review. In: Arai, K., Bhatia, R., Kapoor, S. (eds.) CompCom 2019. AISC, vol. 997, pp. 763–775. Springer, Cham (2019). https://doi.org/10.1007/978-3-030-22871-2_53
29. Coral: Google Coral Dev Board. https://coral.ai/docs/dev-board/datasheet/

30. Puangpontip, S., Hewett, R.: On using deep learning for business analytics: at what cost? In: International Conference on Knowledge-Based and Intelligent Information & Engineering Systems (2022)

31. Li, J.: Research on optoelectronic accelerator based on AI computing. In: 2022 IEEE International Conference on Artificial Intelligence and Computer Applications, pp. 1001–1006 (2022)

32. Li, Y., Nie, J., Chao, X.: Do we really need deep CNN for plant diseases identification? Comput. Electron. Agric. **178**, 105803 (2020)

33. Liu, Y., Yang, C., Jiang, L., Xie, S., Zhang, Y.: Intelligent edge computing for IoT-based energy management in smart cities. IEEE Netw. **33**, 111–117 (2019)

34. Mitchell, W., Westberg, S., Reiling, A., Taha, T., Balster, E., Hill, K.: Generalized power modeling for deep learning. In: IEEE NAECON 2018, pp. 391–394 (2018)

35. Horcas, J.M., Pinto, M., Fuentes, L.: Context-aware energy-efficient applications for cyber-physical systems. Ad Hoc Netw. **82**, 15–30 (2019)

An Evaluation of Smart City Models Towards a New Service Design Model

Leonard Walletzký[1], Odonchimeg Bayarsaikhan[1], Mouzhi Ge[2(✉)], and Zuzana Schwarzová[1]

[1] Faculty of Informatics, Masaryk University, Brno, Czech Republic
{wallet,501452,zschwarz}@mail.muni.cz
[2] Deggendorf Institute of Technology, Deggendorf, Germany
mouzhi.ge@th-deg.de

Abstract. Due to the emergence of smart city applications, various smart city models and architectures have been proposed in different domains. Since there are strengths and weaknesses among those smart city models, it is therefore valuable to evaluate the smart city models and use the results to further develop a new service design model in the smart city. This can on the one hand provide an overview of the similarity and differences of smart city models, and on the other hand, it will also help the new smart service design to avoid reinventing the wheel. Therefore, this paper firstly classifies the smart city models with a conceptual and structural view, where the conceptual models focus on the interactions of components and the structural models are featured by layers with processes. Based on the model classification, the paper further evaluates the models by service structure, interoperability, multi-contextuality and adaptability. The evaluation results can be used to compare, select and improve the smart city models and service design. Based on the results, we propose a new model for designing smart services.

Keywords: Smart city model · Smart ecosystem · Interoperability · Adaptability

1 Introduction

Since smart city contains a very large span of stakeholders ranging from citizens, organizations to municipalities, there are various definitions for the concept of smart city [13,26]. From the organizational perspective, today's organizations intend to be flexible in organizing their operations, services, technological solutions, to respond quickly to any changes and challenges, and improve the organizational resources allocation continuously [8,21].

Throughout the last decade, different works have viewed the smart city from various perspectives, and derived different definitions for smart city [12,17,24]. Most of the works are stressing the importance in a local context [23,32] or analyzing existing conceptual views on smart city [10]. For example, from the view of municipality, it is critical for municipalities and city planning experts to understand versatile aspects of the smart city management, including the structure and composition of smart cities, their interrelationships, and how they interact [15,27]. However, gathering this information in a comprehensive and orderly manner is a significant challenge for them, and due

C. Klein et al. (Eds.): SMARTGREENS 2022/VEHITS 2022, CCIS 1843, pp. 47–67, 2023.
https://doi.org/10.1007/978-3-031-37470-8_3

to the incompleteness of the information, it often affects the quality of their decisions and makes it difficult to implement smart city-appropriate management [2].

To understand smart city, various stakeholders may name or interpret one thing differently, especially with terminology. The way to construct Smart City under one dominant domain like Smart Government [3] or urban development [19] means losing the information and links to other domains that might be critical for Smart City development [5,6]. Therefore understanding this diverse terminologies will provide an comprehensive view for the diversity of smart cities and how they interact with each other [33]. Smart cities need to reflect in their smart city management and operations the ability to respond and adapt to changes at all levels of cities with the rapid development of technology [29,30]. The development of a smart city model in line with this situation is important for the development of a smart city. Thus, it is important to implement a smart city model that is compatible, resilient, and adaptable [20].

This paper is therefore to determine whether existing smart city models meet the requirements of smart cities and provide an evaluation study to help develop a model that meets those requirements. In this work, we will select nine smart city models and compare them based on "structure", "interoperability", "multi-contextual view" and "adaptability" to see if they meet today's smart city requirements. The results of this study will determine whether the existing models meet the needs and will serve as a basis for the development of a suitable model.

The rest of the paper is organized as follows. Section 2 selects nine smart city models that are further divided into conceptual models and structural models. Section 3 evaluates the models based on four criteria, which are structure, interoperability, multi-contextual view and adaptability. Based on the evaluation results, Sect. 4 proposes a new model for service design in smart cities. Section 5 concludes the paper and highlights the future research.

2   Smart City Models

To find the papers that are focused on a structural and conceptual model of smart city, we have used Google Scholar and searched the literature by using the following keywords: smart city, conceptual model, structural model, and architecture. We considered that Google Scholar is more up-to-date with including new papers and combining the paper sources from various libraries such as IEEE, ACM and Springer. Based on the research results we have manually selected the 9 most relevant papers and divided them into two groups: conceptual and structural. The conceptual models focus on the smart city framework and the interactions between different conceptual terminologies. On the other hand, the structural models are mostly layer-based and focused on different stages of smart cities.

2.1   Conceptual Smart City Models

[22] aims to suggest a framework connecting conceptual variants of the smart city label, key elements for being a smart city, and strategic principles for making a city smart. For defining smart city, a variety of the labels can be categorized into three dimensions: technology, people, and community. The conceptual variants are mutually connected

with substantial confusion in definitions and complicated usages rather than independent on each other.

From the discussion of conceptual variants of smart city that set of fundamental factors which make a city smart, the author identifies and clarifies key conceptual components of smart city, and re-categorises and simplifies them into three categories of core factors: technology (infrastructures of hardware and software), people (creativity, diversity, and education), and institution (governance and policy). Given the connection between the factors, a city is smart when investments in human/social capital and IT infrastructure fuel sustainable growth and enhance the quality of life, through participatory governance. The author offers strategic principles for making a city smart in order to realize the various visions specified for diverse policy domains, aligning to the three categories of core components. First, integration of Technology Factors: integrates technologies, systems, infrastructures, services, and capabilities into an organic network that is sufficiently complex for unexpected emergent properties to develop. Second, learning for Human Factors such as social learning and education. And third, governance of Institutional Factors such as collaboration, cooperation, partnership, citizen engagement, and participation (Fig. 1).

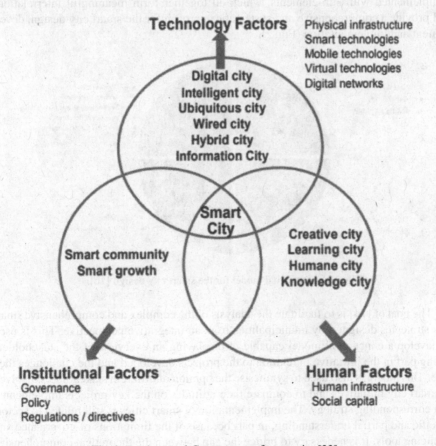

Fig. 1. Fundamental Components of smart city [22].

The research objective of [16] is to present a smart city conceptual model (SCCM) that assists cities and their stakeholders to carry out robust smart city initiatives and enhance sustainable smart city ecosystem design and development. Foundation for SCCM is derived from the systematic literature review of the smart city ecosystems and value networks. SCCM originates from a perception that design and management of complex smart city is not a trivial task and many smart city initiatives have failed it due to weak smart city governance, ecosystem orchestration and insufficient digital technology knowledge and capabilities. Thus, SCCM aims to clarify complex smart city governance, ownership, orchestration and decision-making procedures and advance technological compatibility and correct skills and resource allocation in cities. Furthermore, SCCM aims to provide tools to accelerate competitiveness, transparency and economic growth in cities.

The paper proposed a smart city conceptual model that aims to assist smart city practitioners to form long-term smart city vision and strategy, facilitate the governance of the heterogeneous stakeholder relations and digital technologies, and assist to evaluate risks and funding needs. Smart city conceptual model considers four primary dimensions: strategy, technology, governance and stakeholders. Each primary dimension is complemented with sub-elements, which all together form meaningful interrelations and provide a comprehensive and systematic approach for the smart city design, development and implementation (Fig. 2).

Fig. 2. A conceptual model for the smart city design [16].

The goal of [14] is to facilitate the analysis of the complex and comprehensive smart city strategies designed by municipalities from an integrative perspective. This is used to develop a conceptual model capable of displaying an overview of the stakeholders taking part in the initiative in relation to the projects developed and the challenges they face. This model is also used to synthesise the opinion of different stakeholders involved in smart city initiatives and to compare their attitudes on the key projects implemented in a corresponding strategy. The implementation of smart cities is still related to sector-specific and partial understanding, in part because of the limitations of governance and financing tools. It is necessary to bridge the gap between the theoretical comprehensive perspective and the sector-wide implementation of the smart city concept.

Stakeholders' involvement and engagement in decision-making is essential for Smart governance and it's the key element to becoming a smart city. However, stakeholders reveal different visions of the smart city in their discourses. There are also differences between the image of the smart city and its implementation and between the vision of the stakeholders in smart city development and the initiatives carried out. It can therefore be assumed that narrowing the gap between the stakeholders' vision of smart city initiatives and the implementation of certain projects may make a decisive difference to the success of smart city strategies.

The author further proposed a new model based on analysis of the usage of conceptual models in the scientific literature on smart cities. This research understands the smart city as an integrated and multi-dimensional system that aims to address urban challenges based on a multi-stakeholder partnership. The proposed conceptual model follows a comprehensive and integrative approach to smart cities that links the three main issues identified: (a) the key role of governance and stakeholders' involvement; (b) the importance of displaying a comprehensive vision of smart city projects and dimensions; and (c) the understanding of smart city as a tool to tackle the urban challenges. Finally, the three parts of the conceptual model are shown interrelated. The model is described from the centre to its outer limits, but not necessarily in a linear sequence, in order to aid its understanding (Fig. 3).

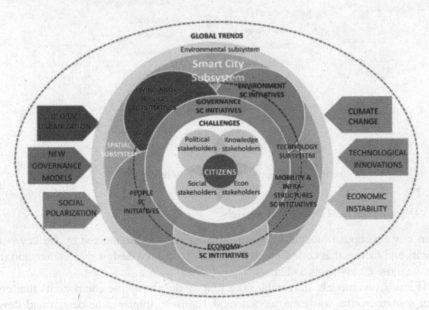

Fig. 3. Smart city implementation and discourses: An integrated conceptual model [14].

[4] aims to produce a new approach and concept, which is the "smart and resilient city". The authors explored five smart city models, and proposed a new model which contains especially resilience concepts in the context of natural disasters. The smart and resilient city model has 25 characters that are integrated and embedded within the scope of smart and resilient city concept: (1) the six characteristics (smart governance, smart

economy, smart environment, smart living, smart mobile and smart people) can lead to a multi-dimensional strategy to synergize and support each other; (2) the four dimensions - the smart and resilient city concept; and (3) the components of the city are divided into physical and non-physical components: resources, processes, and technologies included into the physical group; people, institutions, and activities entered into non-physical groups. This model is developed to serve as a guide on building smarter and more resilient cities for planners and decision-makers, and to increase capacity responses from complex urban systems in facing climate change (Fig. 4).

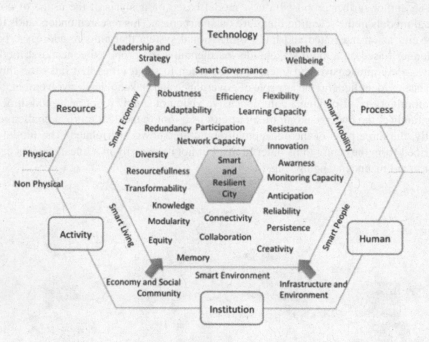

Fig. 4. Smart and resilient city model [4].

2.2 Discussions for Conceptual Models

Smart city conceptual models are multi-dimensional and are defined by the key components and factors that contribute to a smart city, and are designed to understand and manage those components and factors.

The first two models are similar, The first model shows the components that construct a smarter city, while the second model aims to improve the design and development of a smart city ecosystem and is represented by 4 dimensions with its sub-elements. These two models serve more as general outlines and are suitable for providing an overview for the components in a smart city.

The next two models are designed to help smart city planners and decision-makers build smarter and more flexible cities and support smart cities to accomplish the challenges they face. The third model is designed to show smart city stakeholders, their involvement in smart city initiatives, as well as smart city challenges. The fourth model is designed for serving as a guide for smart city planners and decision-makers on how to build smarter and more resilient cities, and to increase capacity responses from complex urban systems in facing the climate change.

For interoperability, some of these conceptual models of a smart city define the interoperability between the components that make up a smart city, but they are not clear. The interoperability in these papers is not detailed on how to help manage smart city components. For multi-contextual view. These conceptual models of smart cities are developed in general or in a specific context. In other words, they cannot be transformed into multi-contextual and cannot be changed. For adaptability, most of these models are not designed to be responsive to change. The fourth model may be able to respond to changes, but only partially.

Although these smart city conceptual models provide a comprehensive understanding of the components in a smart city, they stays in an abstract level. As such, it is important to propose a more detailed model to provide an understanding of the smart city services structure and implementation in order to manage smart city services in a multi-contextual environment.

2.3 Structural Smart City Models

[9] proposes the model of smart city Ecosystem Frameworks. This model provides a comprehensive understanding of the smart city ecosystem framework as shown in Fig. 5. The author develops this model for planning smart cities and considers that a vibrant and sustainable city is an ecosystem comprised of people, organizations and businesses, policies, laws and processes integrated together to create the desired outcomes such as government efficiency, sustainability, health and wellness, mobility, economic development, public safety and quality of life. This city is adaptive, responsive and always relevant to all those who live, work in and visit the city. A smart city integrates technology to accelerate, facilitate, and transform this ecosystem. The author defines four types of value creators in the smart city ecosystem: city, businesses and organizations, communities, and residents; and capability layers.

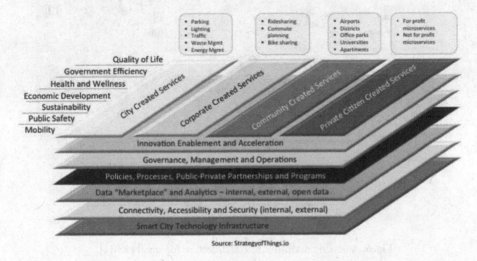

Fig. 5. The smart city ecosystem framework [9].

[1] aims to define a general smart city architecture, which serves governance purposes for innovation and sustainability, while it utilizes experiences from practical cases and corresponding theoretical context. The authors focused on answering the question "What is the structure of a smart city architecture that could define a corresponding standard?" and proposed a generic multi-tier ICT architecture based on the analysis of smart city dimensions, categories, development stages, components, and existing smart city architecture approaches. The generic multi-tier ICT architecture for smart cities is proposed as follows:

– **Layer 1 - Nature Environment:** it concerns all the environmental features where the city is located such as landscape, rivers, lakes, sea, and forests.
– **Layer 2 - Hard Infrastructure (Non-ICT-based):** it contains all the urban features which have been installed by human activities and which are necessary for city operation (buildings, roads, bridges, energy-water-waste utilities etc.).
– **Layer 3 - Hard Infrastructure (ICT-based):** it concerns smart hardware that the SSC services are offered with (datacenters, supercomputers and servers, networks, IoT, sensors etc.).
– **Layer 4 - Services:** all the smart city services are grouped in the smart city sic dimensions and organized according to the international urban key-performance indicators.
– **Layer 5 - Soft Infrastructure:** individuals and groups of people living in the city, as well as applications, databases, software and data, with which the SSC services are realized (Fig. 6).

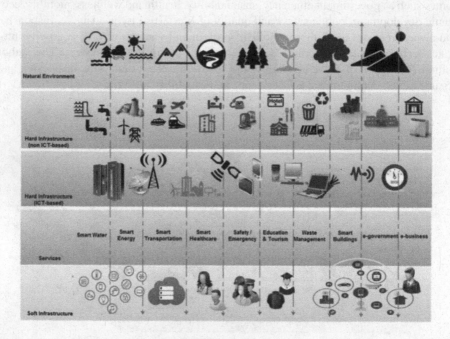

Fig. 6. A generic multi-tier ICT architecture for smart city [1].

[11] defines the concepts of digital twins and digital twin cities, discusses the relationship between digital twins and smart cities, analyzes the characteristics of smart cities based on digital twins, and focuses on the five main applications of smart cities based on digital twins. One of findings is the smart city operation brain (SCOB). The authors described the SCOB and its infrastructure that serves as the Public Information Cloud Service Platform.

Once the public information cloud service platform is established, the office of SCOB is able to start to operate, and the officials could use the applications on the platform to conduct management activities in the smart city. Figure 7 shows the structure of the public information cloud service platform. The platform is composed of an infrastructure layer, software development and operation platform layer, and an application layer. The platform uses infrastructure such as servers, networks, and sensor equipment to acquire data, and uses cloud infrastructure, data, platforms and software as services, and finally achieves the applications of cloud service platforms in various fields such as smart urban management, smart public security, and smart tourism. The platform can create an ecological chain for data collecting, processing, storing, cleaning, mining, applying, and feedback.

[18] describes the key supporting technologies of smart cities (i.e. digital cities, Internet of Things, and cloud computing). From the geomatics perspective, the fundamental and operational issues for smart city are addressed, including geo-referencing and 3D spatial-temporal modeling, integration of global position system (GPS), remote sensing and GIS in mobile platforms, devices and structures for ubiquitous sensing and communication, and service capabilities in cloud environments. The author defines the main framework of a smart city based on the Internet of Things. The Internet of Things shown in Fig. 8 has a hierarchical structure of four layers: distributed sensor layer, ubiquitous network layer, service-oriented middle-ware layer and intelligent application layer.

[31] identifies the benefits of an integrated view that not only interconnects the services, but also identifies joint layers that they rely on, which helps us to understand the impact of the underlying IT services and the infrastructure they rely on. At the same time, we extend our view to the Smart Citizen, who plays an essential role in the value creation process within the smart city.

2.4 Discussions for Structural Models

As for the structural model, most of the models have provided a comprehensive understanding of the smart city and its structure, which are built based on the information and communication technology infrastructure.

A majority of the models in this group provides a deep understanding of the structure of the smart city. Each model is usually built with 4–5 layers. The first two models show a smart urban environment and non-technological infrastructure than other models in this second group. For example, [9] proposed a smart city ecosystem framework compared to other models, and provides important insights regarding how to build a smart city ecosystem through this model. It identifies the layers of smart city services in terms of service coverage, value and innovation, management and policy systems, data and privacy, security, and technology infrastructure, all of which together constitute a smart city ecosystem. The model is valuable in identifying the key components

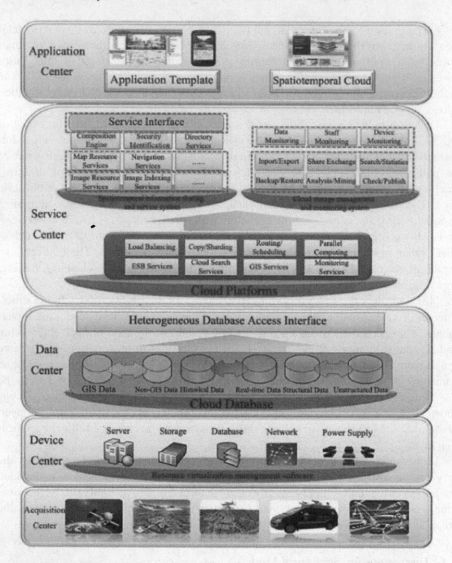

Fig. 7. Schematic diagram of the structure of a smart city public information cloud service platform based on digital twins [11].

of a smart city ecosystem integrated with technology. However, we still need to identify the services that construct a smart city and how those services interconnect to create a smart city.

The smart city model in [1], unlike other models, is designed to create innovation and sustainability, with a smart city architecture that includes the natural environment and non-technological infrastructure. The model has layers called natural environment, services and soft infrastructure and we can obtain an understanding of the possible types that are covered by each layer.

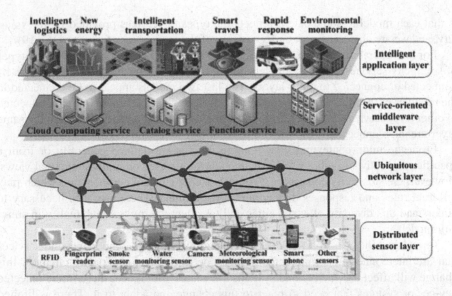

Fig. 8. A framework of the smart city based on the Internet of Things [18].

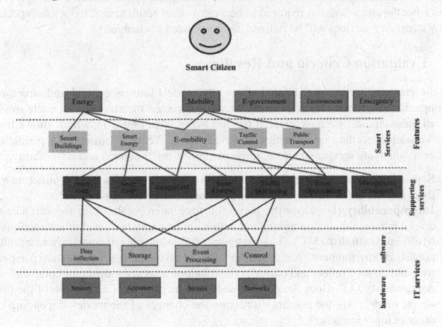

Fig. 9. The structure of smart city layers [31].

The rest of the smart city models are based on information and communication technology infrastructure, and some of these models are more focused on specific technology features, such as IoT and Digital Twin. The common advantage of these models is that each model to some extent reflects the types of services provided by the smart city, and we are able to gain an understanding of the main types of services (Fig. 9).

For interoperability – most of the models in this group provide insights of the types of smart city services, but most models do not fully show how those services are interconnected or connected to other layers. The last two models appear to be connected to the modules of the other layers. In particular, the latest model shows how it is connected to other layer services. However, this model does not show how the services in the same layer are interconnected.

From the multi-contextual view – these models are defined generally or from a specific perspective. In other words, the models are focused on multi-contextual views. However, the smart city consists of various stakeholders and components, which play different roles and responses depending on the context. Therefore, it is necessary to understand this diversity of smart cities and to reflect the multi-contextuality in smart city model.

For adaptability – a smart city is constructed by multiple components and services that are interconnected or interacted. When one device in a smart city changes, this change will affect the devices and systems associated with it, and these interconnected devices or systems that need to react to this change and adapt to it. There is limited description of how these changes will affect other parts of the model. Although [18] describes the characteristics required to become a smart resilient city, it does not specify how smart city services will be defined and responded to changes.

3 Evaluation Criteria and Results

In the previous section, we divided smart city models into conceptual and structural groups, based on their characteristics. We also discussed the character of each group. From these studies, we have created the following table (Table 1), which shows how each model meets the characteristics we have defined. We have considered 4 evaluation criteria, which are service structure, interoperability, multi-context and adaptability.

- **Service Structure (S)** - Is the paper suggesting the view of services' structure? Is there any insight on how to design or analyze the structure of services?
- **Interoperability (I)** - Does the paper illustrate interoperability of the services or does it present the service as isolated with none or a very low level of interactions?
- **Multi-contextuality (MC)** - Does the paper follow the idea of smart city as a multi-contextual environment? Are the authors familiar with the multi-contextual perspective, and do they reflect and consider the relations among the different contexts?
- **Adaptability (A)** - Does the paper count with the process of adaptation of the presented model? Are the authors discussing the changes of the model, depending on outer or inner impulses?

Smart city covers a wide range of stakeholders, advanced technologies and devices such as IoT devices. The diversity of smart cities should be addressed in order to achieve sustainable development of smart cities, whereby we have identified a few key features needed to ensure this diversity, and aim to evaluate if those key features are met by the existing smart city models. Based on the results of the above smart city models review, the evaluation based on each feature will be discussed in the next sections.

Table 1. Evaluation Results of Smart City Models [28].

	Group	Literature name/model	S	I	MC	A
1	Conceptual	Conceptualizing smart city with Dimensions of Technology, People, and Institutions [22]	N	N	N	N
2	Conceptual	Improving Smart City Design: A Conceptual Model for Governing Complex smart city Ecosystems [16]	N	N	N	N
3	Conceptual	Smart City Implementation and Discourses: An Integrated Conceptual Model. The case of Vienna [14]	N	P	N	N
4	Conceptual	Towards Smart and Resilient City: A Conceptual Model [4]	N	N	N	N
5	Structural	The Smart City Ecosystem Framework - A Model for Planning smart cities [9]	F	N	N	N
6	Structural	Defining Smart City Architecture for sustainability [1]	F	N	N	N
7	Structural	Smart City based on Digital Twins [11]	F	N	N	N
8	Structural	Geomatics for smart cities - Concept, Key Techniques, and Applications [18]	F	P	N	N
9	Structural	Smart City Layered Model [31]	F	P	N	N

Legend: "F" - Fulfilled; "P" - Partially; "N" - Not Fulfilled

3.1 Service Structure

As indicated in [25], the key features that are used to determine the structure of services are the interconnections of intelligent systems and smart service designs. We have divided all the selected models into two main groups: conceptual and structural, which depends on the characteristics of the models. In terms of the "structure" key feature, the structural group model provided more smart city services at the structural level, which was convenient with this key feature. Most of the models in the structural group showed smart services in general, while models 7 and 9 showed the structure of services more clearly. Although models 7 and 9 show the structure of smart city services, the relationship between them has not been clearly defined.

3.2 Interoperability

This key feature is one of the important factors to help understand the structure of smart city services, such as the interactions between smart city services, how they work together, and what impact they have. From the above smart city models, models 8 and 9 show interoperability and can see how the design of smart city model's layers and their services are connected to each other. Although these models show interoperability between layers, they do not show interoperability of services on a single layer. By defining the services at that layer, it is possible to understand the structure of smart city services, how services are interconnected as well as their interrelationships. We found that understanding their interoperability can significantly impact the organization of smart city services and optimize the structure of smart city services.

3.3 Multi-contextuality

Smart city includes different stakeholders such as organizations, governments, individuals, and industry professionals, and their perspectives vary depending on their work experience, skills, and work environment. Smart city services also play different roles, which depend on the specifics of each sector, environmental impact factors, stakeholders, and contexts. Smart city governments and experts need to take into account the diversity of smart cities when creating a smart city. Therefore, the smart city service model also needs to be developed by taking into account the versatility and multi-contextuality. The models are based on general and specific perspectives such as IoT, data twin, ICT, etc. Thus it can be seen that it is necessary to develop a multi-contextual model.

3.4   Adaptability

It is critical that smart city models are organized in a way that is adaptable and responsive for service changes. Smart city services are interconnected and affecting each other mutually. If the changes in one part of a service can affect another part, it is important to consider this effect when designing a smart city service. The models we have chosen rarely take this point into account. Thus, it is valuable to develop a flexible model that can adapt to service change.

4   New Model for Smart City Service Design

With regard to the previous analyses, we have developed a new model for Smart City design (Fig. 10). This model was created based on [7,31], with reflection of findings in [8] and the four criteria defined in the above chapters. We've developed this model with the aim to tackle most of the issues related to a multi-contextual and fast changing environment and to mitigate difficulties that smart cities face such as diversity, uncertainty, incomplete information and different perspectives. In this paper, we will introduce the general concept of the new model. Its deeper research and implementation analysis are still in progress.

The model will cover all services of the smart city and enable the implementation of their centralized management. It was developed as a 3-dimensional (3D) layered model and clearly shows the smart city structure and its interconnections of services. We grouped the services vertically based on the context and horizontally based on their functionalities.

4.1   Types of Smart City Services: Background Services and Customer-Facing Services

We've divided the smart city services into two types of services: background services and customer-facing services. First, we've focused on the Background services, because although they are not visible for end users, they are a key feature for creating the base of a smarter environment. It is necessary to improve their visibility to understand the whole complexity of the smart city model environment. The Background services contain all services from the Supporting service layer and the Infrastructure layer in our smart city layered model. These services produce data, processes, information and all the support for customer-facing services that serve end users. Even though they are not creating

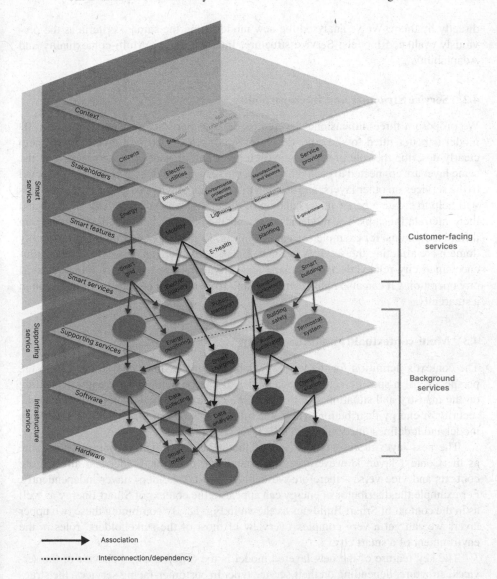

Fig. 10. The new design of smart city services layered model. Based on [7].

the value independently, they are directly affecting the final value the customers get by using Customer-facing services.

The customer-facing services type is a well-established concept and it can be categorized for example, according to the general sector directions defined by the government, as urban planning, energy, mobility, emergency, e-Health, and e-Government. These concepts are very similar in any country or city, and also in all the models we have explored. The Customer-facing services are visible to the end users and can be used directly by them. We've analysed the new model using the same 4 criteria as the previously evaluated models: Service structure, Interoperability, Multi-contextuality and Adaptability.

4.2 Service Structure and Interoperability

We propose a three-dimensional layered model of smart city services, because a 3D model is better fitted to show the design of smart city services in layers. It will help clearly describe the role of services in each layer and present how the services on the same layer are connected to each other. Also, the services on one layer can be connected to the services on other layers, and shifting to a 3D model will easily illustrate that. This will help to create a better understanding of the complexity of smart city services and their interrelationships. The model also presents the relations between the services from different domains, for example, we can see in Fig. 11 that services from Smart Mobility domain are affecting the services in Smart Energy domain, etc. This will further influence smart city-related decision-making and provide an opportunity to improve smart city operations. It can also reduce errors arising from the lack of specific information in a smart city.

4.3 Multi-contextuality and Adaptability

The context's definition for the top layer is based on the smart city strategy from the perspective of a specific actor or stakeholder. It can be defined differently depending on the industry and situation. For example, the context can be Urban development, IT security or energy distribution. The context layer is added in the top of the smart city model and it defines the design of all the layers.

The next layer represents the view of the stakeholder. The meaning is the same as the Context layer. However, we understand that one stakeholder can affect more contexts and vice versa - therefore we defined the stakeholders' layer independently. For example the distributor of energy can appear in the context of Smart Energy as well as in the context of Smart Buildings as shown in Fig. 12. By combining these two upper layers we can get a very complex overview of most of the stakeholders' roles in the environment of a smart city.

The key feature of the new layered model is the difference in behavior of the services' structure, depending on their service type. In customer-facing services, the structure of the services remains unchanged when the context or stakeholders view change. Whereas the background services are fully dependent on the context and stakeholders - they are changing dynamically with the view, defined by context or stakeholder. This enables very clearly to catch, analyse and describe possible overlaps of the services from one domain to another. For example a service that provides information of the charging station's capacity is affecting not only the Mobility, but also the Energy context. This feature also allows researchers and architects to add or modify the model without the necessity to redefine the whole structure. The possibility to add another context or stakeholder or whole service structure is a part of the model. This enables the model to obtain maturity.

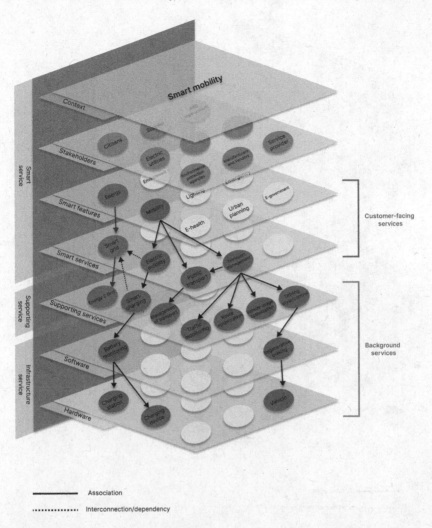

Fig. 11. Smart city services layered model - Mobility context. Based on [7,8].

4.4 Further Development of the Model

We intend to tackle the need to adapt to the multi-contextual environment of the smart city and be flexible to possible changes. Our model is fulfilling all the key criteria we defined for a successful model of a multi-contextual environment. The main challenge is understanding that the smart city is a very dynamic environment and therefore the model must also be dynamic or should have the flexibility to adapt to the changes. The next step in the development is to use the model practically in the municipalities - to get the data about the real development of their services, their interconnections and multi-contextual overlaps, as described in [8]. According to this, we can see the change of the structure in background services during the context change, while the structure of customer facing services remains the same in given time.

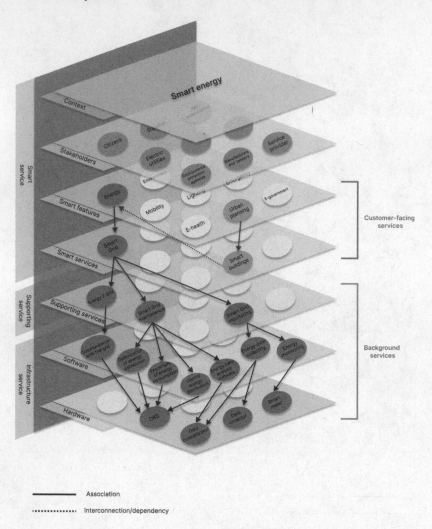

Fig. 12. Smart city services layered model - Energy context. Based on [7,8].

The new model shows that development of the services as isolated solutions is not possible. Even though we do not see their relations at the customer level, they are affecting each other in the background, for example by sharing the same infrastructure, using the same processes or procedures. Ignoring that, the municipalities are risking to cover unexpected costs based on the issues formed in other contexts such as security. The main role of the model is to explore these interconnections and show how to predict such situations.

5   Conclusions

In this paper, we have conducted an evaluation on a variety of literature on smart city models. The research has been focused on nine smart city models. In order to organize the models, we have classified the models into conceptual and structural categories. The conceptual models focused on the smart city framework and interactions among various conceptual components, whereas the structural models are mostly layer-based and focused on different processes for smart cites. Based on this classification, we have further discussed the features of each model group. In order to further understand the models, we have evaluated the models based on their service structure, interoperability, multi-contextuality and adaptability. The evaluation results have shown that the smart cities models can be improved and work collaboratively. Also, the results indicate how to build smart city models in the future. Based on the evaluation results, we have proposed a new model for service design in smart cities, which are further demonstrated in the context of smart mobility and smart energy.

As future work, we will further develop the evaluation criteria into quantitative form, so that the models can be automatically evaluated. Also, we plan to include more smart city models and architectures into the evaluation to observe the similarity and differences among the models. This can be done by creating an alignment of the smart city models with a reference model.

References

1. Anthopoulos, L.: Defining smart city architecture for sustainability, August 2015. https://doi.org/10.3233/978-1-61499-570-8-140
2. Anthopoulos, L., Janssen, M., Weerakkody, V.: A Unified Smart City Model (USCM) for smart city conceptualization and benchmarking, pp. 247–264, January 2019. https://doi.org/10.4018/978-1-5225-7030-1.ch011
3. Anthopoulos, L., Reddick, C., Sirakoulis, K.: Conceptualizing smart government: interrelations and reciprocities with smart city. Digit. Gov. Res. Pract. (2021). https://doi.org/10.1145/3465061
4. Arafah, Y., Winarso, H., Suroso, D.S.A.: Towards smart and resilient city: a conceptual model. In: IOP Conference Series: Earth and Environmental Science, vol. 158, p. 012045, May 2018. https://doi.org/10.1088/1755-1315/158/1/012045
5. Bangui, H., Ge, M., Buhnova, B.: Exploring big data clustering algorithms for Internet of Things applications. In: Muñoz, V.M., Wills, G.B., Walters, R.J., Firouzi, F., Chang, V. (eds.) Proceedings of the 3rd International Conference on Internet of Things, Big Data and Security, IoTBDS 2018, Funchal, Madeira, Portugal, 19–21 March 2018, pp. 269–276. SciTePress (2018)
6. Bastidas, V., Reychav, I., Ofir, A., Bezbradica, M., Helfert, M.: Concepts for modeling smart cities. Bus. Inf. Syst. Eng. **64**, 359–373 (2021). https://doi.org/10.1007/s12599-021-00724-w
7. Bayarsaikhan, O.: Process of service catalogue creation in smart city. Master thesis, Masaryk Univerzity, Fakulty of informatics, Brno (2021). [cite 15–8–2022]. https://is.muni.cz/th/tku18/. sUPERVISOR : Leonard Walletzký
8. Buhnova, B., Kazickova, T., Ge, M., Walletzky, L., Caputo, F., Carrubbo, L.: A cross-domain landscape of ICT services in smart cities. In: Pardalos, P.M., Rassia, S.T., Tsokas, A. (eds.) Artificial Intelligence, Machine Learning, and Optimization Tools for Smart Cities. SOIA, vol. 186, pp. 63–95. Springer, Cham (2022). https://doi.org/10.1007/978-3-030-84459-2_5
9. Chan, B., Paramel, R.: The smart city ecosystem framework - a model for planning smart cities (2018). https://iiot-world.com/smart-cities/the-smart-city-ecosystem-framework-a-model-for-planning-smart-cities/

10. Chourabi, H., et al.: Understanding smart cities: an integrative framework. In: 45th Hawaii International Conference on System Sciences, pp. 2289–2297, January 2012. https://doi.org/10.1109/HICSS.2012.615

11. Deren, L., Wenbo, Yu., Zhenfeng, S.: Smart city based on digital twins. Comput. Urban Sci. 1(1), 1–11 (2021). https://doi.org/10.1007/s43762-021-00005-y

12. Desouza, K., Flanery, T.: Designing, planning, and managing resilient cities: a conceptual framework. Cities 35, 89–99 (2013). https://doi.org/10.1016/j.cities.2013.06.003

13. Dragoicea, M., et al.: Service design for resilience: a multi-contextual modeling perspective. IEEE Access 8, 185526–185543 (2020)

14. Fernandez-Anez, V., Fernández-Güell, J.M., Giffinger, R.: Smart city implementation and discourses: an integrated conceptual model. The case of Vienna. Cities 78, 4–16 (2018). https://doi.org/10.1016/j.cities.2017.12.004. https://www.sciencedirect.com/science/article/pii/S0264275117306558

15. Ge, M., Chren, S., Rossi, B., Pitner, T.: Data quality management framework for smart grid systems. In: Abramowicz, W., Corchuelo, R. (eds.) BIS 2019. LNBIP, vol. 354, pp. 299–310. Springer, Cham (2019). https://doi.org/10.1007/978-3-030-20482-2_24

16. Hämäläinen, M., Tyrväinen, P.: Improving smart city design: a conceptual model for governing complex smart city ecosystems, pp. 265–277, June 2018. https://doi.org/10.18690/978-961-286-170-4.17

17. Lee, J., Hancock, M., Hu, M.C.: Towards an effective framework for building smart cities: lessons from Seoul and San Francisco. Technol. Forecast. Soc. Change 89, 80–99 (2014). https://doi.org/10.1016/j.techfore.2013.08.033

18. Li, D., Shan, J., Shao, Z., Zhou, X., Yao, Y.: Geomatics for smart cities - concept, key techniques, and applications. Geo-Spatial Inf. Sci. 16, 13–24 (2013). https://doi.org/10.1080/10095020.2013.772803

19. Liu, Q., et al.: Categorization of green spaces for a sustainable environment and smart city architecture by utilizing big data. Electronics 9, 1028 (2020). https://doi.org/10.3390/electronics9061028

20. Lom, M., Přibyl, O.: Smart city model based on systems theory. Int. J. Inf. Manag. 56, 102092 (2020). https://doi.org/10.1016/j.ijinfomgt.2020.102092

21. Mbarek, B., Ge, M., Pitner, T.: Trust-based authentication for smart home systems. Wirel. Pers. Commun. 117(3), 2157–2172 (2021). https://doi.org/10.1007/s11277-020-07965-0

22. Nam, T., Pardo, T.: Conceptualizing smart city with dimensions of technology, people, and institutions, pp. 282–291, June 2011. https://doi.org/10.1145/2037556.2037602

23. Neirotti, P., De Marco, A., Cagliano, A.C., Mangano, G., Scorrano, F.: Current trends in Smart City initiatives: some stylised facts. Cities 38, 25–36 (2014). https://doi.org/10.1016/j.cities.2013.12.010

24. Piro, G., Cianci, I., Grieco, L., Boggia, G., Camarda, P.: Information centric services in smart cities. J. Syst. Softw. 88, 169–188 (2013). https://doi.org/10.1016/j.jss.2013.10.029

25. Stepánek, P., Ge, M.: Validation and extension of the smart city ontology. In: Proceedings of the 20th International Conference on Enterprise Information Systems, ICEIS 2018, Funchal, Madeira, Portugal, 21–24 March 2018, vol. 2, pp. 406–413. SciTePress (2018)

26. Štěpánek, P., Ge, M., Walletzký, L.: IT-enabled digital service design principles - lessons learned from digital cities. In: Themistocleous, M., Morabito, V. (eds.) EMCIS 2017. LNBIP, vol. 299, pp. 186–196. Springer, Cham (2017). https://doi.org/10.1007/978-3-319-65930-5_15

27. Trang, L.H., Bangui, H., Ge, M., Buhnova, B.: Scaling big data applications in smart city with coresets. In: Hammoudi, S., Quix, C., Bernardino, J. (eds.) Proceedings of the 8th International Conference on Data Science, Technology and Applications, DATA 2019, Prague, Czech Republic, 26–28 July 2019, pp. 357–363. SciTePress (2019)

28. Walletzký, L., Bayarsaikhan, O., Ge, M., Schwarzová, Z.: Evaluation of smart city models: a conceptual and structural view. In: Klein, C., Jarke, M. (eds.) Proceedings of the 11th International Conference on Smart Cities and Green ICT Systems, SMARTGREENS 2022, 27–29 April 2022, pp. 56–65. SciTePress (2022)

29. Walletzký, L., Carrubbo, L., Ge, M.: Modelling service design and complexity for multi-contextual applications in smart cities. In: 23rd International Conference on System Theory, Control and Computing, ICSTCC 2019, Sinaia, Romania, 9–11 October 2019, pp. 101–106. IEEE (2019)

30. Walletzký, L., Romanovská, F., Toli, A.M., Ge, M.: Research challenges of open data as a service for smart cities. In: Ferguson, D., Helfert, M., Pahl, C. (eds.) Proceedings of the 10th International Conference on Cloud Computing and Services Science, CLOSER 2020, Prague, Czech Republic, 7–9 May 2020, pp. 468–472. SciTePress (2020)

31. Walletzky, L., Buhnova, B., Carrubbo, L.: Value-driven conceptualization of services in the smart city: a layered approach. In: Barile, S., Pellicano, M., Polese, F. (eds.) Social Dynamics in a Systems Perspective. NEW, pp. 85–98. Springer, Cham (2018). https://doi.org/10.1007/978-3-319-61967-5_5

32. Wey, W.M., Hsu, J.: New urbanism and smart growth: toward achieving a smart National Taipei University District. Habitat Int. **42**, 164–174 (2014). https://doi.org/10.1016/j.habitatint.2013.12.001

33. Yang, Q., Ge, M., Helfert, M.: Analysis of data warehouse architectures: modeling and classification. In: Filipe, J., Smialek, M., Brodsky, A., Hammoudi, S. (eds.) Proceedings of the 21st International Conference on Enterprise Information Systems, ICEIS 2019, Heraklion, Crete, Greece, 3–5 May 2019, vol. 2, pp. 604–611. SciTePress (2019)

Fast Electrical Load Classification Using a Dimmer-Based Smart Plug

Dániel István Németh[✉] and Kálmán Tornai

Faculty of Information Technology and Bionics, Pázmány Péter Catholic University,
Práter utca 50/a, Budapest 1083, Hungary
`nemeth.daniel.istvan@hallgato.ppke.hu`

Abstract. As renewable energy resources become a significant source of electricity production, the stable operation of the electrical grid becomes increasingly difficult. Demand-side control of the electrical grid load solves this problem and enables better utilization of renewable energy such as wind or solar power. Adjusting the grid load to meet the renewable production levels requires knowledge about the composition of the grid load as well as the ability to schedule individual loads. We propose a Smart Plug solution capable of accurately classifying the connected electrical load as well as running the Neural Network-based classification on the Smart Plug. The Smart Plug is WiFi-capable allowing wireless measurements as well as remote control of the connected electrical load. We took measurements with the Smart Plug prototype of common household electrical loads and achieved very high accuracy. This accuracy rate can be achieved with on-device measurement and on-device NN inference in less than 2.5 s. Multiple NN-based classification methods and measurements of different amounts of data were examined (measurement profiles).

Keywords: Smart plugs · Smart grid · Electrical load classification · Edge computing · Machine learning · Smart homes · TinyML

1 Introduction

With the spread of renewable energy sources, load balancing of the grid becomes increasingly tricky. Aside from the constantly changing load of the grid, uncontrollable components such as solar or wind farms appear on the production side as well. In order to maximize the utilization of these renewable energy resources, knowledge about the grid's load composition is required as well as the ability to control or schedule individual loads. Scheduling specific loads enable the grid load to be adjusted to meet renewable energy production levels. Research into energy utilization and savings is especially relevant concerning the European energy crisis.

This paper presents a new prototype device with extended capabilities compared to the authors' previous work published in [12]. The new device also uses a slightly different measurement methodology. New measurements were also taken, and the list of measured loads was extended. This paper focuses on Neural Network-based classification methods. The new prototype device collected all measurement data for the Neural Network-based classification. Fully Connected Neural Networks (FCNN), Recurrent Neural Networks (RNN), and Convolutional Neural Networks (CNN) were examined on the new dataset. The new prototype device is capable of recording more precise measurements as well as communicating over WiFi. All measurements presented in this paper were taken wirelessly. The new prototype device can also run the neural network-based classification on-device, so all the benefits of Edge Computing are available. *Compared to our prototype in* [12], *in this paper we present a new Smart Plug prototype capable of wireless communication and on-device load classification. We also present results for a Long-Short Term Memory-based (LSTM) classification method in addition to the improved versions of the FCNN and CNN methods. The list of measured electrical loads was also extended.*

This paper presents a Smart Plug capable of quickly recognizing the connected load as well as controlling it. With such capabilities, load scheduling becomes possible. Accurate classification of the electrical load can be achieved with less than 10 s of measurement data. Different measurement methodologies (Measurement Profiles) were examined, which enable the adjustment of the measurement to the processing capabilities of the hardware as well as the accuracy and response time requirements. Different Neural Network-based classification methods were tested, also aiming to provide solutions for both high- and low-performance applications.

The structure of the paper is as follows: Sect. 2 summarizes the related publications in literature. In Sect. 3, the Smart Plug prototype and the measurement method is presented. Section 4 introduces measurement profiles, which enable faster measurements with minimal impact on classification accuracy. In Sect. 5 the measured household electrical loads are introduced. The Neural Network-based classification results are shown in Sect. 6. Section 7 describes the Smart Plug's on-device classification capabilities and its performance. Finally, the conclusions are presented in Sect. 8.

2   Related Work

Load scheduling is a critical problem that arises with the introduction of non-controllable electricity producers to the grid. In a smart grid, balancing can be achieved by scheduling loads on the demand side, allowing full utilization of renewable resources. Controlling the smart grid's load is critical for better utilization of renewables [9]. Manar Jaradat et al. in [9], examine the problem of Demand-Side Management and model it as a linear programming problem with the goal of fully utilizing the available renewable energy while also minimizing the total cost of electricity purchased from the grid.

Current smart plugs on the market have only limited capabilities. These devices essentially act as relays that can be turned on or off remotely and in some cases, provide power consumption information. This already has some benefits, especially regarding accessibility [10]. But smart plugs on the market lack load classification capabilities. Industry lags behind research in this area [8]. With current solutions on the market, the user needs to individually input the details of the load connected and also has to control the load manually or, in some cases, provide the scheduling information. In [8], environmental sensor data such as temperature, ambient noise, and humidity is combined with smart plugs to create a shared knowledge-based system. With the data from the environmental sensors, the system can estimate whether the load will be used within the next hour or what its power consumption will be. The proposed system, EnAPlug consists of multiple smart plugs communicating with each other and sharing knowledge.

Load monitoring can be achieved with non-intrusive or intrusive solutions [15]. Non-Intrusive Load Monitoring (NILM) is achieved using Smart Meters. In NILM solutions, the power consumption is measured at a single point, recording the total load of the household. To determine the load composition, disaggregation is required to determine the individual appliances contributing to the total load. Data collected by Smart Meters can help the operation of the Smart Grid by providing load data that can be used to estimate future grid load. Intrusive Load Monitoring (ILM) solutions use multiple measuring devices within the household or building. In [15], ILM is split into three categories: In ILM 1, power consumption levels are measured for each zone within the building or household. In ILM 2, each outlet is measured individually, while in ILM 3, each appliance's load is recorded separately.

The smart home system proposed in [3] features smart plugs which communicate with a central node. By obtaining an Electric Load Signature (ELS) from the power consumption data of the load, the system can accurately classify the connected load. The ELS was obtained by recording each load's active and apparent power, voltage, current, and power factor values for one hour with a one-second resolution. With a Decision Tree-based classification method, 93.5% accuracy was achieved. Using a Naive Bayes algorithm, the accuracy rate was 99.9%.

In [13], a bidirectional triode thyristor-based electrical load classification is presented. By manipulating the voltage supply of the load, a characteristic response can be measured. An Arduino microcontroller was used for controlling the TRIAC and collecting the measurement data. The microcontroller masks the voltage signal of the connected load between ratios of 10% and 95% with 5% increments. The number of consecutive masking cycles also varied between 1 and 20. The load's current, voltage, and power consumption values were measured for each combination. The power measurement values were put into a matrix. A Fully Connected Neural Network (FCNN) is used for load classification with the power measurement matrix as the input. With this method, a 96.5% accuracy rate was achieved. Each measurement took 45 s. This paper presents a similar approach to [13], but with several improvements in the prototype device, measurement speed, data collection, and classification methods, as well as offering new capabilities like on-device load classification, wireless communication, and different measurement profiles.

2.1 Edge Computing

In recent years with the increased processing capabilities of end-user devices as well as microcontrollers, it has become possible to run Neural Network-based classifications on the edge. In [11], several advantages are listed:

- Lower latency and improved real-time processing.
- Increased robustness thanks to decentralization. Network failures or cyber-attacks have less impact.
- Computational requirements on the server-side are reduced, and the volume of data transferred is also decreased.
- Increased privacy and security.

There are several application areas in which edge computing solutions offer advantages over traditional cloud-based solutions:

- Image Processing and Computer Vision tasks can benefit from edge computing in several areas. Decreased latency allows faster reaction times. Increased privacy as only the critical information leaves the device, not the entire frame.
- Fast reaction times and network independence are crucial for fully autonomous self-driving vehicles.
- Speech and keyword recognition benefit from increased privacy as well as reduced network bandwidth usage and fewer computational requirements on the cloud side.
- Smart home systems benefit from all aspects listed previously. Increased response times and reliability can be achieved if the system only relies on local network communication to function.
- Smart infrastructure devices usually communicate over metered networks where data usage reduction can offer significant cost savings, especially with the recent spread of NB-IoT and LTE-M communication technologies. Transmitting fewer data can also offer energy savings, increasing the device's battery life.

In [2] a unified energy management framework is introduced with the goal of maximizing the utilization of renewable energy for an edge computing platform. Four functional modules were running in the edge device: A Weather Forecast module responsible for processing historical as well as current weather data. An Energy Generation Prediction Module is responsible for estimating the solar panel's future output; the Weather Forecast module's output is also used as input. An Energy Scheduler Module is responsible for choosing the power input of the load. The final module is a Data Processing module responsible for load balancing of the Computing Platform. The proof-of-concept system used Raspberry Pi-s and also included batteries to store the output of the solar panels. For the proof-of-concept system, the only loads used were a cluster of Raspberry Pi

Single Board Computers (SBCs). The results published in the paper state that an energy bill reduction of 86% is possible. If their solution were to be extended to household appliances, the smart plug system proposed in this paper could be a key component in estimating the future load of the grid as well as enabling load scheduling.

3   Smart Plug Prototype

The prototype uses two microcontrollers. A Raspberry Pi Pico [14] is used for controlling the measurement and recording the Power, Voltage, and Current values. An ESP32 microcontroller [6] is used for WiFi communication and for running Neural Network-based classification. An off-the-shelf dimmer module with a built-in power supply was used for dimming the load as well as powering the microcontrollers.

3.1   Hardware and Measurement Method

The RP2040 was chosen because of its fast ADC as well as the lack of context switching. The context switching on the ESP32 was problematic when trying to achieve precise, deterministic measurements. With the RP2040, even with 8-sample multisampling, around 360 ADC samples can be taken in one AC period as opposed to the 280 with the ESP32 (without multisampling) used in [12]. The two microcontrollers use serial communication between each other for commands and data exchange.

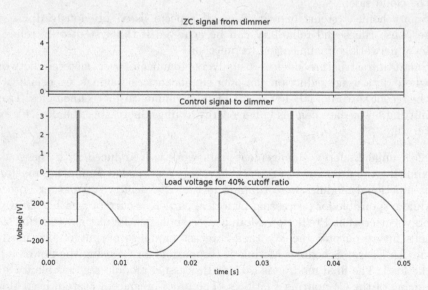

Fig. 1. Dimming method used during the measurement. The ZC and control signals are also shown.

The measurement method is the following: The RP2040 cuts off the connected load's supply voltage and records the load's response. The measurement is synchronized to the AC grid's frequency with the help of the dimmer's Zero Crossing (ZC) output which triggers an interrupt in the microcontroller. The device uses the dimmer's input signal to send a short impulse to the TRIAC inside the dimmer. The TRIAC then stays in a conducting state until the next ZC point. This methodology differs from the one presented in [12] as here, the microcontroller sends only a short impulse instead of leaving the output to the dimmer in a HIGH state until the next ZC event. An example of the cutoff methodology in can be seen in Fig. 1 where the signals are shown for 40% cutoff ratio. During the measurement, different cutoff ratios between 10% and 75% are used. The device records the load's Power, Voltage, and Current consumption for each AC period where some level of dimming is applied. After dimming with one cutoff ratio for the given number of cycles, the load receives power without dimming before measuring its response to the following cutoff ratio.

In our previous work, 14 different cutoff values were used between 10% and 75%. The device would measure with 10% cutoff ratio for 20 cycles, then wait 16 cycles for the load to receive uninterrupted power and then the cutoff ratio is increased by 5% compared to the previous one and an other 20 cycles are measured. One measurement takes 9.76s, and the output is three matrices of size 14 × 20 where each cell represents the measurement of one AC period, and the matrix is filled up in row-major order, so each row contains the measurements with the same cutoff ratio. An example of a power measurement matrix can be seen in Fig. 2.

The Real Power, RMS voltage, and RMS current values are calculated from the ADC measurements of one AC period using the following formulas:

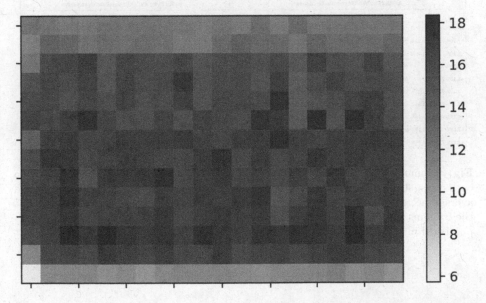

Fig. 2. Power measurement matrix of an LED Light bulb.

Real Power:

$$P = \frac{1}{n} \cdot \sum_{k=1}^{n} U[k]I[k] \tag{1}$$

RMS Voltage:

$$V_{RMS} = \sqrt{\frac{1}{n} \cdot \sum_{k=1}^{n} U[k]^2} \tag{2}$$

RMS Current:

$$I_{RMS} = \sqrt{\frac{1}{n} \cdot \sum_{k=1}^{n} I[k]^2} \tag{3}$$

The data is sent to the ESP32 via a serial connection where it can be classified or transmitted over WiFi.

With the dimmer, the load can also be switched off, allowing the load to be controlled remotely.

4   Complexity Reduction with Measurement Profiles

As we achieved accurate results using SVM-based classification, we examined using simulations how reducing the amount of data collected would affect the classification accuracy. Using smaller measurement matrices reduces the measurement time as well as the computational complexity of the classification.

	RESULTS for WORST classification accuracy:										RESULTS for AVERAGE classification accuracy:									
	2	4	6	8	10	12	14	16	18	20	2	4	6	8	10	12	14	16	18	20
<14,10%-75%>	96.25%	96.56%	97.43%	98.00%	96.95%	97.90%	97.71%	97.62%	98.29%	97.71%	97.89%	98.23%	98.84%	99.04%	98.99%	98.99%	98.97%	98.92%	98.99%	99.00%
<7,10%-70%>	95.14%	96.08%	97.05%	97.05%	96.57%	96.76%	97.52%	96.00%	97.24%	97.14%	96.65%	97.73%	98.34%	98.62%	98.58%	98.52%	98.62%	98.51%	98.61%	98.63%
<5,10%-70%>	93.48%	96.39%	97.28%	97.20%	97.61%	96.86%	97.43%	97.14%	96.85%	96.85%	96.01%	97.79%	98.39%	98.62%	98.57%	98.43%	98.65%	98.45%	98.46%	98.43%
<4,10%-70%>	93.76%	95.34%	96.53%	96.73%	96.65%	97.50%	96.64%	96.56%	96.95%	97.52%	95.43%	97.30%	98.16%	98.52%	98.45%	98.76%	98.62%	98.52%	98.49%	98.79%
<3,10%-70%>	93.65%	95.19%	96.82%	96.86%	97.19%	97.29%	97.41%	97.42%	97.52%	97.52%	95.85%	97.22%	98.21%	98.40%	98.32%	98.70%	98.73%	98.76%	98.78%	98.84%
<2,10%-75%>	92.31%	94.84%	96.59%	97.02%	97.44%	97.96%	97.97%	98.07%	97.87%	97.67%	94.42%	96.54%	98.32%	98.48%	98.83%	99.22%	99.07%	99.19%	99.11%	99.01%
<3,15%-75%>	91.93%	95.50%	96.17%	97.11%	96.93%	97.25%	97.75%	97.08%	98.05%	97.67%	93.65%	96.75%	97.84%	98.37%	98.49%	98.60%	98.82%	98.84%	99.02%	99.03%
<4,15%-75%>	93.44%	96.04%	96.47%	97.18%	97.58%	97.49%	97.01%	96.63%	97.32%	97.79%	95.23%	97.40%	97.84%	98.59%	98.60%	98.43%	98.52%	98.56%	98.65%	98.82%
<5,15%-75%>	95.19%	96.56%	97.38%	97.30%	97.31%	97.51%	98.09%	97.51%	97.80%	98.09%	96.58%	97.68%	98.42%	98.91%	98.94%	98.86%	99.00%	98.97%	98.95%	99.03%
<7,15%-75%>	94.08%	96.60%	97.03%	97.14%	97.61%	97.04%	97.24%	96.37%	97.90%	98.09%	96.40%	97.85%	98.24%	98.74%	98.80%	98.71%	98.72%	98.70%	98.65%	98.88%

Fig. 3. Simulations ran on an early version of the created dataset, 100 samples from each class, 30 used for training. Each simulation was run 100 times, and the worst and average accuracy values were shown. Each row uses the specified cutoff ratios while the columns show the different number of cycles for each cutoff ratio. Figure originally published in [12].

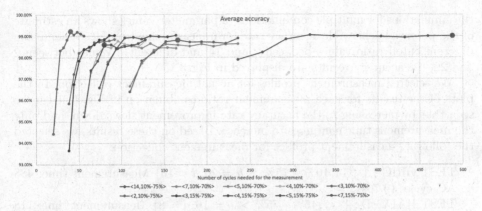

Fig. 4. Average simulation results plotted for each cutoff ratio set. The bigger markers show the measurement profiles chosen. The horizontal axis shows the number of cycles each measurement would take, assuming $d = 16$. The selected measurement profiles are shown with a bigger maker. Figure originally published in [12].

We introduce measurement profiles to generalize the measurement parameters and enable the search for possible optimal measurement matrix parameters. The measurement profile defines the measurement parameters and thus the measurement matrices' size. A measurement profile consists of the following values:

- r - the number of different cutoff ratios
- $percentage\_min$ - the minimal cutoff ratio
- $percentage\_max$ - the maximum cutoff ratio
- h - the number of cycles the AC signal is cut for each cutoff ratio
- d - the number of cycles where the AC signal is not modified between measuring with two cutoff ratios

The cutoff ratios are spaced evenly between $percentage\_min$ and $percentage\_max$. In this paper, measurement profiles are displayed in the following format:

$$\{< r, percentage\_min - percentage\_max >, h, d\} \qquad (4)$$

The required AC periods for a single measurement with a measurement profile can be calculated as follows:

$$N_{cycles} = h \cdot r + d \cdot (r - 1) \qquad (5)$$

We searched for optimal measurement profiles by analyzing the relationship between the amount of data collected within a single measurement and the classification accuracy. To that end, multiple submatrices were extracted from original measurements and used for classification. These extracted submatrices contained the data that the measurement profile would have recorded. (E.g., if $h = 10$, then only the first ten columns of the original matrices would be included.) Running the simulations for multiple combinations of parameter values shows an estimate of the potential achievable accuracy rate for a measurement profile. When using different cutoff ratio values between 2 and 14 and different h values between 2 and 20, the accuracy results are displayed in Fig. 3.

We selected measurement profiles for actual measurement collection. In the plots of the results for each measurement ratio combination in Fig. 4, it can be seen that by increasing h, the accuracy rate improvement slows down, and only the measurement time continues to increase. Based on these results, we selected the following measurement profiles for measurement collection:

- TEST_ORIG : $\{< 14, 10\% - 75\% >, h = 20, d = 16\}$ Measurement time: 488 AC cycles (9.76s)
- TEST_HALVED : $\{< 7, 15\% - 75\% >, h = 10, d = 8\}$ Measurement time: 118 AC cycles (2.36s)
- TEST_FOUR : $\{< 4, 15\% - 75\% >, h = 8, d = 4\}$ Measurement time: 44 AC cycles (0.88s)
- TEST_TINY : $\{< 2, 10\% - 75\% >, h = 12, d = 4\}$ Measurement time: 28 AC cycles (0.56s)

The above labels are used further in this paper to refer to the specified measurement profiles.

5 Measured Devices

A set of common household devices were measured with the Smart Plug prototype. Compared to the list of devices in [12], two additional devices were also measured, an LED Light Bulb and an LED Spotlight. The following list contains the labels used in the paper and the device description:

- ipad10W - A 10W Apple USB adapter for iPad
- usbapple5V1A - A 5W Apple USB adapter
- usb5V1A - A 5W generic USB adapter
- batterycharger4A - A four ampere "smart" lead-acid battery charger
- batterycharger800mA - An 800mA traditional lead-acid battery charger
- fan - A fan
- hairdryer - A hairdryer
- ledbulb - LED Light Bulb
- ledspotlight - LED-based spotlight
- incandescentbulb - An incandescent light bulb
- irlamp - An infrared heat lamp
- laptop - A laptop charger charging the laptop
- monitor - An LCD screen
- solderingiron - A soldering iron

At least 250 measurements were taken with every device for each measurement profile selected in Sect. 4. Examples of measurement matrices of the loads for the

TEST_ORIG and TEST_HALVED measurement profiles can be seen in Figs. 5 and 6.

Some electrical loads listed above are combined into one joint class as distinguishing between electrical loads of the same type is not needed. For electrical load recognition and control, the type of the load is the required information as, based on that, future grid load can be estimated, and the load can be turned off if required. A common *USB* class was created from ipad10W, usbapple5V1A, and usb5V1A. A common *incandescents* class was created from incandescentbulb and irlamp as the infrared heat lamp is also an incandescent lamp.

6   Classification Results

Several Neural Network-based classification methods were examined. The aim of examining different methods is to select the optimal classification method best suited for the computational capabilities and accuracy requirements of the problem.

The classification and evaluation methodology was the following: Of the 250 measurements collected for each measurement profile for each load, 150 were randomly selected for training the model, while the remaining samples were used for evaluating the model's performance after training. In the case of load classes containing more than one measured device (like USB), the 150 and 100 samples were selected evenly from the individual loads' measurements. The training and testing were repeated 100 times for each classification method and measurement profile. The average and worst accuracy rates were calculated along with the average of the individual confusion matrices.

6.1   FCNN

For the FCNN classification, the input was the power measurement matrix. Two hidden layers of neurons 128 and 64 were used with ReLU activation function before the final output layer with SoftMax activation function. The confusion matrices and accuracy rates are shown in Fig. 7 and a summary of the accuracy rates can be seen in Table 1.

We can see that the best accuracy rate is not achieved with the TEST_ORIG profile containing the most data. It is possibly due to the number of neurons which was the same for all four measurement profiles.

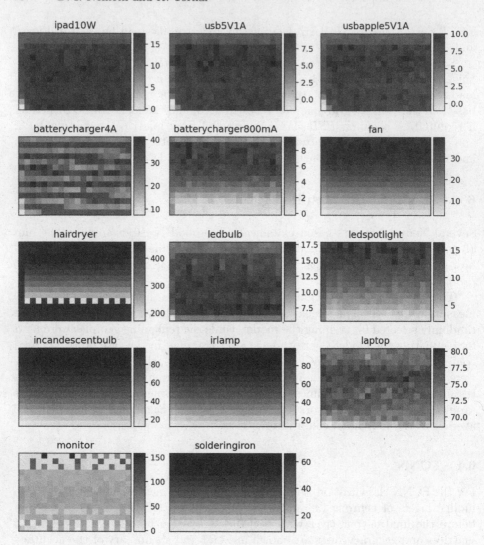

Fig. 5. Power measurement matrices measured with the TEST_ORIG profile.

Table 1. Summary of FCNN-based classification results.

Measurement profile	Average accuracy	Worst accuracy
TEST_ORIG	99.16%	98.00%
TEST_HALVED	99.53%	98.82%
TEST_FOUR	99.57%	98.82%
TEST_TINY	99.04%	95.00%

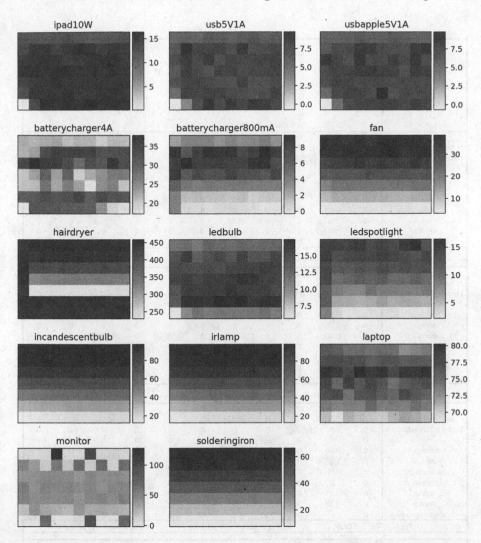

Fig. 6. Power measurement matrices measured with the TEST_HALVED profile.

6.2 RNN

A Long-Short Term Memory cell based Recurrent Neural Network was used for
the load classification. In their structure, long short-term memory Neural Networks differ from traditional Fully Connected networks. The input is not a vector
but a series of vectors for each stage of the LSTM network. The LSTM network's
structure makes it ideal for time-series data classification as the previous inputs
also affect the current stage. Considering the measurement matrices are special

	USB	batterycharger4A	batterycharger800mA	fan	hairdryer	ledbulb	ledspotlight	incandescents	laptop	monitor	solderingiron
USB	100	1.32	0	0	0	0	0	0	0	0.12	0
batterycharger4A	0	93.02	0	0	0	0	0	0	0.24	1.56	0
batterycharger800mA	0	0.01	100	0	0	0	0	0	0	0	0
fan	0	0.01	0	99.98	0	0	0	0.01	0	0.01	0.01
hairdryer	0	0.14	0	0	99.97	0	0	0	0.08	0	0
ledbulb	0	2.17	0	0	0	100	0	0	0	0.2	0
ledspotlight	0	0.01	0	0	0	0	100	0	0	0	0
incandescents	0	0.02	0	0	0	0	0	99.99	0	0	0
laptop	0	1.4	0	0	0.03	0	0	0	99.68	0	0
monitor	0	1.9	0	0	0	0	0	0	0	98.11	0
solderingiron	0	0	0	0.02	0	0	0	0	0	0	99.99
Profile: TEST_ORIG			**Average accuracy: 99.16%**				**Worst accuracy: 98.00%**			
USB	100	0.37	0	0	0	0	0	0	0	0.08	0
batterycharger4A	0	96.52	0	0	0	0	0	0	0.11	1.43	0
batterycharger800mA	0	0	100	0	0	0	0	0	0	0	0
fan	0	0	0	99.98	0	0	0	0	0	0	0
hairdryer	0	0.36	0	0	100	0	0	0	0.01	0	0
ledbulb	0	2.06	0	0	0	100	0	0	0	0	0
ledspotlight	0	0.02	0	0	0	0	100	0	0.01	0	0
incandescents	0	0.01	0	0	0	0	0	100	0	0.01	0
laptop	0	0.17	0	0	0	0	0	0	99.87	0	0
monitor	0	0.48	0	0	0	0	0	0	0	98.48	0
solderingiron	0	0.01	0	0.02	0	0	0	0	0	0	100
Profile: TEST_HALVED			**Average accuracy: 99.53%**				**Worst accuracy: 98.82%**			
USB	100	0.58	0	0	0	0	0	0	0	0.1	0
batterycharger4A	0	95.82	0	0	0.02	0	0	0	0.05	0.23	0
batterycharger800mA	0	0	100	0	0	0	0	0	0	0.02	0
fan	0	0	0	99.97	0	0	0	0	0	0.01	0.09
hairdryer	0	0.09	0	0	99.96	0	0	0	0	0	0
ledbulb	0	3.27	0	0	0	100	0	0	0	0	0
ledspotlight	0	0.02	0	0	0	0	100	0	0.02	0	0
incandescents	0	0	0	0	0	0	0	100	0	0	0
laptop	0	0.04	0	0	0.02	0	0	0	99.93	0	0
monitor	0	0.18	0	0	0	0	0	0	0	99.64	0
solderingiron	0	0	0	0.03	0	0	0	0	0	0	99.91
Profile: TEST_FOUR			**Average accuracy: 99.57%**				**Worst accuracy: 98.82%**			
USB	100	1.15	0	0	0	0	0	0	0	0.01	0
batterycharger4A	0	94.68	0	0	0	0.01	0	0	0.49	0.43	0
batterycharger800mA	0	0	100	0	0	0	0	0	0	0.1	0
fan	0	0	0	99.96	0	0	0	0	0	0	1.07
hairdryer	0	0	0	0	100	0	0	0	2.98	0	0
ledbulb	0	3.99	0	0	0	99.99	0	0	0.01	0.03	0
ledspotlight	0	0.03	0	0	0	0	100	0	0	0.06	0
incandescents	0	0.01	0	0	0	0	0	100	0	0	0
laptop	0	0	0	0	0	0	0	0	96.51	0	0
monitor	0	0.14	0	0	0	0	0	0	0.01	99.37	0
solderingiron	0	0	0	0.04	0	0	0	0	0	0	98.93
Profile: TEST_TINY			**Average accuracy: 99.04%**				**Worst accuracy: 95.00%**			

Fig. 7. Fully Connected Neural Network-based classification results. The confusion matrices are the averages of 100 runs. The worst and average accuracy rates are also shown.

	1	2	3	4	5	6	7	8	9	10	
15%	62.69	62.90	59.70	63.38	62.01	62.06	62.97	62.64	60.99	62.47	X(0)
25%	55.60	60.52	61.32	61.22	61.34	59.41	61.02	60.95	62.02	61.71	X(1)
35%	47.64	54.58	54.82	52.98	55.12	53.83	54.91	54.51	54.31	54.95	X(2)
45%	36.38	44.05	44.04	44.49	37.23	45.59	43.54	45.25	36.30	35.61	X(3)
55%	24.07	30.16	19.20	31.62	19.35	31.71	31.11	19.53	31.17	20.42	X(4)
65%	9.29	9.55	16.81	18.09	8.24	9.89	16.07	17.74	17.93	9.55	X(5)
75%	4.26	6.96	4.23	4.61	4.38	4.55	1.99	3.36	7.68	3.50	X(6)

Fig. 8. Extraction of row vectors from the measurement matrices. The example shows one measurement of the soldering iron with the TEST_HALVED profile. $X(r)$ shows the r-th input of the LSTM network.

time-series data as the matrix is filled in row-major order. Each row of measurements is the load's response to a different level of AC voltage signal manipulation. If we want to interpret the measurement matrix as the input of an LSTM network, there are two possibilities: using the row or column vectors as inputs. Row vectors resemble time-series data as they are in chronological order. After examining both options for the bigger measurement matrices (TEST_ORIG, TEST_HALVED), row vectors provided significantly better results than column vectors. The row vector extraction is also shown in Fig. 8. The LSTM classification results are shown in Fig. 9 and the summary of the accuracy rates can be seen in Table 2. For all measurement profiles, a 40-unit LSTM layer was used.

Table 2. Summary of LSTM-based RNN classification results.

Measurement profile	Average accuracy	Worst accuracy
TEST_ORIG	99.62%	98.73%
TEST_HALVED	99.61%	98.55%
TEST_FOUR	99.63%	99.09%
TEST_TINY	98.72%	89.73%

6.3 CNN

Convolutional Neural Networks are popular solutions in image processing tasks. As in the cases of the TEST_ORIG, TEST_HALVED, and TEST_FOUR measurement profile matrices, we can interpret the task at hand as an image processing task with a low-resolution input image. The inputs of the CNN were the

	USB	batterycharger4A	batterycharger800mA	fan	hairdryer	ledbulb	ledspotlight	incandescents	laptop	monitor	solderingiron
USB	100	0.02	0	0	0	0	0	0	0	0.27	0
batterycharger4A	0	99.68	0	0	0	0.01	0	0	0	1.55	0
batterycharger800mA	0	0	100	0	0	0	0	0	0	0.01	0
fan	0	0	0	100	0	0	0	0	0	0.12	0
hairdryer	0	0	0	0	99.69	0	0	0	0.12	0.15	0
ledbulb	0	0.09	0	0	0	99.99	0	0	0	0.2	0
ledspotlight	0	0	0	0	0	0	100	0	0	0.06	0
incandescents	0	0.07	0	0	0	0	0	100	0	0.36	0
laptop	0	0	0	0	0.31	0	0	0	99.88	0.37	0
monitor	0	0.11	0	0	0	0	0	0	0	96.58	0
solderingiron	0	0.03	0	0	0	0	0	0	0	0.33	100

Profile: TEST_ORIG   Average accuracy: 99.62%   Worst accuracy: 98.73%

	USB	batterycharger4A	batterycharger800mA	fan	hairdryer	ledbulb	ledspotlight	incandescents	laptop	monitor	solderingiron
USB	100	0	0	0	0	0	0	0	0	0.02	0
batterycharger4A	0	99.48	0	0	0	0	0	0	0.02	1.36	0
batterycharger800mA	0	0	100	0	0	0	0.01	0	0	0	0
fan	0	0	0	100	0	0	0	0	0	0.03	0
hairdryer	0	0.01	0	0	100	0	0	0	0.02	0.06	0
ledbulb	0	0.07	0	0	0	100	0	0	0	0.09	0
ledspotlight	0	0	0	0	0	0	99.99	0	0	0.11	0
incandescents	0	0.14	0	0	0	0	0	100	0	0.29	0
laptop	0	0	0	0	0	0	0	0	99.93	0.22	0
monitor	0	0.22	0	0	0	0	0	0	0.03	96.33	0
solderingiron	0	0.08	0	0	0	0	0	0	0	1.49	100

Profile: TEST_HALVED   Average accuracy: 99.61%   Worst accuracy: 98.55%

	USB	batterycharger4A	batterycharger800mA	fan	hairdryer	ledbulb	ledspotlight	incandescents	laptop	monitor	solderingiron
USB	100	0	0	0	0	0	0	0	0	0.02	0
batterycharger4A	0	99.48	0	0	0	0	0	0	0.02	1.36	0
batterycharger800mA	0	0	100	0	0	0	0.01	0	0	0	0
fan	0	0	0	100	0	0	0	0	0	0.03	0
hairdryer	0	0.01	0	0	100	0	0	0	0.02	0.06	0
ledbulb	0	0.07	0	0	0	100	0	0	0	0.09	0
ledspotlight	0	0	0	0	0	0	99.99	0	0	0.11	0
incandescents	0	0.14	0	0	0	0	0	100	0	0.29	0
laptop	0	0	0	0	0	0	0	0	99.93	0.22	0
monitor	0	0.22	0	0	0	0	0	0	0.03	96.33	0
solderingiron	0	0.08	0	0	0	0	0	0	0	1.49	100

Profile: TEST_FOUR   Average accuracy: 99.63%   Worst accuracy: 99.09%

	USB	batterycharger4A	batterycharger800mA	fan	hairdryer	ledbulb	ledspotlight	incandescents	laptop	monitor	solderingiron
USB	100	0.17	0	0	0	0	0	0	0	2.46	0
batterycharger4A	0	95.14	0	0	0	0	0	0	0.01	2.49	0
batterycharger800mA	0	0	100	0	0	0	0	0	0	0.02	0
fan	0	0	0	100	0	0	0	0	0	0.3	0
hairdryer	0	0	0	0	98.99	0	0	0	0	0.18	0
ledbulb	0	0.74	0	0	0	100	0	0	0	0.59	0
ledspotlight	0	0	0	0	0	0	100	0	0	0.57	0
incandescents	0	3.25	0	0	0	0	0	100	0.01	0.45	0
laptop	0	0.06	0	0	1.01	0	0	0	99.98	0.39	0
monitor	0	0.29	0	0	0	0	0	0	0	91.84	0
solderingiron	0	0.35	0	0	0	0	0	0	0	0.71	100

Profile: TEST_TINY   Average accuracy: 98.72%   Worst accuracy: 89.73%

Fig. 9. LSTM-based Recurrent Neural Network classification results. The confusion matrices are the averages of 100 runs. The worst and average accuracy rates are also shown.

	USB	batterycharger4A	batterycharger800mA	fan	hairdryer	ledbulb	ledspotlight	incandescents	laptop	monitor	solderingiron
USB	100	0	0	0	0	0	0	0	0	0.23	0
batterycharger4A	0	99.93	0	0	0.01	0	0	0	0	0.02	0
batterycharger800mA	0	0	100	0	0	0	0	0	0	0	0
fan	0	0	0	100	0	0	0	0	0	0	0
hairdryer	0	0	0	0	99.92	0	0	0	0	0	0
ledbulb	0	0.03	0	0	0	100	0	0	0	0.08	0
ledspotlight	0	0	0	0	0	0	100	0	0	0	0
incandescents	0	0	0	0	0	0	0	100	0	0	0
laptop	0	0	0	0	0.07	0	0	0	100	0	0
monitor	0	0.04	0	0	0	0	0	0	0	99.67	0
solderingiron	0	0	0	0	0	0	0	0	0	0	100

Profile: TEST_ORIG   Average accuracy: 99.96%   Worst accuracy: 99.73%

	USB	batterycharger4A	batterycharger800mA	fan	hairdryer	ledbulb	ledspotlight	incandescents	laptop	monitor	solderingiron
USB	100	0	0	0	0	0	0	0	0	0	0
batterycharger4A	0	99.98	0	0	0	0	0	0	0	0	0
batterycharger800mA	0	0	100	0	0	0	0	0	0	0	0
fan	0	0	0	100	0	0	0	0	0	0	0
hairdryer	0	0	0	0	99.89	0	0	0	0	0	0
ledbulb	0	0	0	0	0	100	0	0	0	0	0
ledspotlight	0	0	0	0	0	0	100	0	0	0	0
incandescents	0	0	0	0	0.02	0	0	100	0	0	0
laptop	0	0	0	0	0.09	0	0	0	100	0	0
monitor	0	0.02	0	0	0	0	0	0	0	100	0
solderingiron	0	0	0	0	0	0	0	0	0	0	100

Profile: TEST_HALVED   Average accuracy: 99.99%   Worst accuracy: 99.82%

	USB	batterycharger4A	batterycharger800mA	fan	hairdryer	ledbulb	ledspotlight	incandescents	laptop	monitor	solderingiron
USB	100	0.01	0	0	0	0	0	0	0	0	0
batterycharger4A	0	99.9	0	0	0.01	0	0	0	0.07	0	0
batterycharger800mA	0	0	100	0	0	0	0	0	0	0	0
fan	0	0	0	100	0	0	0	0	0	0	0
hairdryer	0	0	0	0	98.76	0	0	0.01	0.04	0	0
ledbulb	0	0.04	0	0	0	100	0	0	0	0	0
ledspotlight	0	0	0	0	0	0	100	0	0	0	0
incandescents	0	0	0	0	1.01	0	0	99.99	0	0.01	0
laptop	0	0	0	0	0.22	0	0	0	99.89	0	0
monitor	0	0.05	0	0	0	0	0	0	0	99.99	0
solderingiron	0	0	0	0	0	0	0	0	0	0	100

Profile: TEST_FOUR   Average accuracy: 99.87%   Worst accuracy: 90.82%

Fig. 10. Convolutional Neural Network-based classification results. The confusion matrices are the averages of 100 runs. The worst and average accuracy rates are also shown.

three measurement matrices: Power, Current, and the Voltage matrix divided by 230. Two convolutional layers with 3×3 kernels were used with 40 and 20 channels, followed by one hidden, fully connected layer with 20 neurons before the final layer. Between the convolutional and fully connected layers, SoftMax provided normalization was used. The network's size is significantly smaller than the one used in [12], and a sixfold reduction of trainable parameters was achieved. Figure 10 shows the confusion matrices and the classification results. A summary of the accuracy rates can be seen in Table 3. The CNN-based classification results are the best of the three NN-based methods examined.

Table 3. Summary of CNN-based classification results.

Measurement profile	Average accuracy	Worst accuracy
TEST_ORIG	99.96%	99.73%
TEST_HALVED	99.99%	99.82%
TEST_FOUR	99.87%	90.82%

7   On-Device Electrical Load Classification

7.1   TinyML – Machine Learning on Microcontrollers

TinyML is a relatively new topic. Training and running the inference of Neural Networks requires significant computational capabilities and thus is traditionally run on computers with powerful CPUs and GPUs. The recent advancements in low-power machine learning solutions such as for smartphones and the increased computational capabilities of microcontrollers paved the way for machine learning on microcontrollers.

In [5], several benefits of TinyML are presented. The large amount of sensor data generated on the device can fully be processed, so data which previously could not be transmitted due to bandwidth or cloud-side processing limitations can be used. Data usage reduction can offer huge cost savings both on the server side and on the transmission side as well. The required network bandwidth is also reduced which can be beneficial both in terms of power usage and network congestion especially if there are a large number of IoT devices on the network. The data that is transmitted to the cloud is of less sensitive nature which means that the consequences of that data being captured by a third-party are less severe. In safety critical systems such as in healthcare or autonomous vehicles, the latency of cloud-based ML is unacceptable and can have serious consequences. TinyML offers independence from network communication and eliminates the latency caused by communicating with a remote server. An other advantage is increased reliability. If the cloud-provided services are offline, this impacts the IoT devices running in different households. TinyML solutions have increased independence from the cloud-based parts of the system and if designed correctly, can function even without those services. TinyML can operate even in remote areas where there is no network connectivity. TinyML can also enhance the energy efficiency of the system as some cases, the power used for transmitting the data is more than the power required for the microcontroller to run the classification. If data processing is done on the IoT device, then transmitting irrelevant data can be avoided. An example given in [5] is a surveillance system used to detect anomalies. Most frames captured by the cameras contain no relevant information, so sending them to the server would be a waste of network bandwidth.

7.2   Smart Plug with TinyML Capabilities

Running the electrical load classification on the Smart Plug offers several benefits. Network traffic can be reduced as sending the raw measurement over WiFi
is not required. It also reduces WiFi congestion and wireless radio usage, which
reduces power consumption. Running the classification on-device also improves
system reliability since the Smart Plug does not rely on a central infrastructure
for load classification to work. Server-side infrastructure requirements are also
reduced.

Considering the edge computing scenario, we designed the new Smart Plug
around an ESP32 board featuring a 4MB PSRAM module to ensure there is
enough memory for the NN inference. On the ESP32, we used TensorFlow Lite
Micro [4] (TFLite Micro), a popular library for running exported TensorFlow
Lite [1] models on microcontrollers. The structure of the TFLite Micro library
is modular, allowing vendors to provide optimized versions of certain operations, thus optimizing the NN inference speed. Espressif, the manufacturer of
the ESP32 board, offers such an optimized version of the TFLite Micro library,
and we used that version [7]. Unfortunately, LSTM support in TFLite Micro
is still in progress at the time of writing this paper, but the FCNN and CNN
models were evaluated on the microcontroller.

We were interested mainly in the inference times and model sizes as those
impact the system's performance the most. TFLite Micro requires the model to
be loaded into memory, so the model has to fit both into the flash storage of
the ESP32 as well as to the memory. The file copy time from flash to memory
impacts the startup time of the Smart Plug. The model files were stored in the
SPI Flash FileSystem (SPIFFS) partition of the flash.

The model loading and NN inference times for the FCNN and CNN models
are shown in Tables 4 and 5. The achievable classification accuracy results from
Sect. 6 are plotted for each examined NN model in Fig. 11. We can see that the
CNN-based methods' increased accuracy comes at the cost of a much longer
inference time, but the inference times are still significantly shorter than the
time required for the measurement. Table 6 summarizes the total time requirements for each model examined. If we take into account the combined total
classification time (measurement and NN inference), then we can see in Fig. 12
that the optimal method in terms of accuracy and time requirement seems to
be the TEST_HALVED measurement profile with CNN classification method.
In 2.431s, the Smart Plug can run the measurement and the CNN inference and
thus accurately determine the type of electrical load connected.

Table 4. Performance of FCNN classification on the Smart Plug.

Measurement profile	Model input size	Model size	File load time	Inference time
TEST_ORIG	14×20	182 KB	2985 ms	20 ms
TEST_HALVED	7×10	74 KB	1277 ms	7 ms
TEST_FOUR	4×8	55 KB	900 ms	5 ms
TEST_TINY	2×12	51 KB	833 ms	5 ms

Table 5. Performance of CNN classification on the Smart Plug.

Measurement profile	Model input size	Model size	File load time	Inference time
TEST_ORIG	$14 \times 20 \times 3$	383 KB	6287 ms	272 ms
TEST_HALVED	$7 \times 10 \times 3$	101 KB	1722 ms	72 ms
TEST_FOUR	$4 \times 8 \times 3$	57 KB	991 ms	20 ms

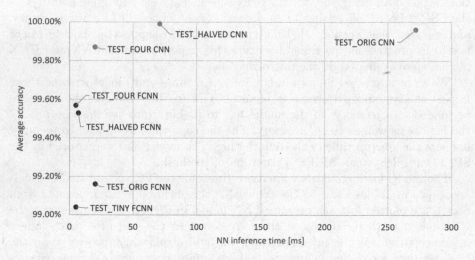

Fig. 11. Plot of average classification accuracy scores and on-device inference times for the different NN models examined.

Table 6. Total classification (measurement and NN inference) time requirements of each NN model.

Measurement profile	Measurement time	NN type	Inference time	Total time
TEST_ORIG	9760 ms	CNN	272 ms	10032 ms
		FCNN	20 ms	9780 ms
TEST_HALVED	2360 ms	CNN	71 ms	2431 ms
		FCNN	7 ms	2367 ms
TEST_FOUR	880 ms	CNN	20 ms	900 ms
		FCNN	5 ms	885 ms
TEST_TINY	560 ms	FCNN	5 ms	565 ms

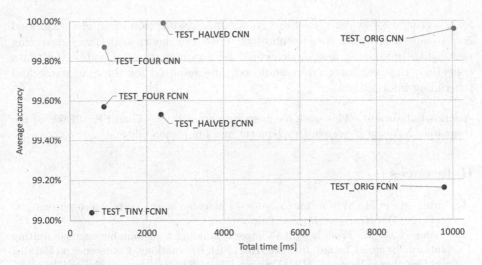

Fig. 12. Plot of average classification accuracy scores and total on-device load classification (measurement and NN inference) time.

8 Conclusions and Future Work

In this paper, we presented a fast method for electrical load classification. The Smart Plug prototype measures the response of the connected electrical load to manipulating its voltage supply signal. We have shown that within 10 s, it is possible to take measurements and classify the load connected with above 99.9% accuracy. With the TEST_HALVED measurement profile and Convolutional Neural Network-based classification, 99.99% accuracy is possible on-device within 2.5 s. With such a system, the Smart Grid can quickly react to the changing load and estimate future grid load. With the Smart Plug, control of the load is also possible, so the grid load can be controlled if a temporary shutdown of the load is allowed. Compared to our previous results in [12], we presented a new prototype device that is capable of running the classification on-device. New measurement data were collected as well, and two new electrical loads were added. Current Smart Plugs on the market lack load detection capabilities and the load classification methods presented in the literature either require long measurement times (time-series data) or require a desktop-performance computer for load classification and; thus, fast on-device classification is not possible. The Smart Plug we presented solves these problems and offers an accurate method to correctly detect the type of electrical load within just a few seconds.

8.1 Future Work

In the future, we plan on measuring new electrical loads. In addition, NN-based Open Set recognition methods will be examined. Detecting a previously unseen load is crucial for system reliability as the misclassification of an electrical load could lead to errors in load estimation. With the device capable of detecting new loads, profiling a new device could be automated. After automated data collection, the user interaction would only be required for the load name and scheduling information.

Acknowledgement. This work has been supported by the Fund FK 137 608 of the Hungarian National Research, Development and Innovation Office.

References

1. Abadi, M., et al.: TensorFlow: large-scale machine learning on heterogeneous systems (2015). https://www.tensorflow.org/
2. Chang, X., et al.: From insight to impact: building a sustainable edge computing platform for smart homes. In: 2018 IEEE 24th International Conference on Parallel and Distributed Systems (ICPADS), pp. 928–936 (2018). https://doi.org/10.1109/PADSW.2018.8644647
3. da S. Veloso, A.F., de Oliveira, R.G., Rodrigues, A.A., Rabelo, R.A.L., Rodrigues, J.J.P.C.: Cognitive smart plugs for signature identification of residential home appliance load using machine learning: from theory to practice. In: 2019 IEEE International Conference on Communications Workshops (ICC Workshops), pp. 1–6 (2019)
4. David, R., et al.: Tensorflow lite micro: embedded machine learning for tinyml systems. In: Smola, A., Dimakis, A., Stoica, I. (eds.) Proceedings of Machine Learning and Systems, vol. 3, pp. 800–811 (2021). https://proceedings.mlsys.org/paper/2021/file/d2ddea18f00665ce8623e36bd4e3c7c5-Paper.pdf
5. Dutta, D.L., Bharali, S.: Tinyml meets IoT: a comprehensive survey. Internet Things **16**, 100461 (2021)
6. Espressif Systems: Esp32. https://www.espressif.com/en/products/socs/esp32
7. Espressif Systems: Optimised neural network functions for espressif chipsets. https://github.com/espressif/esp-nn
8. Gomes, L., Sousa, F., Vale, Z.: An intelligent smart plug with shared knowledge capabilities. Sensors **18**(11), 3961 (2018). https://doi.org/10.3390/s18113961
9. Jaradat, M., Jarrah, M., Jararweh, Y., Al-Ayyoub, M., Bousselham, A.: Integration of renewable energy in demand-side management for home appliances. In: 2014 International Renewable and Sustainable Energy Conference (IRSEC), pp. 571–576 (2014)
10. Mtshali, P., Khubisa, F.: A smart home appliance control system for physically disabled people. In: 2019 Conference on Information Communications Technology and Society (ICTAS), pp. 1–5 (2019)
11. Murshed, M.G.S., Murphy, C., Hou, D., Khan, N., Ananthanarayanan, G., Hussain, F.: Machine learning at the network edge: a survey. ACM Comput. Surv. **54**(8) (2021). https://doi.org/10.1145/3469029
12. Németh., D., Tornai., K.: SP4LC: a method for recognizing power consumers in a smart plug. In: Proceedings of the 11th International Conference on Smart Cities and Green ICT Systems - SMARTGREENS, pp. 69–77. INSTICC, SciTePress (2022). https://doi.org/10.5220/0010982800003203

13. Petrović, T., Morikawa, H.: Active sensing approach to electrical load classification by smart plug. In: 2017 IEEE Power Energy Society Innovative Smart Grid Technologies Conference (ISGT), pp. 1–5 (2017)
14. Raspberry Pi Foundation: RP2040. https://www.raspberrypi.com/products/rp2040/
15. Ridi, A., Gisler, C., Hennebert, J.: A survey on intrusive load monitoring for appliance recognition. In: 2014 22nd International Conference on Pattern Recognition, pp. 3702–3707 (2014)

Vehicle Technology and Intelligent Transport Systems

Solving the Dial-a-Ride Problem for Railway Traffic by Means of Heuristics

Christoph Grüne[1]([✉]) [iD] and Stephan Zieger[2]([✉]) [iD]

[1] Department of Computer Science, RWTH Aachen University, Aachen, Germany
gruene@algo.rwth-aachen.de
[2] Institute of Transport Science, RWTH Aachen University, Aachen, Germany
zieger@via.rwth-aachen.de

Abstract. Railway services in many rural areas were scaled down or suspended, in the 1960s and 1970s. Nowadays, the accessibility and availability of public transport in the countryside is becoming more important again. As demand in rural areas is very dispersed, both temporal and spatial, demand-responsive transport services with small highly automated trains are a possible solution. The basic idea of the classic Dial-a-Ride Problem (DARP) is used and extended to the railway system.

The extension of the DARP is then denoted as Dial-a-Ride Problem for Railway Traffic (DARPRT). In the DARPRT, railway vehicles serve transportation requests of passengers who specify their pickup and delivery location and time windows in a rail network. The goal is to optimize schedule, routing and energy management of trains to serve all passenger requests under a set of constraints. Thus, the main addition of the DARPRT to the classical DARP are the rail infrastructure constraints, e.g. headway and dwell times of the trains.

Based on a brief complexity analysis which shows hardness for this problem, an algorithmic framework is developed. This framework is implemented as a multi-level insertion heuristic considering the different aspects of the problem in a hierarchical order. Subproblems with a higher impact, such as scheduling, are solved first, while subproblems with lower impact on the solution, such as routing, are solved last.

The heuristic is evaluated in a computational study on generated instances based on real partially abandoned railway networks in rural areas. The feasibility study shows the general applicability of the methods under mild assumptions. Furthermore, possible improvements are discussed.

Keywords: Dial-a-Ride Problem · Railway Traffic · Insertion Heuristic · Timetabling · Railway Scheduling · Rural Railway Networks

1 Introduction

In many countries with long-standing rail systems, some rural railway lines have been discontinued [29] or are threatened by decommissioning [10] due to political decisions

This work is funded by the Deutsche Forschungsgemeinschaft (DFG, German Research Foundation) — 2236/1. Simulations were performed with computing resources granted by RWTH Aachen University under project 4178.

C. Klein et al. (Eds.): SMARTGREENS 2022/VEHITS 2022, CCIS 1843, pp. 93–133, 2023.
https://doi.org/10.1007/978-3-031-37470-8_5

and economic constraints. On the one hand, there is the question of the economic viability of some of these lines, but on the other hand, in the "Year of the Rail" (2021) proclaimed by the European Union [9], there has been a lot of political attention to realize possibilities for reactivation or continued operation. Besides environmental aspects, accessibility and availability of public transport in rural areas play a major role. In addition, traffic from rural areas is a major congestion generator in the neighboring cities.

One possibility to tackle the challenge is the implementation of demand-responsive operation by highly automated small rail vehicles. Vehicle concepts for these have been proposed by Schlaht et al. [27] and Schindler [26]. The idea of demand-responsive transport is currently solely used for rubber-tyred systems. In both cases, the process involves collecting requests from passengers and calculating a timetable based on them considering a set of constraints. The railway vehicles should have at least Grade of Automation (GoA) Level 3, preferably Level 4 [28] which means that most or all of the operations are automatized. This has two advantages. On the one hand, the use of personnel is reduced or obsolete, which makes up a large proportion of costs, especially on railway lines with low revenues. On the other hand, crew scheduling aspects, which are complex in the case of constantly changing timetables, are avoided.

With the help of suitable communication technology, conventional external signaling can be dispensed and the vehicles can also move by means of a virtual moving block. In fact, one such model is currently being tested in a trial phase in France under the name *Taxirail* [1, 10] and under review in Germany under the acronym *JuLiA* [15]. There are many related challenges such as technical implementation, economic efficiency or passenger related benefit estimation which are partly answered by Zieger and Nießen [31] as well as Ritzer et al. [25]. In the context of the paper, we will focus exclusively on the algorithmic piece in the complex puzzle.

The paper examines the underlying transportation problem and its complexity in detail. One natural approach for the mathematical handling is using the Dial-a-Ride Problem (DARP) as a basis. The DARP is a problem in the realm of Pickup and Delivery Problems (PDP), whereby mostly passengers are transported. Furthermore, the DARP can be categorized into the area of Vehicle-Routing-Problems (VRP), in which the routing of vehicles is optimized subject to certain constraints.

The DARP consists of a graph $G = (V, A)$, k vehicles and p passengers that want to be transported from a point $a_i \in V(G)$ to a point $b_i \in V(G)$, for $1 \leq i \leq p$, in the network G. If passengers also have the possibility to choose a time window for the departure or arrival in the considered time horizon T', the problem is referred to as the Dial-a-Ride Problem with Time Windows (DARPTW) in the literature. The aim is to minimize a set of objective functions relating to vehicles and/or passengers, such as traveling time of vehicles, waiting time of passengers or traveling time of passengers.

In this paper, we focus on the Dial-a-Ride Problem for Railway Traffic (DARPRT), which is a generalization of DARPTW. That is, the vehicles considered are trains that are routed over a railway network. In contrast to rubber-tyred DARPs, the degrees of freedom are lower but interdependencies are higher due to the signalling and routing constraints. These establish further constraints such as the need for spatial separation of trains, i.e. headway times. In the scope of the paper, only double-track systems are assumed which helps in designing the algorithms, but needs to be extended in the future to allow for single-track sections as well. Furthermore, boarding the vehicles is only allowed at specific stations and a dwell time for boarding and alighting is given. Moreover, the DARPRT introduces operational constraints such as limited access to energy for trains (fuel tank, battery) such that they have to recharge their energy supplies, which may be only possible at specific stations as well with a minimum recharging time. As the recharging processes vary between simply changing a battery and classical refuelling, the model allows for automated recharging while passengers are on board.

Related Work. In contrast to the classical railway planning procedure (demand estimation, line planning, timetabling, platform and track assignment, rolling stock planning, crew scheduling, shunting and maintenance planning) [11], the focus in this setting is on the passengers and their travel demands. That is, the whole planning procedure reacts adaptively on the passenger demands and needs to be performed dynamically. The classical DARP provides the framework for a rather bottom-up instead of a top-down approach and attracted much attention as it is a basic problem on which many derived applications rely, e.g. taxi, medical transport or meals on wheels. Hence, much related work can be found as it is an extensively studied area. Cordeau and Laporte [6,8] gave an overview on the underlying model and its variations as well as known algorithms for the DARP. A more recent literature review on the DARP was performed by Molenbruch et al. [22].

One of the first algorithmic contributions was developed by Psaraftis [23]; it is a dynamic program which solves the DARP for single vehicles exactly. Jaw et al., [17] introduced an insertion heuristic for the DARP. Based on this Madsen et al. [19] built up the REBUS framework for firefighting departments. In the further process, the surveyed DARP variants got more complex concerning the constraints and objective functions. Therefore, e.g. Cordeau and Laporte [7] introduced a tabu search for multi-objective DARP which was refined by Berbeglia et al. [2].

Additionally, there are many search heuristic approaches to solve the DARP and its variants. Recent contributions are from Jain et al. [16] and Gschwind et al. [13] who introduce a large-scale neighborhood search. Moreover, a genetic search approach was provided by Jorgensen et al. [18]. Further search heuristic contributions that specialize on the energy constraint of such problems were developed. One recent work by Masmoudi et al. [21] considers the DARP with electric vehicles and battery swapping stations.

Besides the offline problem in which the requests is known beforehand, the online variant is an important practical problem as well. In a practical setting, it is possible that passengers want to be included ad-hoc and on-demand into an existing schedule. For example in taxi settings, the passenger calls the taxi office and a taxi is routed to the passenger while it possibly transports further passengers. This variant was already algorithmically examined by Psaraftis [23]. Furthermore, Xin and Ma [3] investigated the online competitiveness of the problem as well.

The Dial-a-Ride idea in the railway setting has not gained a lot of research attention yet. Cats and Haverkamp [4,5] examine the effect of implementing automated demand-responsive operation in mainline traffic with a macroscopic model. With it, they research the optimal station and line capacity and find that the line capacity becomes much more crucial in contrast to conventional operation. More recently, two optimization approaches have been proposed by Zieger and Nießen [30] as well as Grüne and Zieger [12]. The former uses the ideas of a network flow problem while the latter relies on time-expanded network graphs with tracker variables. Both approaches only allow for limited number of vehicles and passengers such that for real-world implementations a faster solution with approximations is necessary. Such a simulation framework has been presented by Zieger and Nießen [32], but the approach does neither include a complexity analysis of the problem nor the energy management aspect. The energy management is also omitted by Ritzer et al. [24] who focus specifically on one region and tailor their algorithms accordingly. To the best of the authors knowledge, these are the only sources dealing with the DARPRT.

Contribution. The DARPRT is thus a novel and highly relevant problem, especially with the underlying combination of scheduling, energy management and routing. Specifically, the inclusion of railway infrastructure constraints, such as deadlock prevention and headway time, into a DARP has only been studied recently.

This paper examines the offline version of the problem. Thus, full knowledge about the problem is given, i.e. the passenger requests are known upfront. We restrict the problem to subdivided trees as railway network which is a common infrastructure layout in rural areas, however, with the restriction of double-track sections. The subdivision of the paths between the stations represents the block structure of the signaling system. Therefore, most of the instances can be processed by our heuristic, while providing adequate structure for solving the instances faster.

Furthermore, the paper adds a complexity analysis for the DARPRT and presents algorithms in much more detail for solving the DARPRT. We prove that the DARPRT (with fixed time horizon) is NP-hard and not approximable within polynomial time. Thus a heuristical approach is the most promising approach to solve real-world instances with many passenger requests.

The proposed algorithm is a (randomized) hierarchical multi-stage insertion heuristic. The stages of the heuristic are the partitioning and scheduling of passengers on trains, the insertion of charging stops for the energy management and the routing of the trains on the railway infrastructure. For this, we combine several techniques and algorithms to develop the heuristical framework. The charging stop insertion encoded in an improvement graph such that a modified shortest path algorithm finds an optimal solution on a given schedule. The routing is solved by a heuristical threshold algorithm.

Furthermore, the insertion heuristic enables handling the online version of the problem in general as it allows inserting passengers one after another by definition. Thus, the heuristical framework is usable as black-box framework for decision support tools and infrastructure evaluations. The computational study also shows that medium instances (70 passengers) can be evaluated on a single node computer. The parallelization of the framework, however, enables processing a higher number of passenger requests as well.

Paper Outline. In Sect. 2, we start with a precise definition of the DARPRT and classify the problem with a short complexity analysis in Sect. 3. Based on the complexity analysis, we develop algorithms solving the DARPRT, which we describe and analyze in Sect. 4. We evaluate the corresponding results in a computational study in Sect. 5. Finally, we conclude the paper by summarizing the results in Sect. 6.

2 Problem Definition and Notation

The DARPRT problem has many different mathematical objects as input. We derive the notation and the parameters from the practical setting by analyzing the infrastructure and the necessary parameters of the trains. We begin with the analysis of the railway infrastructure. Thereby, the railway infrastructure is modeled based on a mesoscopic view as a graph.

Railway Infrastructure. The railway infrastructure consists of many components and dependencies which makes it complex to concept and operate. To allow for abstraction the infrastructure can be modelled with different granularity. A more detailed view of an exemplary infrastructure is depicted in Fig. 1. The important components are the depot, stations and lines connecting the stations and the depot. Switches are modelled as well. However, this view can be made more detailed by modelling exact signal or train stop positions and further components into the microscopic view.

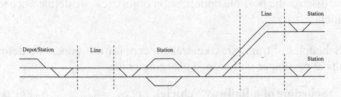

Fig. 1. Rail infrastructure with four stations and double-track lines in between.

In the context of the paper, less abstraction as in a macroscopic model would not be sufficient for the proposed algorithms in the scope of a feasibility study. The lines are subdivided by blocks. We, therefore, use a mesoscopic view on the rail infrastructure. Thus, mathematically speaking, we solely focus on the DARPRT on graphs that are subdivided directed trees with forward and backward arcs. The railway system is a double-track railway system. The exemplary railway infrastructure from Fig. 1 is rendered into the infrastructure in Fig. 2. In this figure, the black vertex is the depot D, the gray vertices are stations S and the white vertices are points $V \setminus S$ at which passengers cannot board or alight any train. The subdivision of the tree models the block structure of the signalling system. Only one train can be inside one block at a time. Thus, the blocks have a sufficient size to always ensure enough headway time and the location of the trains are always accurately defined, which is a necessity for the routing algorithms.

Problem Input Definition. The input to the DARPRT is (1) a directed graph $G = (V, S, E, D, A, (\ell_a)_{a \in A}, (f_a)_{a \in A})$ with vertices V and arcs A, where $S \subseteq V$ are train stations, $E \subseteq V$ are energy charging points, $D \in E$ is the depot, $\ell : A \to \mathbb{N}_0$ is the travel time function and $f : A \to \mathbb{N}_0$ is the energy consumption function. The direction of an arc defines the possible travel direction on the corresponding track. Further input is (2) a time horizon T' (encoded in unary or constant). Moreover, we have (3) a set $P = \{1, \ldots, p\}$ of passengers, each of them has (4) a demand $D_p = (s_1, s_2) \in S^2$

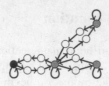

Fig. 2. The subdivided directed path with forward and backward arcs modeling the infrastructure from Fig. 1.

with start station s_1 and end station s_2 and (5) a time window $W_p \in T'^2 \times S$ corresponding where $s \in S$ denotes the station according to the time window. Then, we have (6) a set $R = \{1, \ldots, r\}$ of trains whereby each of them has (7) a vehicle capacity $(c_r)_{r \in R} \in \mathbb{N}_0^R$ and (8) an energy capacity $(e_r)_{r \in R} \in \mathbb{N}_0^R$. At last, there are parameters (9) w_{dwell}, which is the dwell time for dwelling at a train station, and (10) w_{charge}, which is the necessary time to charge energy; for the sake of simplicity, both are assumed to be constant.

Before we discuss the possible optimization objectives, we define a schedule S_r for a railway vehicle r.

Schedules. Schedules of trains are a central concept for this paper. We define these by a tuple of halts at passenger stations and charging points.

Definition 1 (Schedule of a Railway Vehicle). *Let $S_r = (h_1, \ldots, h_n)$ be the schedule of railway vehicle r, with $h_1, \ldots, h_n \in E \cup S$. A halt h_i can be a charging point if $h_i \in E$ and r recharges at h_i or a passenger station if $h_i \in S$ and r halts for passengers. If h_i is a charging point and a passenger station vehicle r has to wait the maximum of w_{dwell} and w_{charge}.*

Optimization Criteria and Constraints. The objective of the DARPRT is to minimize a weighted sum of the total travelling time of vehicles (TTTV) or the total travelling time of passengers (TTTP).

(i) *Total Traveling Time of Vehicles (TTTV) - the sum of the usage time for every vehicle.* Formally, let $S_r = (h_1, \ldots, h_{n_r})$ be the schedule for railway vehicle $r \in R$:

$$TTTV = \sum_{j=1}^{r} \sum_{i=1}^{n_r-1} \left(\ell(h_i, h_{i+1}) + \begin{cases} w_{dwell}, & \text{if } h_i \text{ is passenger station} \\ w_{charge}, & \text{if } h_i \text{ is charging point} \end{cases} \right)$$

(ii) *Total Traveling Time of Passengers (TTTP) - the sum of the time needed to travel from the start station to the destination station over all passengers.* Formally, let $S_r = (h_1, \ldots, h_{n_r})$ be the schedule for railway vehicle r and $P_i^{\#}$ the number of passengers at station in railway vehicle r at h_i:

$$TTTP = \sum_{j=1}^{r} \sum_{i=1}^{n_r-1} P_i^{\#} \cdot \left(\ell(h_i, h_{i+1}) + \begin{cases} w_{dwell}, & \text{if } h_i \text{ is passenger station} \\ w_{charge}, & \text{if } h_i \text{ is charging point} \end{cases} \right)$$

The optimization criteria are optimized subject to the following set of constraints. First, we have passenger constraints. (a) All passengers arrive at their destinations without violating the time windows and (b) have w_{dwell} time steps to board and alight. (c) The number of passengers for the trains does not exceed their capacity $(c_r)_{r \in R}$ for all points in time. Furthermore, (d) the passengers are allowed to use only one train on their journey. This is motivated by the complexity of the algorithms and resulting passenger dissatisfaction if changing of vehicles within their journey is included. Then, we have energy constraints. (e) No train runs out of energy, (f) the energy charging procedure needs w_{charge} time steps, charges the train completely and the train is chargeable only at charging stations. At last, we have further train and routing constraints. (g) The timetable is conflict-free and trains comply with the designated headway time at all time stamps, that is, no two trains use the same arc at the same time with the exception that (h) arbitrarily many trains may dwell at one station. Finally, (i) all schedules start and end at the depot.

3   Complexity of DARPRT

We briefly analyze the complexity of the DARPRT. For this, we first show that the decision variant of the DARPRT is in NP.

Theorem 1. *The decision variant of the DARPRT is in NP.*

Proof. The DARPRT solution can be encoded as a partition of passengers over trains. This can be done by a mapping from the trains to the passenger set, which is clearly at most linear in the size of the input. Furthermore, the schedule for each train can be encoded by an ordering of the passengers in the train, which is linear in the number of passengers. At last, the route of the train over time and space has to be encoded. This can be done by an ordered list of pairs containing the arc which is traveled and the time stamp at which it is traveled. Furthermore, we store in the route when the train dwells to let passengers board or alight. This is linear in the number of time stamps, too.

Thus, we have a certificate for every instance which is at most polynomial in the size of the input. Furthermore, we can check the certificate in polynomial time. First, we check that the partition is a correct partition. Following, we check the feasibility of the schedules. At last, we check the connectivity and feasibility of the routes and that the schedule is correctly mapped into the route. This is doable by iterating over the partition, the schedules and the routes, which is in polynomial time in length of the certificate. Therefore, the decision variant of the DARPRT is in NP.

Secondly, we show the hardness of the problem for which we survey the hardness on a subset of constraints.

Lemma 1. *The DARPRT on paths restricted only to the ride-sharing constraint and TTTV as optimization criterion is NP-hard.*

Proof. Guan [14] proved the NP-hardness of routing one vehicle with capacity greater than one on a path via reduction from 2/3-SAT. To provide a reduction, we use the reduction of [14] to encode the 2/3-SAT instance into a DARPRT instance. Furthermore, all DARPRT constraints can be relaxed such that only one train is used and only the vehicle capacity constraint is used together with the normal DARP constraints. That is, DARPRT is simply a generalization to the routing of one vehicle with passenger capacity greater than one.

The implications of the analysis on the DARPRT problem can be summarized in the following theorems.

Theorem 2. *The DARPRT on paths, trees and general graphs is NP-complete.*

Proof. The restricted problem routing one vehicle with passenger capacity greater than one is already NP-hard. DARPRT on paths, on trees and on general graphs are a generalization of it. The completeness follows from Theorem 1.

The following theorem provides a stronger statement on the hardness of the DARPRT. It also shows that solutions to the DARPRT are not efficiently computable in general.

Theorem 3. *If $P \neq NP$, then DARPRT on paths is not polynomially time approximable within a polynomial factor.*

Proof. Suppose there is a polynomial time $poly(n)$-approximation algorithm for DARPRT with approximation factor p. Then, we can decide arbitrary 2/3-SAT instances in polynomial time with the following family of DARPRT instances. Consider the reduction of Lemma 1. Instead of defining the reduction over the length of the arcs, we can use the energy consumption over the arcs. Let F be the instance family defined by the reduction from 2/3-SAT.

First, we add a new vertex d in front of vertex s_0 as new depot. The arc length of (d, s_0) and (s_0, d) are set to 0. We further redefine all other arcs by setting the length to be 0 and set the energy consumption to 1. Thus, every route, optimal or not, has a length of exactly 0 corresponding to the total traveling time vehicles.

In conclusion, the approximation algorithm has to decide whether the energy constraint is satisfied or not, which is as hard as solving 2/3-SAT, while the approximation does not yield any simplification as the length of all possible routes is 0. Thus, we have $P = NP$ if there is an algorithm which guarantees any approximation factor which is polynomial in the input. This is a contradiction.

4   Algorithms

We use a hierarchical structure to introduce an insertion heuristic which finds an (optimized) solution that may be randomized as well. The hierarchical structure consists of a partition of the passengers into the trains as first level. The second level is the scheduling of trains based on the partition. The third level consists of the insertion of charging stops and as last level there is the collision-free routing of the trains. The solution provided by the insertion heuristic is part of the partition and scheduling levels and uses a charging stop insertion algorithm for the third level and a time-disjoint path algorithm for the last level as a subroutine to compute an overall solution to the DARPRT. In order to have a structured view on the current solution, we define

- S_r^{IH} as the provisional schedule resulting from the Insertion Heuristic,
- S_r^{CS} as the provisional schedule resulting from the Charging Stop Insertion algorithm, whereby the input is some S_r^{IH},
- S_r^{DR} as the provisional schedule resulting from the Disjoint Routing algorithm, whereby the input is some S_r^{CS}.

4.1 Insertion Heuristic

We start with the description of the main algorithm, the insertion heuristic. The insertion heuristic covers the partition of passengers into trains as well as the schedules of the trains. It is presented in Algorithm 1 as pseudocode. The heuristic adapts the algorithms from Jaw et al. [17] and Madsen et al. [19] to the DARPRT. The basic idea is to insert a passenger set P', $|P'| \geq 1$, into the schedule S_r^{IH} by trying out all possible insertions of the passengers P' into S_r^{IH} one after another for all trains $r \in R$, i.e. the order of stops in the original schedule S_r^{IH} is not changed. We denote the ordering corresponding to the scheduling tuple of S_r^{IH} as $x_i \preceq_{S^{IH}} x_j$ iff $i \leq j$. A feasible insertion is an insertion that is able to satisfy all constraints. In this paper, the feasibility is evaluated by finding a feasible solution using the charging stop insertion algorithm in Sect. 4.2 and the time-disjoint path algorithm in Algorithm 3 as subalgorithms. Observe that the for loop in line 4 of Algorithm 1 handles the partition part of the subproblem and Algorithm 2 handles the scheduling part of the subproblem.

Algorithm 1. Insertion Heuristic.

Input   : Graph G, Demands $(D_i, W_i)_{i_p \in P}$
Output: Feasible DARPRT routing schedules S_r^{DR} for all $r \in R$
1 Set $R = \emptyset$ // R is the set of railway vehicles
2 Map $S = \emptyset$ // S is the mapping between $r \in R$ and the schedule S_r^{IH} of r
3 **for** $(s_i^{start}, t_i^{end}) \in D_i$ **do**
4   **for** $r \in R$ **do**
5   Call Algorithm 2 for finding feasible insertion I into S_r^{IH}
6   **if** *there is no insertion I* **then**
7   Add train r^{new} to R
8   Insert s_i^{start} and s_i^{end} into $S_{r^{new}}^{IH}$
9   **else**
10   Insert s_i^{start} and s_i^{end} according to I into S_r^{IH}.
11 **for** $r \in R$ **do**
12   Calculate charging stops for S_r^{IH} and insert into S_r^{CS}
13   Calculate feasibility and costs of new schedule S_r^{CS} to schedule S_r^{DR}
14 **return** S_r^{DR} *for all* $r \in R$

There is an important optimization that may improve the practical running time. Consider the time windows of the passenger.

Observation 4. *Let S_r^{IH} be a schedule for $r \in R$, p_1, p_2 be passengers with demands (s_1^{start}, s_1^{end}) for p_1 and (s_2^{start}, s_2^{end}) for p_2 with w.l.o.g. start time window $[t_{1,1}, t_{1,2}]$*

for p_1 and $[t_{2,1}, t_{2,2}]$ for p_2. If s_2^{start} is inserted after s_1^{start} in the schedule S_r, i.e. $s_1^{start} \prec_{S_r} s_2^{start}$, then $t_{1,1} \leq t_{2,2}$. This is valid analogously for all combinations of start and end time windows as well.

With this observation, the first and last possible insertion can be calculated in linear time by iterating over the schedule once. This can reduce the number of steps by $\mathcal{O}(i \cdot p^{3i})$ for the insertion of i passengers. The passenger insertion subroutine is presented in Algorithm 2.

Algorithm 2. Passenger Insertion Subroutine.

Input : Graph G, Schedule S_r^{IH}, Demand $(s_i^{start}, s_i^{end}, W_i)$
Output: Schedule $S_{r,1}^{IH}$ with best insertion of $(s_i^{start}, s_i^{end}, W_i)$ into S_r^{IH}

1 **for** $s_1 \in S_r^{IH}$ **do**
2   **for** $s_2 \in S_r^{IH}$ with $s_1 \prec_{S_r^{IH}} s_2$ **do**
3   Insert s_i^{start} into S_r^{IH} behind s_1
4   Insert s_i^{end} into S_r^{IH} behind s_2
5   Check validity of S_r^{IH} per Obs. 4 $S_r^{CS} \leftarrow S_r^{IH}$
6   Calculate charging stops for S_r^{IH} and insert into S_r^{CS}
7   Calculate feasibility and costs of new schedule S_r^{CS} to schedule S_r^{DR}
8   Store S_r^{IH} if S_r^{DR} is cost-minimal and feasible
9   or **return** S_r^{IH} *if it is feasible and first insertion is requested*

10 **return** *Cost-minimal feasible insertion into* S_r^{IH}

Variants. It is possible to alter the heuristic in various ways. The following considerations are implemented. First, there is the possibility to insert more than one passenger at once. This increases the running time of the insertion subroutine (Algorithm 2) corresponding to the number of inserted passengers. For every additional passenger, a quadratic overhead is produced because for every passenger both, the start and end point, have to be inserted. For the simultaneous insertion of i passengers, Algorithm 2 calculates up to p^{2i} insertions. Furthermore, it is possible not to use the best insertion but a random insertion. This can be a hybrid approach as well. From the best k insertions, one insertion can be chosen randomly. For this paper, we only use the non-randomized insertion of one passenger because of time considerations that are revealed in the computational study.

Further, we can use this heuristic as starting point for search heuristics as well as a standalone algorithm combined with algorithms that refine the partition or the schedules of the trains.

4.2   Charging Stop Insertion Algorithms

Based on the schedule from the insertion subroutine, charging stops have to be inserted in order to ensure that the train has enough energy. We model this subproblem with a graph that has arcs between all reachable charging stops with costs on the arcs that correspond to the cost generated for travelling between the charging stops. Thus, a shortest path algorithm provides an optimal charging stop regime.

Model. Let $S_r^{IH} = (h_1, h_2, \ldots, h_m)$ be a schedule of $r \in R$, where $h_i \in S_r^{IH}, i \in [m]$, are stations. Let s_j, s_k be a charging stop or a station in the network. We define $E(s_j)$ to be the set of charging points in the network that are reachable from s_j with one energy filling based on the shortest distance from s_j. We further define $E_p(s_j, s_k)$ to be the set of charging points in the network that are reachable from s_j with one energy filling, whereby the train is strictly following the path p beginning at s_j leading to s_k. At last, we define $E(s_j, s_k)$ to be the set of charging points in the network that are reachable from s_j or s_k with one energy filling or are on the path from s_j to s_k.

Let $G(S_r) = (V, A)$ be the directed optimization graph. We define

$$V := \{(v, i) \mid v \in E(h_i, h_{i+1}), i \in [m]\},$$
$$A_1 := \{((v', i), (v'', i)) \mid v' \in E(h_i) \cup E_p(h_i, h_{i+1}),$$
$$v'' \in (E_p(h_i, h_{i+1}) \cup E(h_{i+1})) \cap E(v')\}$$
$$A_2 := \{((v', j), (v'', i)) \mid v' \in E(h_j, h_{j+1}), v'' \in (E(h_i, h_{i+1}) \cap E_p(v', v'')) \cap E(v')$$
$$\text{for } p = (v', h_{j+1}, \ldots, h_i, v''), j < i\}$$

and

$$A := A_1 \cup A_2.$$

The cost on the arcs are the travel time (or other objective functions) that are induced by travelling according to the schedule with charging stops. The cost function TTTV and TTTP are only locally dependent on the schedule. Thus, the costs on the arcs are fixed and easily computable based on the given schedule. The specific definition of the cost functions is presented in Sect. 4.2.1.

Let us review the definition with the following considerations. The vertices in V represent the possible charging stops for the schedule S_r^{IH}. If a vertex $v \in V$ belongs to the shortest path p, the corresponding charging stop is used in S_r^{CS}. The charging stops are inserted in the order of the path p, whereby vertex $v = (u, i)$ is inserted between h_i and h_{i+1} in schedule S_r^{CS}.

The arc set A_1 models charging stops in between two consecutive halts h_i and h_{i+1}. That is, A_1 models the connection of h_i with all reachable charging points as well as all reachable charging on the path from h_i to h_{i+1}. Observe that it is possible to recharge at a charging point in front of h_i in order to recharge before travelling to h_{i+1} as well as overshooting h_{i+1} to recharge and travelling back to h_{i+1}.

The arc set A_2 on the other hand models skipping charging stops between two consecutive halts in the schedule S_r^{SC}. The logic behind it is the same as in A_1 but in between the halts of h_i and h_j with $i < j$, no charging stop takes place.

The arc sets A_1 and A_2 are defined such that a directed acyclic graph results. This is possible because cyclic arcs in A_1 and A_2 can be ruled out by optimality considerations. For this, consider the path $p_{S_r^{IH}}$ that is given by traveling over the direct connections in schedule $S_r = (h_1, \ldots, h_m)$. Let $sp(h_i, h_j)$ be the shortest path between h_i and h_j. Then $p_{S_r^{IH}} = (sp(h_1, h_2), sp(h_2, h_3), \ldots, sp(h_{m-1}, h_m))$. A vehicle would never leave $p_{S_r^{IH}}$ if it is not necessary because of charging. Thus, the starting point of one level i is always (h_{i-1}, i). Then, the vehicle might deviate from $p_{S_r^{IH}}$ to find a charging stop nearby to charge and travel to h_i. Thereby, h_{i-1} and charging stops, which are not in between the path of h_{i-1} to h_i, cannot be visited again for charging because the vehicle would recharge at h_{i-1} before instead of leaving $p_{S_r^{IH}}$. This holds for all levels such that arcs which are not on $p_{S_r^{IH}}$ can be eliminated.

The set A_2 models the same structure with the difference that it supports not just the charging in between all consecutive stops but gives the train the possibility to skip them. Thus, the arcs can go from some (v', j) to some (v'', i) such that over the whole distance of $v', h_{j+1}, h_{j+2}, \ldots, h_{i-1}, v''$ the train takes no charging stop.

In order to provide a better understanding, we present a tangible short schedule in Example 1.

Example 1. Let $S_1 = (0, 5, 0)$ be the schedule, in which charging points have to be inserted for the railway infrastructure in Fig. 3 with charging stops $\{0, 2, 3, 6\}$. The charging capacity of train $r = 1$ is four stations, whereby the stations are equidistant. Station 0 is the depot.

Fig. 3. The simplified infrastructure for Example 1 with charging stops $\{0, 2, 3, 6\}$.

From the infrastructure from Fig. 3, the schedule $S_1^{IH} = (0, 5, 0)$, the charging stops $\{0, 2, 3, 6\}$ and the charging capacity of four stations, the charging stop insertion graph $G(S_1^{IH})$ can be derived as in Fig. 4.

The schedule begins in depot 0 and ends in depot 0. This is modeled by vertex 0_0 for the start and 0_3 for the end. The two layers of vertices $\{0_1, 1_1, \ldots, 6_1\}$ and $\{0_2, 1_2, \ldots, 6_2\}$ model the routes between the stops of the schedule. These are in this case 0 to 5, which is modeled in the first layer, and then 5 to 0, which is modeled in the second layer.

Let h_i, h_{i+1} be the halting points of layer i. Then, the arcs within one layer define the trip from the out-going charging point to the in-going charging point, where a recharge takes place at the in-going charging point. Thereby, the train does not halt at passenger station h_{i+1}. An arc a going from a higher layer to lower layer encodes that the train halts at passenger stations h_{i+1} to h_{i+j}, where j is the lowest layer that is bypassed by arc a, before charging at the in-going charging point.

The charging capacity is four stations. Thus, the train may travel from 0 to 0, 2 or 3 to recharge. From 2 or 3 the train is able to travel to 6 and from 2 to 3. If the train recharges at 3, it is able to travel to 5 and then back to 3 or to 6, but not 0. If the train recharges at 2, it is only able to travel 5 and then to 6 but not back to 2 or 3. If the train, however, travels first to 6 to travel to passenger halt 5, the train is able to travel to charging stops 2 and 3 and back to 6. Thus, the arcs between the layers are $(2, 6), (3, 3), (3, 6), (6, 2), (6, 3)$ and $(6, 6)$. At last, the train is able to travel from 0, 2 and 3 to 0, whereby a recharge at 0 is not necessary as the schedule ends. Thus, arcs to 0_3 are valid as well.

Based on the graph, it is now possible to calculate paths from 0_0 to 0_3 in order to calculate the charging stop insertions. Two exemplary feasible schedules are $S_{1,1}^{CS}$ and $S_{1,opt}^{CS}$. The schedules are tuple of the station number and the filling level of the energy

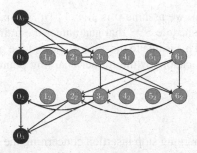

Fig. 4. The charging stop graph $G(S_1^{IH})$ for schedule S_1^{IH} with charging capacity of four stations, where the set of charging stops is $\{0, 2, 3, 6\}$.

container. A charging stop is indicated by two energy containers with an arrow:
$S_{1,1}^{CS} = (0 \blacksquare, 2 \square \mapsto \blacksquare, 5 \square, 6 \square \mapsto \blacksquare, 3 \square \mapsto \blacksquare, 0 \square)$ calculated from path $(0_0, 2_1, 6_2, 3_2, 0_3)$ in $G(S_1)$ and $S_{1,opt}^{CS} = (0 \blacksquare, 3 \square \mapsto \blacksquare, 5 \blacksquare, 3 \square \mapsto \blacksquare, 0 \square)$ calculated from shortest path $(0_0, 3_1, 3_2, 0_3)$ in $G(S_1^{IH})$.

Variants. Overall, we can use this model in combination with a shortest path algorithm to find the best possible charging stop insertion for a given schedule. However, the best charging stop insertion may lead to an infeasible routing subproblem. Therefore, we establish a heuristic that takes up to k shortest paths into account by iterating from the best to the worst solution until a feasible solution is found. Alternatively, the best combination of the k shortest paths for all trains can be calculated.

Completeness of the Model. Based on this model, we can argue that all possible charging stops insertions that lead to a feasible schedule based on schedule S_r^{IH} are encoded in graph $G(S_r^{IH})$.

Lemma 2. *Let $S_r^{IH} = (h_1, h_2, \ldots, h_m)$ be a schedule in which $h_i \in S^{IH}, i \in [m]$, are stations and $G(S_r^{IH})$ is the corresponding charging stop insertion graph. Then $G(S_r^{IH})$ encodes all possible charging stop insertions for schedule S_r^{IH}.*

Proof. For the first direction, assume we have a valid schedule with charging stops S_r^{CS} based on schedule S_r^{IH}. Then, S_r^{CS} may have the following charging stop configurations:

(1) $S_r^{CS} = (\ldots, e, e', \ldots)$ is encoded in $G(S_r^{IH})$ by definition of A_1 by arc $((e, i), (e', i))$,
(2) $S_r^{CS} = (\ldots, e, h_k, e', \ldots)$ is encoded in $G(S_r^{IH})$ by definition of A_2 by arc $((e, k-1), (e', k))$,
(3) $S_r^{CS} = (\ldots, e, h_k, \ldots, h_l, e', \ldots)$ is encoded in $G(S_r^{IH})$ by definition of A_2 by arc $((e, k-1), (e', l))$.

These are all possible configurations S_r^{CS} because the depot is a charging point and an arbitrary number of halts in between two charging points can be made. Thus, all possible configurations are encoded in $G(S_r^{IH})$.

For the other direction, we assume p is a $(v, 1)$-(v', m)-path in $G(S_r^{IH})$. Then, p corresponds to a correct schedule S_r^{CS} that guarantees the train to have enough energy over the whole schedule. This is due to the construction of the graph arcs that exist only if the charging point is reachable by the former charging point as per definition of the arcs.

4.2.1 Cost Functions.

In order to find the best charging stop insertion concerning the optimization criteria we have to define a proper cost function on the arcs of the graphs. For this, we assume that the optimization criteria are only based on the current state of the train, i.e. they only depend on the current position (e.g. station or track) of the train, the current passenger number or the current energy level. Here, we only consider the optimization criteria TTTV and TTTP which fulfill these criteria. We let $c : A \to \mathbb{Z}$ be the cost function on the arcs of $G(S_r^{CS})$ and $P_i^{\#}$ the number of passengers after stop h_i. Then for $a = ((v', i), (v'', i)) \in A_1$, we have

$$c(a) = \begin{cases} \ell(v', v'') & \text{for TTTV} \\ \ell(v', v'') \cdot P_i^{\#} & \text{for TTTP} \end{cases}$$

and for $a' = ((v', j), (v'', i)) \in A_2$, we have

$$c(a') = \begin{cases} \ell(v', h_{j+1}) + \sum_{x=j+1}^{i-1}(\ell(h_x, h_{x+1}) + w_{dwell}) + (\ell(h_i, v'') + w_{charge}) \\ \quad \text{for TTTV} \\ \ell(v', h_{j+1}) \cdot P_{j+1}^{\#} + \sum_{x=j+1}^{i-1}(\ell(h_x, h_{x+1}) + w_{dwell}) \cdot P_x^{\#} + \\ (\ell(h_i, v'') + w_{charge}) \cdot P_i^{\#} \text{ for TTTP} \end{cases}$$

Lemma 3. *Let $S_r^{IH} = (h_1, h_2, \ldots, h_m)$ be a schedule in which $h_i \in S_r^{IH}$, $i \in [m]$, are stations and $G(S_r^{IH})$ is the corresponding charging stop insertion graph. There is a one-to-one cost correspondence between a path p in $G(S_r^{IH})$ and the schedule with charging stops S_r^{CS} based on S_r^{IH}.*

Proof. First of all, Lemma 2 holds, i.e. the schedule S_r^{CS} is valid. For the proof of the cost correspondence consider the cost function on the arcs of the graph $G(S_r^{IH})$ for schedule S_r^{IH}. Let S_r^{CS} be a schedule with charging stops based on S_r^{IH}. Because the cost function is only dependent on the current state of the vehicle we can independently sum up the costs between the stops of S_r^{CS}.

First, consider two charging stops $(\ldots, a, b, \ldots)$ in an arbitrary schedule S_r^{CS} and the corresponding arc $((a, i), (b, i))$. Then, the vehicle stops for the charging point a and travels from a to b. Thus, the cost has to be $c(a, b) + w_{charge}$ for this situation. This is correct by definition of $G(S_r^{IH})$ and S_r^{CS}. For the TTTV case we have $c(a, b) = w_{charge} + \ell(a, b)$ and for TTTP $c(a, b) = w_{charge} + \ell(a, b) \cdot P_i^{\#}$.

Second, we may have two charging stops $(\ldots, a, \ldots, b, \ldots)$ in an arbitrary schedule S_r' and the corresponding arc $((a, i), (b, j))$. Then, again the cost has to be $c(a, b) + w_{charge}$ for this situation. This is correct by definition of $G(S_r^{IH})$ and S_r^{CS} again with the difference that the vehicle travels from a over different stations and then to b. Therefore, the cost for traveling from a over the stations to b has to be summed up. Thus, $c(a')$ for $a' \in A_2$ is the correct cost function for TTTV and TTTP. Because those are all possibilities, the one-to-one cost correspondence holds.

4.3   Time-Disjoint Path Algorithms

At last, we have to route the trains collision-free and with headway time ensured through the railway system. For this, we define time-disjoint paths. Those are paths the trains travel that are disjoint over time, i.e. the trains do not use the same block at the same time. In a practical setting, the travel time through a block is in the range of several minutes determining the headway time between two succeeding trains. In the future, the trains may be additionally allowed to reduce the headway time drastically by means of inter-train communication, e.g. for breaking. Then, the headway time will be in the realm of few dozen seconds. Therefore, it is not very important to route the trains optimally. Thus, the following heuristic solves the problem sufficiently well in a practical setting. For this, we define critical trains and time windows.

Definition 2   (k-critical Time Window). *Let w.l.o.g. $[t_1, t_2] \in T' \times T'$ be a destination time window and r a train to which passenger p is associated with. The time window is k-critical if the route to the station associated with this time window $[t_1, t_2]$ takes at least $t_2 - k$ units of time. In other words, the buffer for the train r for passenger p is at most k time units. For start time windows, k-criticality is defined analogously. We call a train k-critical if it has a k-critical time window.*

Besides the satisfaction of the time windows the actual routing (line 6 of Algorithm 3) is of interest. The algorithm routes the trains by simulating the schedules discretely over every time step. The routing includes all waiting times by freezing the position of the train for w_{dwell} time steps while dwelling or w_{charge} time steps while charging.

The idea of the heuristic based on k-critical time windows is depicted in Fig. 5.

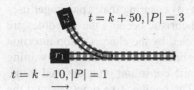

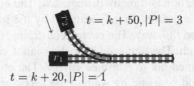

(a) Case 1: Train r_1 is routed first because a time window of its passengers falls below threshold.

(b) Case 2: Train r_2 is routed first because it transports more passengers and no threshold is deceeded.

Fig. 5. The difference in routing trains in the threshold heuristic.

The following heuristic, referred to as Threshold Heuristic (Algorithm 3), uses the criticality of a train to decide which trains are routed first. The rules are to prioritize k-critical trains first for some k and those trains with most passengers second.

4.4   Feasibility Checking of a Schedule

Due to the hierarchy of the different subproblems and -algorithms, the feasibility of the schedules resulting from the insertion heuristic and its subalgorithms is not easy to see. Thus, we survey how the constraints are fulfilled.

Algorithm 3. Threshold Heuristic.

    Input   : Graph G, Time horizon T', Trains R, Train routes inclusive time windows and passenger number $(p_r)_{r \in R}$

    Output: Feasible Time-disjoint-Path routing

1 Let $R_{p,t} = \{r \mid r$ is at point p at time stamp $t\}$

2 Let $R_{p,t,d}^{collision} = \{r \mid r \in R_{p,t}$ and there is $r' \in R_{p,t} \setminus \{r\}$ which is moving into direction $d\}$ for $d \in \{left, right\}$

3 **for** $t \in T', p \in V(G), d \in \{left, right\}$ **do**

4   **if** $|R_{p,t,d}^{collision}| \geq 2$ **then**

5   **if** *there is* $r \in R_{p,t,d}^{collision}$ *that is k-critical, where k is minimal* **then**

6   route train r first

7   **else**

8   route train with most passengers (or in general the train producing the most cost)

The time window constraint (a) is at first loosely ensured by the insertion heuristic. by modification of the schedule by the charging stop insertion algorithm and possible routing restrictions, which are calculated in the threshold heuristic, the time windows have to be checked after calculating the complete routing. Thus at the end, the time windows are checked again. If the time windows are not satisfied, the insertion is dismissed. The dwell time constraint (b) is ensured while calculating the routing in the threshold heuristic. The passenger capacity constraint (c) is ensured by the insertion heuristic. If a demand is inserted such that the number of passengers exceed the train capacity, the insertion is directly disregarded. The constraint (d) ensuring that a passenger uses only one train is directly satisfied by the insertion heuristic because the schedules are designed this way. The energy constraint (e) is satisfied by the charging stop insertion algorithm. The threshold heuristic cannot violate the energy constraint because waiting is assumed not to consume energy. The charging-time constraint (f) is ensured in the threshold heuristic by waiting the necessary time. The conflict-free timetable and the headway time, constraint (g), are satisfied by the routing simulation over time in the threshold heuristic. Constraint (h), which states that arbitrary many trains are able to dwell at one station is ensured by the insertion heuristic. At last, the schedule has to start and end at the depot, as in constraint (i). This is ensured by the insertion heuristic. If a new train is added, the schedule contains two stops at the depot. Further insertions into the schedule may not be inserted at the front or at the end of the schedule.

4.5   Running Time

To conclude the algorithm description, we analyze the running time of the insertion heuristic that uses the presented algorithms as subalgorithms.

First of all, we analyze the running time of the Insertion Heuristic itself. Overall, we have to insert p passengers. For every insertion, we have up to $\mathcal{O}\binom{S_r}{2} = \mathcal{O}\binom{2p}{2}$ possibilities. Furthermore, the charging stops and the route for each insertion have to be evaluated. Thus, the running time is $\mathcal{O}(p^3 f((S_r^{IH})_{r \in R})$ where $f((S_r^{IH})_{r \in R})$ is the running time for the charging insertion algorithm and Time-disjoint Path algorithm combined.

Next, we analyze the Charging Stop Algorithm. Let G be the base graph and $S_r^{IH} = (h_1, \ldots, h_m)$ be the schedule to insert charging stops for. Then, we have $\mathcal{O}(|S_r^{IH}| \cdot |V(G)|)$ vertices in the charging stop model G'. Furthermore $|A_1| = \mathcal{O}(|S_r^{IH}| \cdot |V(G)|^2)$ and $|A_2| = \mathcal{O}((|S_r^{IH}| \cdot |V(G)|)^2)$. Therefore, the construction of the graph is possible in $\mathcal{O}((V(G) + E(G))(|S_r^{IH}| \cdot |V(G)|)^2)$ including the calculation of the arc cost. Furthermore, we can use the Bellman-Ford algorithm for DAG, which runs in linear time on the graph. Thus, the overall running time is in $\mathcal{O}((|S_r^{IH}| \cdot |V(G)| + |S_r^{IH}| \cdot |V(G)|)^2)(m|V(G)|)^2) = \mathcal{O}((|S_r^{IH}| \cdot |V(G)|)^4)$. This estimate, however, is rather pessimistic, because the number of arcs is limited by the set of reachable charging stops. Especially if the number of needed charging stops is low, then the Bellman-Ford algorithm finds a solution quickly due to the low number of arcs. Thus, the number of needed charging stops is a better estimate for a practical setting than the rather pessimistic theoretical worst-case analysis.

At last, we analyze the Threshold Heuristic. The algorithm runs in time $\mathcal{O}(|R| \cdot |S_r^{CS}|_{r \in R} \cdot |A(G)| \cdot |T'|)$ where R is the set of vehicles and $A(G)$ is the set of arcs of base infrastructure graph G and time horizon T'. This is justified by the calculation of the criticality, which is linear in the schedule size for each train and the actual routing which is also linear for each train.

Overall, the running time of the algorithm is

$$\mathcal{O}(p^3 \cdot (\mathcal{O}((|V(G)|)^4 \cdot |S_r^{IH}|_{r \in R}) + \mathcal{O}(|R| \cdot |S_r^{CS}|_{r \in R} \cdot |A(G)| \cdot |T'|))$$

$$= \mathcal{O}(p^3 \cdot |S_r^{CS}|_{r \in R} \cdot ((|V(G)|)^4 + |R| \cdot |A(G)| \cdot |T'|))$$

5   Computational Study

In the computational study, the performance of the insertion heuristic with all its subalgorithms is evaluated. First, we present the empirical instances that are used as basic networks. After this, we describe the instance generator and all its parameters that are used to generate the input. Third, we take a look at the parameterization of the instances that are surveyed in the study. At last, we present the results of the study in form of general performance analysis together with a sensitivity analysis concerning the parameters of the instances, an analysis on the performance of the separate base networks and a special case analysis for the Eifelquerbahn. The latter is selected as its network length has a large influence on the insertion heuristic.

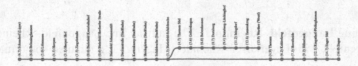

Fig. 6. Route map of Bielefelder Kreisbahnen.

5.1   Empirical Graph Instances

In the following, the infrastructures of some currently disused rural railway lines in North Rhine-Westphalia, Germany, are presented.

Bielefelder Kreisbahnen. The Bielefelder Kreisbahnen were a railway line located in- and outside of Bielefeld. In Fig. 6, a detailed route map can be found.

Eifelquerbahn. The Eifelquerbahn is a railway line between Andernach and Gerolstein in the German low mountain range Eifel. In Fig. 7 a detailed route map can be found.

Fig. 7. Route map of the Eifelquerbahn.

Gummersbacher Kleinbahnen. The Gummersbacher Kleinbbahnen were a railway system in Gummersbach connecting the urban core and some outer districts of Gummersbach. In Fig. 8, a detailed route map can be found.

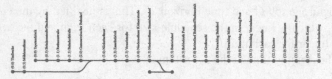

Fig. 8. Route map of Gummersbacher Kleinbahnen.

Railway Line Köln-Sülz–Berrenrath. The railway line Köln-Sülz-Berrenrath connects the inner district of Cologne to Hürth, a town in the south-west of Cologne. A detailed route map can be found in Fig. 9.

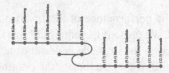

Fig. 9. Route map of the railway line Köln-Sülz–Berrenrath.

Krefeld Eisenbahn-Gesellschaft. The railway system Moers-Hüls-Krefeld of Krefeld Eisenbahn-Gesellschaft is situated in Krefeld. In Fig. 10, a detailed route map can be found.

Railway Line Langenfeld–Rheindorf. The railway line Langenfeld–Rheindorf connects Langenfeld with Leverkusen-Rheindorf. In Fig. 11, a detailed route map can be found.

Fig. 10. Route map of Krefeld Eisenbahn-Gesellschaft.

Railway Line Solingen–Wuppertal-Vohwinkel. The railway system Solingen-Wuppertal-Vohwinkel connects the towns Solingen and Wuppertal. In Fig. 12, a detailed route map can be found.

5.2 Study Setup

The study consists of three parts. In all parts, we use the following six measures to evaluate the performance of the algorithm: run time performance in each iteration, the number of trains used for the solution, the overall solution cost, the solution cost for TTTP in particular, the solution cost for TTTV in particular, and the overall run time performance. The overall solution cost is the mere sum of TTTP and TTTV. The first part provides an evaluation for the overall performance of the algorithm including the sensitivity of the parameters in the instances. In the second part, the results for the different base networks are compared. The third and last part presents the performance on a specific setting that can be seen as an extreme: the Eifelquerbahn with hub Gerolstein. It is the instance with the greatest length and is thus more sensitive to a stricter time horizon and energy capacity. But first, we will have a look on the different parameters that can be adjusted for all instances.

5.2.1 Parameters.

The following parameters are adjustable. If not stated otherwise they are fixed to the following values.

- Time horizon T': 72,000 s (20 h)
- Time buffer: 14,400 s (4 h) - time for trains to set up from the depot
- Time window W_p size: 900 s (15 min)
- Dwell time w_{dwell}: 61.2 s (approx. 1 min)
- Charging time w_{charge}: 900 s (15 min)
- Energy capacity of trains e_r: 25,200 s (7 h) travel time
- Block Size: 50 m – the partition of the line
- Number of passengers: (35, 35)

The number of passengers are generated by two different distributions. The tuple (a, b) means that a passengers are generated by the uniform distribution over time and

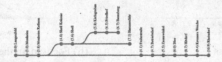

Fig. 11. Route map of the railway line Langenfeld–Rheindorf.

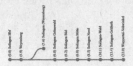

Fig. 12. Route map of the railway line Solingen–Wuppertal-Vohwinkel.

stations and b passengers are generated by a hub distribution. The hub location is not necessarily the same as the depot location. The hub generation is characterized by the central position of the hub. In real demand distributions, the railway network is often connected to a station which has an important role in the network. This hub or central station usually has a high demand on workdays in a way such that passengers travel to the central station in the morning and back in the afternoon. Thus, we model this behavior by generating demand time windows based on two Gaussian distributions, one generating the morning demands and one generating the afternoon demands, as presented in Fig. 13. The morning demands have the hub as destination (blue curve) and the afternoon demands (red curve) have the hub as origin. The generation of the other stations is done via a uniform distribution over all other stations.

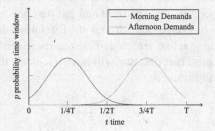

Fig. 13. The hub distribution of passenger demands. (Color figure online)

5.3   Results

All calculations were conducted on cluster nodes with 2 sockets and 384 GB RAM. The CPUs on both sockets are Intel Skylake Platinum 8160 with 2.1 GHz clock speed and

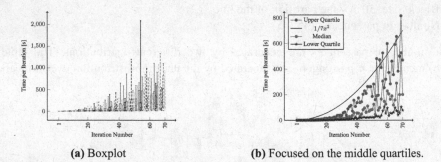

(a) Boxplot   (b) Focused on the middle quartiles.

Fig. 14. The evolution of the computation time for increasing iteration numbers over all infrastructures (first feasible insertion).

24 cores. Every single instance can use the resources of 8 cores, 16 threads, and 28 GB RAM and at most 24 h of computation time. In order to provide a concise analysis of the data we only show selected graphs to support our analysis. Further data and diagrams can be found in Appendix A.

There is no significant difference between data, which results from instances with one charging stop at the depot, and the data, which results from instances in which charging stops are allowed at all stations, if not stated otherwise. Thus, only the results for the instances with charging stops at all stations are presented in the following graphs.

General Time Performance Results. Before we analyze the data for the best passenger insertion, we outline the performance of finding feasible insertions with the passenger insertion heuristic. For this, we use the first found feasible insertion by the passenger insertion heuristic. In Fig. 14, the time for each iteration can be found.

After we depicted the running time capabilities of the first feasible passenger insertion, we continue with the analysis of the insertion heuristic iteration time in Fig. 15.

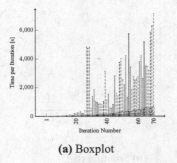

(a) Boxplot

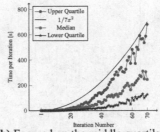

(b) Focused on the middle quartiles.

Fig. 15. The evolution of the computation time for increasing iteration numbers over all infrastructures (best insertion).

In Fig. 14a and in Fig. 15a, the time performance for all instances and every iteration is depicted. As there are some significant outliers, the running time for the lower quartile, median and upper quartile is displayed once more in Fig. 14b and in Fig. 15b. Furthermore, the function $f(x) = 1/7 \cdot x^2$ is plotted, because the theoretical worst

Table 1. Mapping of Labels: Parameters.

x P.	x Passengers
B 100 m	Block Size 100 m
D Hub	Hub Passenger Dist
D Rand	Uni. Rand. Passenger Dist
Red. Energy	Energy Capacity: 3.5 h
T 2 h	Time Horizon 2 h
T 4 h	Time Horizon 4 h
T 8 h	Time Horizon 8 h
ZControl	Control Group (Standard Parameterization)

case analysis suggests that the time for one iteration execution is squared based on the number of existing passengers. The practical data supports this running time analysis of the algorithms. The insertion time for one passenger grows quadratically with the number of insertions. Nevertheless, there are significant outliers that exceed the upper quartile time by a factor of 10. Overall, we can conclude that the running time of the insertion heuristic is cubic in expectation in the number of passengers to insert. In order to compare the insertion time for the first feasible insertion and the best insertion, we first compare the upwards outliers. These are significantly lower for the first feasible insertion algorithm. The median, upper and lower quartile are generally lower, however, there is more variance and more upward outliers for the first feasible insertion algorithm in contrast to the best insertion algorithm.

Figure 16a displays the number of trains necessary for all instance configurations. The parameters are set as described in Sect. 5.2.1 up to the mentioned parameter, which is changed according to the specification in Table 1.

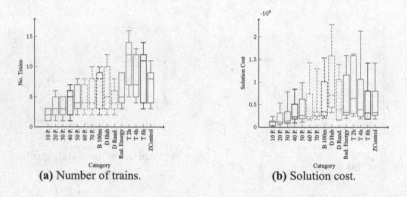

(a) Number of trains.   (b) Solution cost.

Fig. 16. Analysis over different passenger distributions.

The number of trains in Fig. 16a is highly dependent on the number of passengers, as expected. Furthermore, the density of the passenger demands is an important factor. It is observable that the number of trains is generally the higher the smaller the time horizon is (T 2 h, T4 h, T 8 h).

In Fig. 16b the solution cost for the different variations is displayed. The solution cost of TTTP are about one magnitude higher than those of TTTV. This is mainly due to the passenger number multiplicator in the TTTP formula. Thus, the costs are highly dependent on the local density of the passenger requests and the distance between the origin and destination of the demand. Conclusively, *D Hub* and *T 2h* have higher solution costs than *D Rand.* respectively *T 4h*, *T 8h* or *ZControl*.

Comparison of Base Networks. In this section, the data for all calculations is separated according to the base networks from Sect. 5.1. This increases the granularity and allows for more specific observations. The mapping of the labels can be found in Table 2

Table 2. Mapping of Labels: Infrastructure.

Andernach	Eifelquerbahn w/ Hub Andernach
Bielef.Kreisbhf	Bielefelder Kreisbahnen w/ Hub Bielefelder Kreisbahnhof
Gerolstein	Eifelquerbahn w/ Hub Gerolstein
Gummersb.Bhf	Gummersbacher Kleinbahnen w/ Hub Gummersbacher Bahnhof
Kaiseresch	Eifelquerbahn w/ Hub Kaiseresch
KoelnSuelz	Railway Line Köln-Sülz–Berrenrath w/ Hub Köln-Sülz
KrefeldNord	Krefeld Eisenbahn-Gesellschaft w/ Hub Krefeld Nord
Langenfeld	Railway Line Langenfeld–Rheindorf w/ Hub Langenfeld
Rheindorf	Railway Line Langenfeld–Rheindorf w/ Hub Rheindorf
SolingenHbf	Railway Line Solingen–Wuppertal-Vohwinkel w/ Hub Solingen Hbf

In Fig. 17a and 17b, the number of trains respectively the solution costs are plotted against the instance settings. The values concerning the number of trains and the solution costs strongly correlate to the length of the networks. The Eifelquerbahn generates the most extreme results due to its lengthy network structure. Here, especially the number of trains and the solution cost are much higher compared to the other instances.

Furthermore, the running times in Fig. 17c give some insight into the data. Here, especially the Gummersbacher Kleinbahnen and Bielefelder Kreisbahnen and to a lesser extent the railway line Langenfeld–Rheindorf seem to require more time for the computation. In contrast, the other instances and especially the Eifelquerbahn seem to be less complex in terms of finding solutions. The complexity of the network has an influence on the performance of the algorithm in the sense that a tree network is more complex than a path network. The computational results on the different infrastructures and variations support the observation.

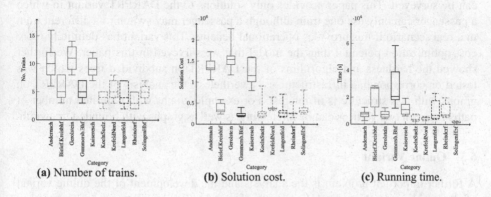

(a) Number of trains.   (b) Solution cost.   (c) Running time.

Fig. 17. Analysis over different infrastructures.

In conclusion, the data shows expected correlations and dependencies that were already analyzed from a theoretical point of view. Furthermore, it is possible to find best insertions in a reasonable amount of time for most settings. Nevertheless, optimizations have to be implemented into the algorithms to be fully practically usable in a setting of hundreds of passengers. Additionally, more hardware can be used to enhance the parallelization in the insertion heuristics. Small railway networks with small distances between the stations seem to provide the best structure for the algorithm, whereas more complex structures and more lengthy instances seem to be more problematic for finding good solutions. An important problem are the outliers for insertions with higher passengers numbers. The algorithmic reason is that most of the insertion possibilities are enumerated. Thus, the performance can be improved by trading off solution quality. By making use of the randomization in the insertion heuristic, the number of overall insertions can be capped for each iteration. Thus, those outliers are ruled out completely.

6 Prospect

6.1 Summary

The complexity analysis shows that the DARPRT is generally hard to solve. The problem has many constraints and possible optimization criteria.

We further developed and analyzed algorithms to solve the DARPRT or its subproblems. The analysis of the DARPRT algorithms showed that small instances of the DARPRT are solvable reasonably fast. Optimizations can be found in improving the parallelization to make better use of more hardware.

6.2 Extensions and Variants of the DARPRT

This paper surveys only a limited area on the DARPRT and its variants. Particularly, the analysis of further optimization criteria is of interest, e.g. minimization of waiting time for passengers. Furthermore, variations in the constraints or additional constraints can be surveyed. This paper provides only solutions to the DARPRT variant in which a passenger can only use one train although a passenger may switch to a different train in a real scenario if this provides operational benefits. This variant has definitely more cost optimization potential than the model that we surveyed in this paper. We further showed the hardness and algorithms of the DARPRT on subdivided trees which was tested on corresponding infrastructures. Nevertheless, the analysis of the DARPRT on graphs with less structure is of interest. For example graphs with a limited number of paths between two vertices can be interesting as well as graphs with bounded treewidth.

6.3 Online Variant

A further important problem is the analysis and the development of the online variant of the problem. In the online variant, the demands of the passengers are revealed in the process of computation, i.e. demands may be inserted after calculating a route for a train. Of course this is very relevant for practical scenarios of the DARPRT.

A good starting point for the competitiveness analysis may be the k-SERVER problem and its extension the k-TAXI problem. Both problems are at least k-competitive as shown by Manasse et al. [20] and Xin and Ma [3]. The DARPRT is a generalization of these problems and may be harder because of the set of additional constraints. However, the practical setting provides information on the demands in a network as we have modeled in the hub distribution for passenger requests. Thus, a probabilistic model of the DARPRT, which models this information into a distribution on potential further demands may be a better approach. With this approach, the algorithms which were developed in this paper may be reused in an probabilistic algorithmic framework.

A   Appendix

A.1   General Performance Results

The diagrams in Figs. 18, 19, 20, 21, 22, 23, 24, 25, 26 and 27 show the accumulated data over all instances. This allows a general view on the performance of the algorithm. The labels are the same as presented in Table 1.

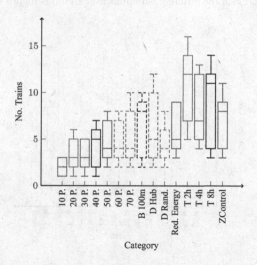

Fig. 18. Number of trains for the different variations over all infrastructures. Charging everywhere.

Comparison of Base Networks. In this section, the data on all calculations is compared to the base networks. The data is depicted in the diagrams of Fig. 28, 29, 30, 31, 32, 33, 34, 35, 36 and Fig. 37 The values are as expected corresponding to the length of the networks, whereby the Eifelquerbahn with its lengthy network structure results in the most extreme results. Here, especially the number of trains and the solution cost are much higher compared to the other instances.

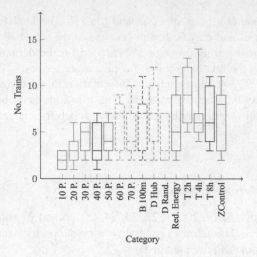

Fig. 19. Number of trains for the different variations over all infrastructures. Charging at depot.

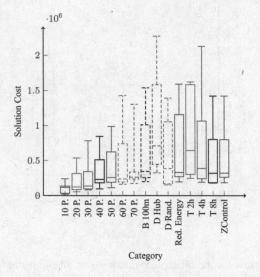

Fig. 20. The solution cost for the different variations over all infrastructures. Charging everywhere.

Special Case: Eifelquerbahn with Hub Gerolstein. This section focusses on the data for the Eifelquerbahn with Gerolstein as Hub. The parameterization is same as in Sect. 6.3.1 up to the mentioned parameter in the chart, which is changed to the mentioned value. All data is shown in Figs. 38, 39, 40, 41, 42, 43, 44, 45, 46 and Fig. 47. The most important difference is the number of trains for the smaller time horizons (2 h, 4 h, 8 h compared to 16 h in Control) and for reduced energy capacity in the scenario, in which only the hub has the energy restoring property.

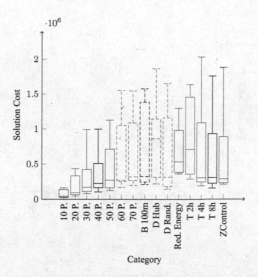

Fig. 21. The solution cost for the different variations over all infrastructures. Charging at depot.

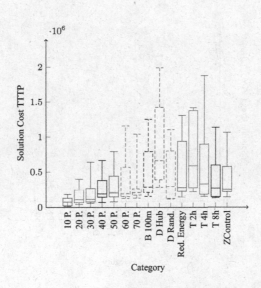

Fig. 22. The TTTP part of the solution cost for the different variations over all infrastructures. Charging everyhwere.

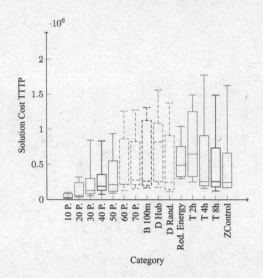

Fig. 23. The TTTP part of the solution cost for the different variations over all infrastructures. Charging at depot.

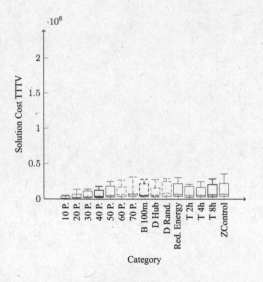

Fig. 24. The TTTV part of the solution cost for the different variations over all infrastructures. Charging everyhwere.

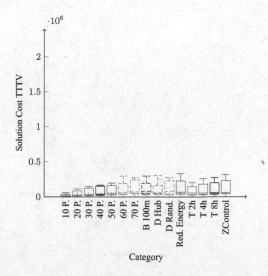

Fig. 25. The TTTV part of the solution cost for the different variations over all infrastructures. Charging at depot.

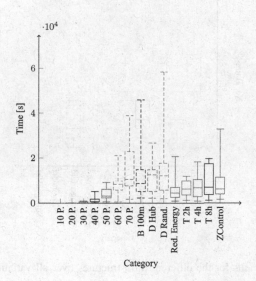

Fig. 26. Computation time for different categories. Charging everywhere.

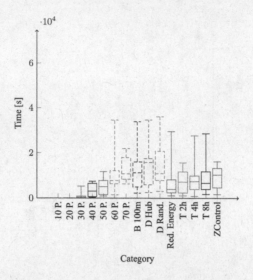

Fig. 27. Computation time for different categories. Charging at depot.

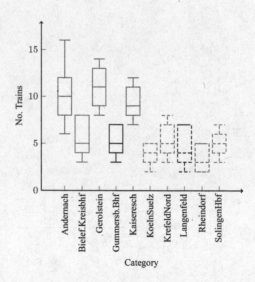

Fig. 28. Number of trains for the different infrastructures over all variations. Charging everywhere.

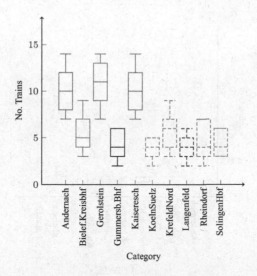

Fig. 29. Number of trains for the different infrastructures over all variations. Charging at depot.

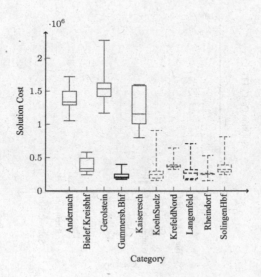

Fig. 30. Solution cost for the different infrastructures over all variations. Charging everywhere.

124 C. Grüne and S. Zieger

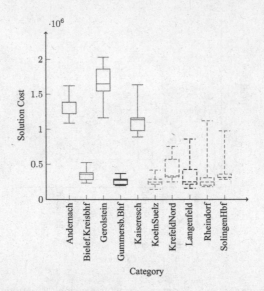

Fig. 31. Solution cost for the different infrastructures over all variations. Charging at depot.

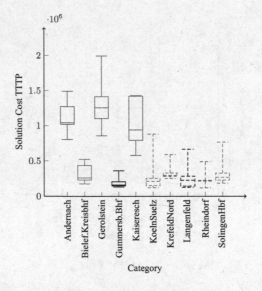

Fig. 32. Solution cost TTTP for the different infrastructures over all variations. Charging everywhere.

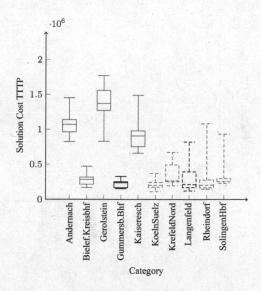

Fig. 33. Solution cost TTTP for the different infrastructures over all variations. Charging at depot.

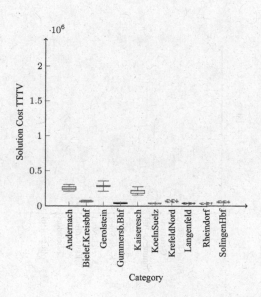

Fig. 34. Solution cost TTTV for the different infrastructures over all variations. Charging everywhere.

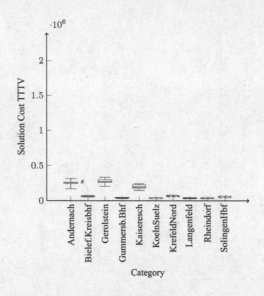

Fig. 35. Solution cost TTTV for the different infrastructures over all variations. Charging at depot.

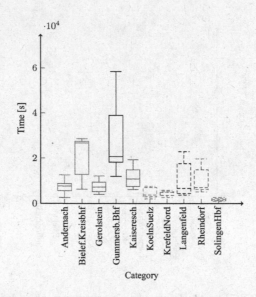

Fig. 36. Running time for the different infrastructures over all variations. Charging everywhere.

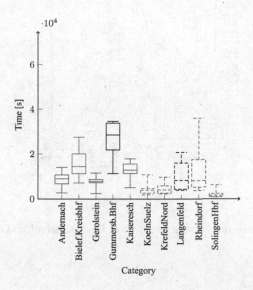

Fig. 37. Running time for the different infrastructures over all variations. Charging at depot.

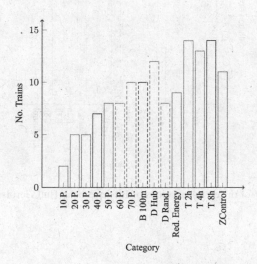

Fig. 38. Number of trains for different variations of Eifelquerbahn Hub Gerolstein. Charging everywhere.

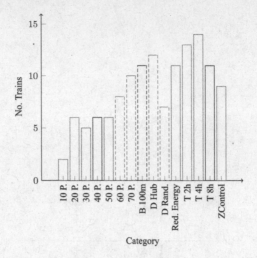

Fig. 39. Number of trains for different variations of Eifelquerbahn Hub Gerolstein. Charging at depot.

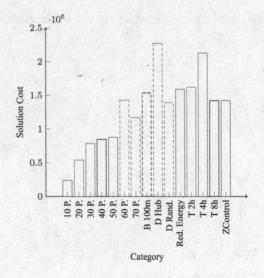

Fig. 40. Solution cost for different variations of Eifelquerbahn Hub Gerolstein. Charging everywhere.

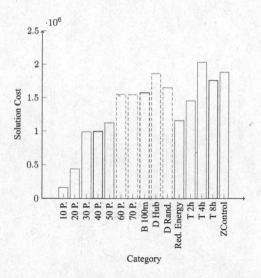

Fig. 41. Solution cost for different variations of Eifelquerbahn Hub Gerolstein. Charging at depot.

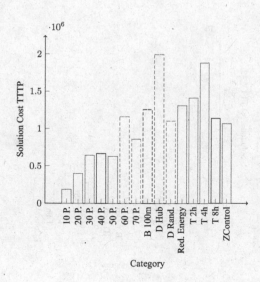

Fig. 42. Solution cost TTTP for different variations of Eifelquerbahn Hub Gerolstein. Charging everywhere.

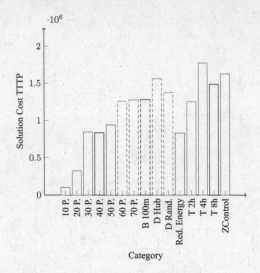

Fig. 43. Solution cost TTTP for different variations of Eifelquerbahn Hub Gerolstein. Charging at depot.

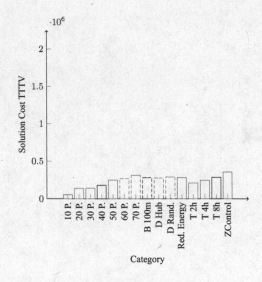

Fig. 44. Solution cost TTTV for different variations of Eifelquerbahn Hub Gerolstein. Charging everywhere.

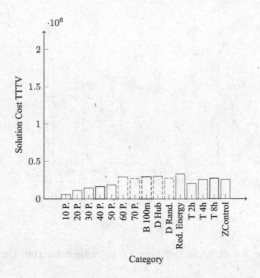

Fig. 45. Solution cost TTTV for different variations of Eifelquerbahn Hub Gerolstein. Charging at depot.

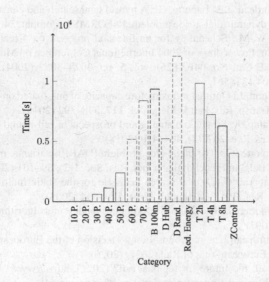

Fig. 46. Running time for different variations of Eifelquerbahn Hub Gerolstein. Charging everywhere.

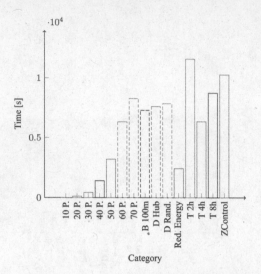

Fig. 47. Running time for different variations of Eifelquerbahn Hub Gerolstein. Charging at depot.

References

1. La solution pour les petites lignes — Taxirail. https://www.taxirail.fr/
2. Berbeglia, G., Cordeau, J.F., Laporte, G.: A hybrid tabu search and constraint programming algorithm for the dynamic dial-a-ride problem. INFORMS J. Comput. **24**(3), 343–355 (2012)
3. Xin, C.-L., Ma, W.-M.: Scheduling for on-line taxi problem on a real line and competitive algorithms. In: Proceedings of 2004 International Conference on Machine Learning and Cybernetics (IEEE Cat. No. 04EX826), vol. 5, pp. 3078–3083 (2004). https://doi.org/10.1109/ICMLC.2004.1378561
4. Cats, O., Haverkamp, J.: Optimal infrastructure capacity of automated on-demand rail-bound transit systems. Transp. Res. Part B Methodol. **117**, 378–392 (2018)
5. Cats, O., Haverkamp, J.: Strategic planning and prospects of rail-bound demand responsive transit. Transp. Res. Rec. **2672**(8), 404–410 (2018)
6. Cordeau, J.F., Laporte, G.: The dial-a-ride problem (DARP): variants, modeling issues and algorithms. Q. J. Belgian French Italian Oper. Res. Soc. **1**(2), 89–101 (2003)
7. Cordeau, J.F., Laporte, G.: A tabu search heuristic for the static multi-vehicle dial-a-ride problem. Transp. Res. Part B Methodol. **37**(6), 579–594 (2003)
8. Cordeau, J.F., Laporte, G.: The dial-a-ride problem: models and algorithms. Ann. Oper. Res. **153**(1), 29–46 (2007)
9. Council of the European Union: Proposal for a Decision of the European Parliament and of the Council on a European Year of Rail (2021) (2020)
10. Geerts, E.: Taxirail: the future for regional rail? (2021). https://www.railtech.com/rolling-stock/2021/07/27/taxirail-future-for-regional-rail/?gdpr=accept
11. Goossens, J.W.: Models and algorithms for railway line planning problems. Ph.D. thesis (2004)
12. Grüne, C., Zieger, S.: Demand-responsive scheduling in railway transportation. In: Proceedings of the 8th International Conference on Vehicle Technology and Intelligent Transport Systems (VEHITS2022), pp. 239–248 (2022)

13. Gschwind, T., Drexl, M.: Adaptive large neighborhood search with a constant-time feasibility test for the dial-a-ride problem. Transp. Sci. **53**(2), 480–491 (2019)
14. Guan, D.J.: Routing a vehicle of capacity greater than one. Discrete Appl. Math. **81**(1), 41–57 (1998)
15. Impacts, R.R.: Jülich: Testbetrieb mit autonomem Zug startet (2022). https://www.eurailpress.de/railimpacts/forschung/detail/news/juelich-testbetrieb-mit-autonomem-zug-startet-2022.html
16. Jain, S., Van Hentenryck, P.: Large neighborhood search for dial-a-ride problems. In: Lee, J. (ed.) CP 2011. LNCS, vol. 6876, pp. 400–413. Springer, Heidelberg (2011). https://doi.org/10.1007/978-3-642-23786-7_31
17. Jaw, J.J., Odoni, A.R., Psaraftis, H.N., Wilson, N.H.M.: A heuristic algorithm for the multi-vehicle advance request dial-a-ride problem with time windows. Transp. Res. Part B Methodol. **20**(3), 243–257 (1986)
18. Jorgensen, R.M., Larsen, J., Bergvinsdottir, K.B.: Solving the dial-a-ride problem using genetic algorithms. J. Oper. Res. Soc. **58**(10), 1321–1331 (2007)
19. Madsen, O.B.G., Ravn, H.F., Rygaard, J.M.: A heuristic algorithm for a dial-a-ride problem with time windows, multiple capacities, and multiple objectives. Ann. Oper. Res. **60**(1), 193–208 (1995)
20. Manasse, M.S., McGeoch, L.A., Sleator, D.D.: Competitive algorithms for server problems. J. Algorithms **11**(2), 208–230 (1990)
21. Masmoudi, M.A., Hosny, M., Demir, E., Genikomsakis, K.N., Cheikhrouhou, N.: The dial-a-ride problem with electric vehicles and battery swapping stations. Transp. Res. Part E Logist. Transp. Rev. **118**, 392–420 (2018)
22. Molenbruch, Y., Braekers, K., Caris, A.: Typology and literature review for dial-a-ride problems. Ann. Oper. Res. **259**, 295–325 (2017). https://doi.org/10.1007/s10479-017-2525-0
23. Psaraftis, H.N.: An exact algorithm for the single vehicle many-to-many dial-a-ride problem with time windows. Transp. Sci. **17**(3), 351–357 (1983)
24. Ritzer, P., Flamm, L., Scheier, B., Mönsters, M.: Demand Responsive Rail Transport auf Regionalstrecken - Konzept, Machbarkeit und Wirtschaftlichkeit. Eisenbahntechnische Rundschau **70**(6) (2021)
25. Ritzer, P., Mönsters, M., Flamm, L., Weik, N.: Demand Responsive Transport im Schienenverkehr - Eine Analyse des Systemdesigns. ETR-Eisenbahntechnische Rundschau **71**, 35–39 (2022)
26. Schindler, C.: The Aachen rail shuttle ARS-autonomous and energy self-sufficient feeder transport. J. Rail Transp. Plann. Manag. **21**, 100299 (2022)
27. Schlaht, J., Frink, L., Laumen, P., Pfeifer, A., Schindler, C., Nießen, N.: Automated Nano Transport System - Ansatz zur Entwicklung autonomer Schienenfahrzeuge. In: Proceedings of the 1st International Railway Symposium Aachen, pp. 60–77 (2018). https://doi.org/10.18154/RWTH-2018-222698. https://publications.rwth-aachen.de/record/720242
28. UITP: Metro Automation Facts, Figures and Trends. International Association of Public Transport (2012)
29. Der Verband Deutscher Verkehrsunternehmen (VDV): Auf der Agenda: Reaktivierung von Eisenbahnstrecken 2020 (2020). https://www.vdv.de
30. Zieger, S., Nießen, N.: The dial-a-ride problem in railways. In: 9th International Conference on Railway Operations Modelling and Analysis (RailBeijing2021), (2021)
31. Zieger, S., Niessen, N.: Opportunities and challenges for the demand-responsive transport using highly automated and autonomous rail units in rural areas. In: 2021 IEEE Intelligent Vehicles Symposium (IV), pp. 77–82. IEEE (2021)
32. Zieger, S., Nießen, N.: A simulation framework for the operation of automated small rail vehicles in rural areas, 6 p. 13th World Congress on Railway Research, Birmingham (UK), 6 June 2022–10 June 2022 (2022). https://publications.rwth-aachen.de/record/850350

Intelligent Roadside Infrastructure for Connected Mobility

Shiva Agrawal[1]([✉])(iD), Rui Song[2,3](iD), Kristina Doycheva[2](iD), Alois Knoll[3](iD), and Gordon Elger[1,2](iD)

[1] Institute of Innovative Mobility, Technische Hochschule Ingolstadt, Ingolstadt, Germany
{shiva.agrawal,gordon.elger}@thi.de
[2] Fraunhofer IVI, Ingolstadt, Germany
{rui.song,kristina.doycheva,gordon.elger}@ivi.fraunhofer.de
[3] Technical University of Munich, Garching, Germany
{rui.song,knoll}@tum.de

Abstract. Intelligent roadside infrastructure units are crucial for connected mobility applications, smart traffic flow optimization, road condition monitoring, emergency vehicle routing during accidents or traffic jam situations, and for various autonomous driving use cases. Although significant achievements in the development of roadside infrastructure units have been accomplished in recent years, challenges still remain open. Advanced sensors, algorithms, and communication technology are required to design robust and reliable systems. To face these challenges, the work presented in this paper aims at developing an intelligent roadside infrastructure unit that can easily be adapted to various applications and locations. The unit is comprised of advanced sensors, i.e. camera, radar (Radio Detection and Ranging), and lidar (Light Detection and Ranging) sensors for efficient environment perception, and one V2X (Vehicle-to-Everything) communication module for sending the required information to nearby road users. A sensor data fusion module and communication technologies constitute the core of the intelligent roadside infrastructure unit. The development involves mechanical and electrical design as well as methods for the synchronization of multiple sensors and joint sensor calibration. Moreover, an auto-labelling framework for training data annotation and a multi-sensor monitoring framework is implemented. To test the work presented in this publication, a case study was conducted. Preliminary tests at a pedestrian crossing junction show that the intelligent roadside unit can successfully be applied for smart traffic light control.

Keywords: Intelligent roadside infrastructure · Connected mobility · Sensor fusion · V2X communication · Traffic light control · Camera · radar · Lidar

---

S. Agrawal and R. Song—These authors contributed equally.

C. Klein et al. (Eds.): SMARTGREENS 2022/VEHITS 2022, CCIS 1843, pp. 134–157, 2023.
https://doi.org/10.1007/978-3-031-37470-8_6

1   Introduction

The self-driving industry has advanced in recent years with the aim to bring more reliable, safe, and autonomous vehicles to the market. According to the SAE (society of automotive engineers) levels of driving automation as described in SAE J3016 [1], autonomous vehicles are classified from level 0, which means no automation, to level 5, which means full automation. As the level of automation increases beyond SAE level 2, a high number of sensors is required by such vehicles due to safety, redundancy, and high-speed processing requirements, and to obtain information from many real-time sources. With this information, vehicles can perform real-time path planning and obstacle avoidance to navigate from point A to point B. But even after adding so much technology to the vehicle, it is still difficult for any vehicle to acquire all the required information about the surrounding in real-time solely based on its own sensors and processing units.

One solution to this issue is to allow vehicles to communicate with each other on the road so that their individual systems can use real-time information from other vehicles to improve their perception [36] or plan their trajectories [21]. This solution is further enhanced by designing and deploying smart infrastructure units on the side of the roads which usually comprise multiple cameras, radar, lidar sensors, and communication modules. These intelligent roadside infrastructure units can perceive the traffic well in advance and with a much wider field of view compared to vehicles. The sensor data can be processed to extract useful information and then critical warnings and alerts can be sent to passing by vehicles and other road users through the communication module based on V2X (*Vehicle-to-Everything*), V2I (*Vehicle-to-Infrastructure*) and V2N (*Vehicle-to-Networks*) communication technologies.

Apart from assisting vehicles on the road, intelligent roadside infrastructure units play a vital role in the development of smart cities. Numerous new application areas like traffic monitoring, traffic flow optimization using smart traffic light control, pothole detection, construction area detection, routing emergency vehicles smartly in case of road closure or accident, road condition monitoring, pedestrian counters at specific zones, etc. are actively getting recognition as new research topics.

Despite a large number of possible applications in the domain of intelligent roadside infrastructure, the research and outcomes available in the literature are still limited. In addition, state-of-research approaches do not explore the benefits of raw-level sensor fusion for enhanced environment perception and also do not focus on smart traffic light control systems based on intelligent roadside infrastructure.

Although raw-level sensor fusion has increasingly been considered in the literature, the presented approaches are not within the intelligent roadside infrastructure domain. Also, the available work mainly focuses on two-dimensional (2D) radar fusion with a camera and is limited to the improvement of camera-based 2D image detection using radar as an additional input source, while the work presented in this paper focuses on using 3D radar with mono-cameras to generate fused objects in a 3D coordinate system and also aims at tackling the challenges in intelligent roadside infrastructure applications, specifically smart traffic light control.

This paper is an extended version of [3]. The use cases, a concept for an intelligent roadside infrastructure unit, and a short overview of the basic components of such a unit are described in [3]. In this extended paper, an updated system architecture of an intelligent roadside infrastructure unit, sensor selection, and specification, a hardware design of an experimental mast (including mechanical and electrical designs), methods for sensor synchronization, joint calibration of sensors, an auto-labelling framework for training data generation for artificial intelligence (AI) based sensor fusion, brief insights of sensor fusion and validation and a sensor monitoring framework are described in detail. Further, intermediate results and findings are provided. Additionally, a software architecture for vehicular communication including a hybrid communication framework is provided.

This paper is structured as follows: Sect. 2 details related work with other similar test field projects, provides technical background and a literature survey on various sensor fusion, sensor synchronization, and calibration methods. Section 3 covers the high-level system architecture of the presented work and describes the major parts of the system. Section 4 details the hardware design and development of the intelligent roadside infrastructure of the described work. Section 5 provides insights about sensor synchronization, calibration, sensor fusion and validation, and sensor monitoring approaches for the intelligent roadside infrastructure unit. Section 6 details the communication modules using ETSI (European Telecommunications Standards Institute) V2X messaging and ERTICO (European Road Transport Telematics Implementation Coordination Organisation) SENSORIS (SENSOR Interface Specification). Section 7 describes a case study and then a conclusion and an acknowledgment are provided.

2   Related Work

2.1   Test Fields with Roadside Infrastructure

The development of smart infrastructure for connected mobility is a comparatively new trend, but it has taken exponential growth in recent years. Many research institutes and companies from different regions are actively working in this area and some of these works are listed in this section.

The work described in [22] provides a relatively simple, wireless data collection system. In this work, thirty-one sensors are deployed at different locations along the road and they use a Raspberry Pi as a processing module. The described system is inexpensive, but it is not appropriate for connected mobility and advanced traffic monitoring and control because this system does not use any advanced sensors for the detection of road users. A test-bed described in [32] is part of research from the University of Tennessee at Chattanooga and comprised eleven infrastructure units. Each such unit is equipped with air quality sensors, cameras, lidar and radar sensors, an audio recording facility, and networking modules. Data from multiple units are further collected at a central system for further processing and information extraction. The work in [19] comprised multiple small testbeds between the cities of Aachen and Dusseldorf in Germany. The main focus is to conduct cooperative tests and development between infrastructure units and autonomous vehicles. The project presented in [24] describes a test bed in Lower Saxony, Germany for automated driving and connected mobility. The sensors and perception module of the test bed detect all vehicle positions with high precision to provide an accurate traffic situation. The work described in [10] is also in the direction of connected mobility and autonomous driving. It is developed to cover various types of public roads like highways, state and federal roads, inner-city routes with bicycles, pedestrians and streetcars, residential areas, and parking garages. This test field is located between Karlsruhe, Bruchsal, and Heilbronn in Germany. A test field presented in [6,18] is located in Munich, Germany. It is developed for traffic monitoring and connected mobility on highway A9. The project uses a vast number of cameras and radar sensors for accurate traffic monitoring. The work described in [2] focuses on the development of a large test field comprised of 11 intelligent infrastructure units which the authors refer to as roadside units. The aim of this test field is to assist and conduct various tests together with autonomous driving technology development.

The presented work in this paper focuses on the use cases of connected mobility and smart traffic light control for traffic flow optimization.

2.2 Sensor Fusion

In an intelligent roadside infrastructure unit, accurate detection, classification, and accurate motion prediction of road users are necessary under all weather and light conditions. But with only one type of sensor with currently available technology, this task is not feasible. Every sensor has some strengths and some weaknesses as stated in [33] and hence to enhance perception and to overcome the limitations of each sensor, data from multiple sensors (two or more sensors) is fused together.

As stated in [33,35,38], multi-modal sensor fusion can be performed at different levels in the perception pipeline. It is broadly classified as data-level fusion, decision-level fusion, and feature-level or target-level fusion. In data-level fusion, regions of interest (ROI) are generated from the radar or lidar points and then these points are projected on the camera image. Then the corresponding regions from the images are extracted. Finally, these regions of interest are passed through a feature extractor and a classifier.

In decision-level fusion, object detection is carried out at individual sensors independent of other sensors in the system. Later all the objects from different sensors are associated and fused together to generate a common track object list. This fusion approach is widely known and common in practice. Further, there are two variants of this fusion approach. One is object-level fusion [7,27], where object lists from multiple sensors are fused to generate one track object list. Another approach is track-to-track fusion [9] where track objects are generated from each sensor and then they are fused together to create a fused track object list.

The last approach is feature-level fusion [37] and it is comparatively new. The work in this domain is still limited and some of the work specifically for camera and radar fusion is given in [4,5,17,23]. In this kind of fusion, raw data from two or more sensors are fused together at an early stage after extracting high-level features. Mostly AI-based approaches are involved and the final result is a fused object list with class information. The work described in this paper also focuses on this category of sensor fusion.

2.3 Sensor Synchronization

In any multi-sensor system setup, each sensor measures and sends data usually at a different frequency and in its own coordinate frame. To overcome these challenges, appropriate methods and algorithms for sensor synchronization and sensor calibration are used respectively. This sub-section describes the sensor synchronization and the next sub-section describes the sensor calibration.

As described in [38], sensors can be synchronized at two different levels - hardware level and software level.

Hardware synchronization means that all the sensors are triggered at the hardware level to measure and send data simultaneously. This trigger can be sent either by external hardware as shown in Fig. 1 (top) or by one of the sensors of the system, acting as a master, and other sensors acting as slaves as shown in Fig. 1 (bottom).

Hardware synchronization is difficult because sensors require the hardware-level capability to take trigger signals as input, and setting up such a system is comparatively complex. Another approach is software synchronization. In this approach, all the sensors use software timestamps and share the same reference

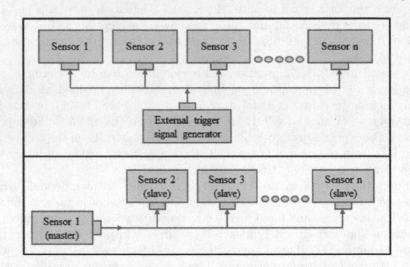

Fig. 1. Hardware trigger methods for sensor synchronization.

clock. For example, coordinated universal time (UTC), global positioning systems (GPS), etc. Then each sensor sends the data at its own frame rate and each frame contains a timestamp. Later, the frames belonging to nearby timestamps from multiple sensors are taken together for fusion. If the sensors provide data at a different frequency, then software synchronization will remove some frames from high-frequency sensors. This is known as sub-sampling.

2.4 Sensor Calibration

The main aim of calibrating a multi-sensor system is to transform the measurements from individual sensor coordinates to a common coordinate system that can represent the external three-dimensional (3D) world in a more intuitive way. There are many methods developed in the past as mentioned in [11,20].

Broadly, the extrinsic calibration of a camera, lidar, and radar-based sensor system, can be categorized as 3D-2D calibration and 3D-3D calibration. 3D-2D calibration includes 3D radar or 3D lidar to camera image calibration and 3D-3D calibration includes 3D radar to 3D lidar calibration or vice-versa.

For 3D-2D calibration, Eq. 1 is used. In Eq. 1, [X, Y, Z] is a vector that represents one 3D sensor point and it is multiplied by the camera intrinsic matrix and transformation matrix to project this point on the 2D camera image. Further in Eq. 1, f_x and f_y are focal lengths in pixel coordinates, (c_x, c_y) are optical centres, t_x, t_y, t_z represent translation parameters and $r_{ij}, i > 0, j > 0$ represents rotational parameters. The final pixel values of u and v for the projected 3D point can be calculated by Eqs. 2 and 3 respectively, where u', v', w' represent intermediate values.

$$\begin{bmatrix} u' \\ v' \\ w' \end{bmatrix} = \begin{bmatrix} f_x & 0 & c_x \\ 0 & f_y & c_y \\ 0 & 0 & 1 \end{bmatrix} \begin{bmatrix} r_{11} & r_{12} & r_{13} & t_x \\ r_{21} & r_{22} & r_{23} & t_y \\ r_{31} & r_{32} & r_{33} & t_z \end{bmatrix} \begin{bmatrix} X \\ Y \\ Z \\ 1 \end{bmatrix} \tag{1}$$

$$u = u'/w' \tag{2}$$

$$v = v'/w' \tag{3}$$

For 3D-3D calibration, Eq. 4 is used. In this Equation, $[X_s, Y_s, Z_s]$ is the point of the source 3D coordinate frame and $[X_d, Y_d, Z_d]$ is the same point transformed to the destination 3D coordinate frame. For example, if one wants to transform a radar to a lidar coordinate frame, then the source is the radar coordinate and the destination is the lidar coordinate frame. As a note, the transformation matrix has different values for different sensor calibration pairs.

$$\begin{bmatrix} X_d \\ Y_d \\ Z_d \\ 1 \end{bmatrix} = \begin{bmatrix} r_{11} & r_{12} & r_{13} & t_x \\ r_{21} & r_{22} & r_{23} & t_y \\ r_{31} & r_{32} & r_{33} & t_z \\ 0 & 0 & 0 & 1 \end{bmatrix} \begin{bmatrix} X_s \\ Y_s \\ Z_s \\ 1 \end{bmatrix} \tag{4}$$

3 Architecture of the Intelligent Roadside Infrastructure Unit

The high-level architecture of the intelligent roadside infrastructure is given in Fig. 2 where hardware components are shown on the left side and software modules are shown on the right side. This architecture is updated and revised from paper [3]. The hardware components are comprised of three red-green-blue (RGB) mono-cameras, three 3D automotive radar sensors, one 360° rotating lidar sensor, one V2X communication module, and two traffic lights acting as a final control element. The software modules include a sensor perception, a communication, a decision maker, and a traffic light control module.

With the help of sensor perception, specifically with sensor fusion, road users including vehicles, pedestrians, and bicycles are detected and tracked. The results of the perception are used as an input to control the traffic lights smartly with the aim to minimize the waiting time of vehicles as well as pedestrians and bicyclists crossing the junction and also to prioritize emergency vehicles.

The architecture in section 3 of paper [3], has a backend that is now updated and revised as the decision maker module which is comprised of a local decision maker and local messaging, and a remote decision maker. The decision maker module is part of the intelligent roadside infrastructure unit and the remote decision maker is in the cloud. The main purpose of the remote decision maker is to remotely monitor the functioning of the system. Further, in case of any system error or failure, it is used for diagnostics and error correction.

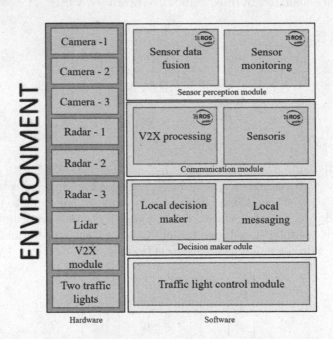

Fig. 2. High-level architecture of the intelligent roadside infrastructure unit.

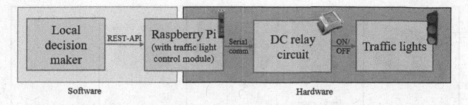

Fig. 3. A block diagram of the traffic light control module.

The **local decision maker** receives the perception data in form of a serialized message structure using the *SENSORIS* [26] protocol. The local decision maker is connected to the messaging infrastructure by an exchangeable adapter to allow different cloud-based message systems like Google Pub/Sub and local-based message systems like RabbitMQ for modular data exchange. The *SENSORIS* road-user tracked object list of each timestamp is converted into an internal road user model by the local decision maker that is extended with functionality to allow different calculations. These road users are stored in a cache to observe them during their travel time in the sensor field of view. Based on the information in the cache representing the current road user situation around the intersection and the current state of the traffic light, a decision algorithm is triggered. The algorithm calculates the optimal state for the traffic light. An event is then sent out to the traffic light control module to change the states of the traffic lights according to the calculated decision.

The **local messaging** service sends data and commands between the local decision maker and the remote decision maker residing in the cloud.

The **traffic light control module** controls the states of the traffic lights.

As shown in Fig. 3, the local decision maker defines the new states for the traffic lights based on the output of the sensor perception module. These new states act as new decisions and are sent to the traffic light control module running on the Raspberry Pi. According to the decision states, the control module sends signals to the direct current (DC) relay circuit via serial communication, and then traffic lights are switched ON or OFF based on the output signal. In case of failure of communication between the decision maker and the traffic light control module, the traffic lights work in standard time-based logic as fail-safe mode.

Details of the **sensor perception module** and **communication module** of the intelligent roadside infrastructure unit are presented in Sect. 5 and 6 respectively.

4 Hardware Design

This section details the hardware design of the intelligent roadside infrastructure unit. The complete hardware setup comprised multiple sensors and one V2X module mounted on a mast in the infrastructure. In the laboratory a tripod, a pole-like mechanical structure is used for flexible mobile set-up. It also contains

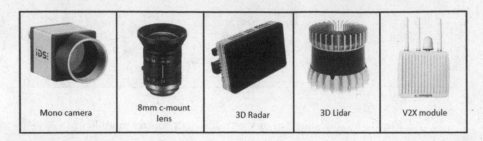

Fig. 4. Sensors and V2X module of the intelligent roadside infrastructure unit [15,16, 25,30,31].

one control cabinet, a small box with all the supporting hardware like switches, protocol converters, DC power supply, DC splitter, cables, relay, etc., and the traffic lights, acting as a final control element.

4.1   Sensors and V2X Module Specifications

The sensors used in this work include RGB mono-cameras from IDS with C-mount 8 mm lens, ARS548 radar sensors from Continental, and an Ouster OS1 lidar sensor with 64 channels. The V2X communication module used is Commsignia ITS-RS4-M roadside unit as shown in Fig. 4.

The **mono-camera** [30] has a complementary metal-oxide semiconductor (CMOS) sensor with 1/1.2" optical class, C-mount type with a resolution of 1936×1216 pixels. The maximum frame rate is 30 frames per second (fps), with a Gigabit interface and power over Ethernet (PoE) capability. Further, an optical lens [31] with an 8 mm focal length is used for the camera.

The **3D automotive radar** [25] is a long-range radar with a detection range of up to 300 m. It has an operating frequency of 77 GHz, a horizontal field of view (HFoV) and a vertical field of view (VFoV) of 100° and 28° respectively, a range resolution of 0.22 m, a horizontal and a vertical angular resolution of 2.3° and 1.68° respectively and a frame rate 20 Hz. The output interface is BRR (BroadR Reach) Ethernet 100 Mbit/s and works at 12 V DC supply.

The **3D automotive lidar** [16] is a digital beam-forming, medium range lidar with a detection range of up to 120 m. It has a horizontal field of view of 360°, a vertical field of view of 22.5° (below the horizon), working frame rates 10 Hz 20 Hz, a Gigabit Ethernet output interface, and a power consumption of 14–20 W at 12 V DC.

The **V2X communication module** [15] has an integrated global navigation satellite system (GNSS) and inertial measurement unit (IMU) based localization system with Wireless connection options of WIFI/BLUETOOTH/CELLULAR (3G/LTE). It has 10/100/1000 Mbps Ethernet PoE capability with different V2X radio variants like autotalks section/NXP TEF5100 (RF transceiver) and SAF5100 (baseband)/Marvell SDIO (88W8987PA)/Qualcomm 9150.

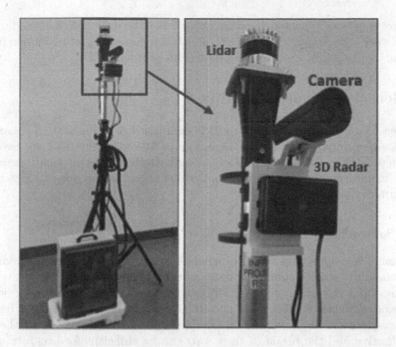

Fig. 5. Laboratory sensor mast.

4.2 Mechanical Design

Figure 5 shows the laboratory setup of the intelligent roadside infrastructure unit that consists of one radar, one camera, and one lidar sensor mounted on an industrial tripod. Customized housings and 3d printed mountings are designed that have the possibility to orient the sensors according to the field of view requirement. All the electrical components are placed inside the small box known as the control cabinet as shown in Fig. 5. For research purposes, only one pair of a camera and a radar is sufficient, hence the present setup is developed accordingly. Later for the final demonstration, additional pairs of camera and radar sensors will be added to detect vehicles and pedestrians passing from different directions on the road. Moreover, one V2X module will be mounted to test the communication between the infrastructure unit and vehicles.

4.3 Electrical Design

Figure 6 highlights the electrical connections of the complete setup (excluding the traffic light controller).

The cameras and the V2X module are powered with PoE, while the lidar and radar sensors are powered with a normal 12 V DC power supply. The application unit is the main computer where all the software modules are running. Hence, each sensor is connected finally to this device either via a PoE switch or via a protocol converter (in the case of the radar). For the automotive 3D radar used in the work, the output is over BRR. It is then converted into commercial 1G Ethernet and data is sent over user datagram protocol (UDP).

5   Sensor Perception Module

The sensor perception module (Fig. 2) is comprised of a sensor data fusion and a sensor monitoring module. The sensor data fusion module outputs real-time motion predictions of dynamic objects along with their class information and the sensor monitoring module keeps a continuous check on the sensor connectivity and data availability.

5.1   Sensor Data Fusion

The complete sensor data fusion pipeline is comprised of multi-sensor synchronization, multi-sensor calibration, data collection and annotation, raw-level sensor fusion and validation, and multi-object tracking. In the presented work, sensor fusion of 3D automotive radar and RGB mono camera is carried out because these two sensors are a very good complement to each other. Also, they are cost-effective and the fusion of these two can be sufficient for accurate object detection and classification. The fused object list is then fed into a Kalman filter-based tracking algorithm to predict the motion of dynamic road users, such as vehicles, pedestrians, and bicycles. In order to make use of the complete sensor data, raw-level sensor fusion is selected instead of object-level or track-level sensor fusion.

The high-level software architecture of the sensor fusion module is given in Fig. 7. The complete perception module is running on a robot operating system (ROS). The numbers highlighted in Fig. 7 are different outputs from each part of the software module. (1) and (2) are the raw output from the mono-camera and 3D radar sensor. (3) is the 3D point cloud of the radar sensor which contains multiple reflections, also known as detections. Each detection is associated with a range, an azimuth angle, an elevation angle, a doppler speed, and a radar cross-section (RCS) value. Further range, azimuth angle, and elevation angle are converted to Cartesian coordinates represented as (X, Y, Z) of radar. (4) is the RGB image from the camera which has a resolution of 1920×1080 pixels. (5) is the pseudo-image of the radar frame. It is a sparse image similar to a camera image but provides information from a radar sensor - like distance, velocity, and RCS. The size of the pseudo-image of the radar is the same as the camera image. (6) is the fused 3D object list from radar and camera after raw-level AI-based sensor data fusion. This fused object list is then given as input to the Kalman filter-based multi-object tracking module to generate dynamic object trajectories or a tracked object list (7).

For associating the data from the 3D radar and the mono-camera, which belongs to the same object in the environment, both sensors are synchronized at the software level to extract the data at almost the same time instance from the

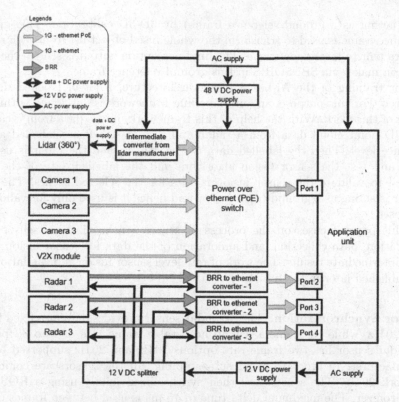

Fig. 6. Electrical design of the intelligent roadside infrastructure unit.

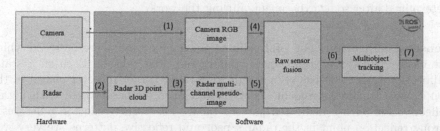

Fig. 7. Software architecture of the sensor data fusion.

radar and the camera. This is a crucial step for raw-level sensor fusion. Once the sensor frames of the same timestamp are available after synchronization, joint calibration is performed using a pre-defined multi-target-based system. In the calibration process, the 3D radar sensor is calibrated spatially with the mono-camera and then the radar point cloud is projected from a 3D coordinate frame to 2D image coordinates to create a radar pseudo image. Additionally, the fused object list generated from the fusion algorithm is in the 3D coordinate frame of the radar sensor which is transformed into an infrastructure coordinate frame (also acting as a ground reference frame) by 3D-3D calibration. This ground reference frame is used to transform the whole fused object list from each radar-camera pair to a common frame. The final perception output is sent to the local decision maker via SENSORIS in this ground reference frame.

For training of the AI-based fusion architecture, a lot of labelled data is required. For this purpose, an auto-labelling framework is developed within the scope of this work. With the help of this framework, image data from a camera and 3D point cloud data from a radar and a lidar sensor are labelled at the instance level. Then the labelled data of the camera and the radar is used to train and test the sensor fusion algorithm and the labelled data of the lidar is used to validate the sensor fusion results for the selected scenes. The lidar sensor is acting as a ground truth sensor and hence it is used only for validation purposes.

This paper focuses on the process of sensor synchronization, sensor joint calibration, data collection, and annotation of the data for sensor fusion along with intermediate results. The work of raw-level sensor fusion and validation will be published later in the future.

Sensor Synchronization. The 3D radar sensor provides data at a fixed frame rate 20 Hz, while the camera has an adjustable frame rate of 1 to 30 fps and the lidar sensor has two frame rate options 10 Hz and 20 Hz supported by the manufacturer. In order to avoid sub-sampling, all the sensors are configured to work 20 Hz. The sensors are then synchronized jointly using a ROS time synchronizer. The maximum delta time of 15 ms is used between frames of two sensors to consider them from almost the same time instance. This value is determined after some experiments during the work.

Sensor Calibration. For joint calibration, unique targets are designed which are easily detected by the camera, radar, and lidar sensors. Each such static calibration target consists of one high RCS radar corner reflector placed in the center of a square Styrofoam. This Styrofoam is further covered with highly reflective foil with a dedicated pattern on it. The corner reflector generates a strong reflection point in the radar sensor and reflective patterns are very well detected by the lidar and camera. In lidar, all the reflected points from each target are clustered together using DBSCAN (density-based spatial clustering of applications with noise) and then the center point is calculated. In the camera, state-of-the-art Mask-RCNN (region-based convolutional neural network) is re-trained using transfer learning to detect and calculate the center point of each target. The process of calibration using this method is detailed in a dedicated research paper which is in the submission phase.

Multiple such static targets are placed at different positions in the field of view and from each target, one unique point is measured (to the best possible accuracy) in each sensor coordinate frame to generate a list of point pairs belonging to the same target but from different sensors. For example, in the camera, the (u, v) values of each point are measured, and in radar and lidar, the (x, y, z) values of each point are measured. The point pairs belonging to the camera and radar, and camera and lidar are processed separately using the PnP-RANSAC algorithm to calculate the transformation matrices. These transformation matrices together with the intrinsic matrix of the camera are then used to project radar points and lidar points on the camera image based on Eqs. 1, 2, and 3. Figure 8a shows the projected lidar points on the camera image and Fig. 8b shows the projected radar points on the camera image.

For transforming the sensor fusion results to an infrastructure coordinate frame (also acting as a ground reference frame), 3D to 3D calibration is performed. To make this calibration simple, the ground reference frame which is associated with the tripod is aligned with the lidar coordinate frame in a way, that there is zero relative rotation between them. The translation in the X and Y direction is also kept zero and the translation along the Z axis is a constant value. As the lidar sensor is mounted on top of the tripod, the origin of the lidar is at height h compared to the origin of the infrastructure coordinate frame which is at the base of the tripod and touching the ground. This height h is the translation value along the Z axis. Now, to transform the fused object list from the radar coordinate frame to the ground reference frame, first it is transformed to the lidar coordinate frame and then to the ground reference frame. For radar to lidar coordinate calibration, point pairs of both sensors are fed into the least square-based algorithm to calculate a transformation matrix as given in Eq. 4.

Data Collection and Annotation. For training and testing of deep learning-based neural network for raw sensor fusion, data is collected from all three sensors for pre-defined scenes to include different object categories. The collected data in form of Rosbag (a file format in robot operating system to store multiple data messages) is processed offline and exported to a hierarchical directory structure. In this exported data, each frame of the camera data is stored in portable network graphics (PNG) file format and each frame of radar and lidar data is stored in point cloud data (PCD) file format along with metadata and timestamps.

This exported data is then fed into an auto-labelling software framework, where first a custom trained Mask R-CNN is used to generate masks of different objects on the camera image, and then the radar and lidar points are projected on the camera image independently. The points belonging to objects of interest are labelled to a corresponding class and other points are discarded. At last, the labelled data is exported in javascript object notation (JSON) file format and stored together with the raw data. Figure 9a and Fig. 9b show the lidar and radar points respectively on the camera images after annotation.

5.2   Sensor Monitoring

For continuous checks of the sensor data, an abstract-level monitoring framework is developed. As stated before, the sensor perception module is running on ROS. So, all sensors, i.e. camera, radar, and lidar, have independent ROS nodes which

(a)

(b)

Fig. 8. Lidar point cloud projected on a camera image (8a) and radar point cloud projected on the camera image (8b).

acquire data from them. Hence, sensor monitoring is implemented at this level in the perception pipeline.

In the ROS environment, every sensor publishes data on a specific topic with a unique name. Sensor monitoring is implemented to run 1 Hz. Three parameters, i.e. active status flag, data status flag, and data publishing rate are used to check and monitor data from each sensor.

As described in Fig. 10, at first all the active topics are scanned and then each individual topic (which is of interest) is searched in the scanned list of active topics. If the topic is found, then the active status flag is set to true. If the topic name is not found in the active topic list, then the active status flag is set to false. This means that the particular sensor's ROS node crashed or stopped working due to an error or an issue and then the further process for this sensor is stopped.

If the active status flag is set to true, then, as a next step, the data available from this topic is checked. If the topic is active and also publishing messages, it means that the sensor is working and the data status flag is set to true. During lab work, it was observed that, sometimes, even though the ROS topic was active,

(a) Lidar points labelled

(b) Radar points labelled

Fig. 9. Annotation generation of lidar data (9a) and of radar data (9b).

it stopped publishing data. This can happen if the sensor power is shut off or connectivity at the hardware level is lost, but the ROS node is still running in the software. Hence, the data status flag helps to monitor such problems. In case no messages are published, the data status flag is set to false.

When both flags are set to true, the data publishing rate is calculated for the topic. In the same way, the topics of all the sensors are checked and the associated parameters are updated once a second. The updated parameters are sent to the local as well as to the remote decision maker and remote monitoring module.

6   Communication Module

6.1   V2X Module

Environmental perception has been successfully deployed in modern vehicles, in order to realize advanced driving assistance systems (ADAS) and autonomous driving (AD). Compared to vehicles, the perception results in the roadside

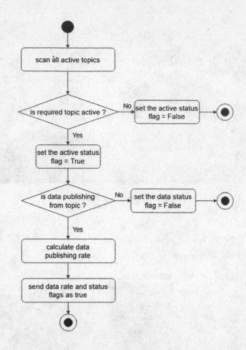

Fig. 10. Sensor monitoring - logic diagram.

infrastructure can provide road environmental information with higher quality, because (*i*) the sensors are fixed on masts, so that perception is not affected
by any movements; (*ii*) the heights and angles of sensors can be specifically
designed for each particular spot and thus provide more accurate perception,
which is especially useful for generating High Definition (HD) dynamic traffic
maps with Bird-Eye-View (BEV). Especially by leveraging hybrid V2X communication technologies, the intelligent roadside infrastructure in the system is
able to broadcast the current traffic dynamic maps via V2X messages and let
connected vehicles be aware of the traffic environment in a larger range with the
extended sensors on the masts.

Figure 11 shows the hybrid V2X module used in the system that consists
of cooperative intelligent transportation stations (C-ITS, including connected
vehicles and roadside infrastructure), traffic lights, and a local decision maker.
The system enables the bi-directional information sharing through I2N and I2V
modules: (*a*) The information obtained by the vehicles are utilized in the sensor
fusion module and enhances traffic services in the local decision maker; (*b*) The
intelligent roadside infrastructure unit results on the masts are shared to connected vehicles. Specifically, two main communication frameworks are applied in
Cooperative Intelligent Transport System (C-ITS) - *ERTICO SENSORIS* [26]
und *ETSI C-ITS V2X messages* [14], which are open, standardized, and commonly accepted. Particularly, *ERTICO SENSORIS* provides a sensor interface
between vehicles and the cloud via cellular communication. The objects detected

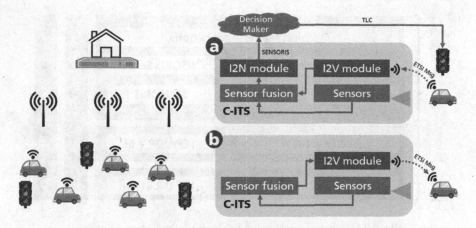

Fig. 11. An overview of the V2X communication module.

Table 1. Mapping between ESTI V2X Message (Msg) types in I2V module and categories of *SENSORIS* data elements in I2N module

I2V Msg	I2N Msg[d]	Content
CAM[a]	Localization	Position, rotation and dynamic status
CPM[b]	Object Detection	Information of movable and static objects
DENM[c]	Traffic Events	Hazard, dangerous slowdown, traffic condition, etc.

[a] CAM: Cooperative Awareness Message, standardized in EN 302 637-2.
[b] CPM: Collective Perception Message, draft-standardized in TS 103 324.
[c] DENM: Decentralized Environmental Notification, standardized in EN 302 637-3.
[d] SENSORIS category messages used in I2N module with respect to SENSORIS specification v1.3.1 public.

by each vehicle equipped with *SENSORIS* software can be uploaded in form of messages encoded using Google protobuf. *ETSI C-ITS V2X messages* are composed of a set of protocols in the facilities layer of the V2X protocol stack [26].

By broadcasting various messages, e.g. *Collective Awareness Messages* (CAM), *Cooperative Perception Messages* (CPM), *Decentralized Environmental Notification Messages* (DENM), the C-ITSs can share sensor information in an ad-hoc network over ITS-G5 or C-V2X in the 5.9 GHz frequency band [8]. As shown in Table 1, the shared V2X messages can be mapped to *SENSORIS* messages for further I2N communication and shared with the local decision maker for more advanced traffic analysis [27] and AI-based services, such as a labeling service for federated learning [28,29], or reinforcement learning-based traffic optimization [12,13,34]. Further details on the hybrid network software architecture using *SENSORIS* and *V2X Messaging*are described in the previous work of Song and Festag [26].

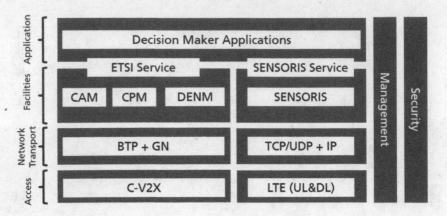

Fig. 12. Proposed protocol stack in communication solution.

6.2   V2X Protocol Stacks

An appropriate communication design enables promising information exchange among all intelligent components in the entire system, which guarantees the performance of intelligent infrastructure-based traffic services and applications. In this paper, the challenges of efficient data sharing in communication networks are specifically tackled, i.e., (i) highly heterogeneous networks for dissemination of various messages using vehicle-to-vehicle (V2V), vehicle-to-cloud (V2C), vehicle-to-infrastructure (V2I) communication, etc. (ii) variety of quality of service (QoS) requirements in miscellaneous traffic services.

To exploit the information in the road traffic and interoperate the systems in hybrid networks together with infrastructure and vehicles, in the paper the protocol stack with both communication frameworks for deployment is used, which is shown in Fig. 12. The main aim to include both types of communication is to consider possible interface compatibility for the future expansion of the project. Further, this will also help to gain sufficient experience in the development of the required software stack.

In addition, as shown in Fig. 12 on the left side, the system is designed for V2X protocol stacks. C-V2X with PC5 interface resides on the access layer. GeoNetworking (GN) distributes the packets in the geographical field and the basic transport protocol (BTP) enables the multiplexing and demultiplexing of messages on the site of C-ITS. In the facilities layer, the CAM, CPM, and DENM with corresponding ETSI Service are employed for sensor data sharing [14]. On the right side, long-term evolution (LTE) with uplink and downlink (UL&DL) is set as the physical interface for communication with the local decision maker. As the first cloud deployment, the TCP/IP-based Google Pub/Sub is integrated for *SENSORIS* message dissemination. Both *ETSI* and *SENSORIS* services are defined as interfaces between application and facilities layers. Consequently, the backend applications can take action depending on the information from the hybrid networks.

6.3   SENSORIS Integration

In this section, the implementation details on the *SENSORIS* integration into the system are provided. In particular, the connection between the intelligent roadside infrastructure unit and the local decision maker is established by the middleware Google Pub/Sub. The coming dynamic maps in object lists can be received by a listening thread in time and then forwarded to the *SENSORIS* message builder. This message builder generates the *SENSORIS* message with respect to a pre-defined configuration file, where the signal mapping between fused object lists and *SENSORIS* are archaically defined. By adjusting the rule of signal mapping in this configuration file, the system is flexibly scalable. As the original *SENSORIS* specification provides multiple methodologies for the same information, only dedicated data elements are selected for the system. Also, in each *SENSORIS* message, only one specific message category is considered.

For instance, to share an object list, the data elements under *ObjectDetectionCategory* are filled in the I2N module as described in the following listing is filled:

```
// One object
event_group.object_detection_category.movable_object
// 3D geometry model
movable_object.rectangular_box_and_accuracy
// Bounding Box
center_orientation_size.size_and_accuracy.metric_vehicle
// Position
center_orientation_size.center_position_and_accuracy.metric_vehicle
// Orientation
center_orientation_size.orientation_and_accuracy.euler_vehicle
// Acceleration
acceleration_and_accuracy.metric_vehicle
```

Afterward, the data are capsuled in one message for applications in the local decision maker.

7   Case Study

The intelligent roadside infrastructure unit described in this publication was designed and developed with the aim of traffic light control for traffic flow optimization and performing specific tests for connected mobility. To evaluate the application of roadside infrastructure unit and communication technology for the aforementioned tasks, a case study was considered. A location in Ingolstadt, Germany was chosen to illustrate a possible installation of a roadside infrastructure unit. The selected location is a pedestrian crossing junction (Fig. 13), where the yellow broad lane is a vehicle lane with a speed limit of 50 km/h and the narrow pink lane is used by pedestrians and bicycles. Both lanes intersect at the crossing and are regulated by traffic lights. The same crossing junction with traffic lights is also shown in the corner of Fig. 13 for better visual understanding.

The first experiments have shown that the roadside infrastructure unit presented in this paper is appropriate for traffic participant data collection in a

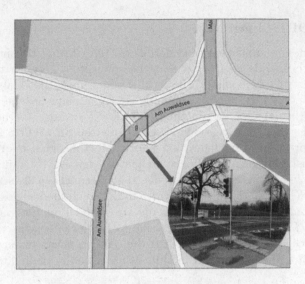

Fig. 13. Case study location and setup [3].

real-world scenario. Since it can be installed in a way such that the sensors' field of view covers the locations relevant for traffic light control, information required for traffic flow optimization, e.g. the number of vehicles that intend to cross the junction, can easily be obtained. By analyzing the traffic situation based on the data provided by the roadside infrastructure unit and communicated through the V2X module, an optimal traffic light state can be determined.

8   Conclusion

In this publication, the benefits of intelligent roadside infrastructure units for the development of autonomous vehicles and for smart cities are discussed along with the details of the development of one such unit for traffic flow optimization. Moreover, various aspects of the development including mechanical and electrical design, high-level architecture, sensors, sensor perception pipeline, and communication methods for I2V and I2N are provided in detail. The described system and the setup are adaptable to various infrastructure-based applications, and hence it provides a strong baseline for research and development for various use cases.

The raw-level sensor fusion framework and its validation are the next steps of the presented work. After the fusion framework is implemented and validated, the system is to be extended with more sensors for demonstration and for future research.

Acknowledgement. This work is supported by the Bavarian Ministry of Economic Affairs, Regional Development and Energy (StMWi) in the project "InFra Intelligent -

Infrastructure". We would also like to thank Continental for providing the 3D automotive radar sensor for this work.

References

1. SAE levels of driving automation homepage. https://www.sae.org/blog/sae-j3016-update. Accessed 3 Oct 2022
2. Agrawal, S., Elger, G.: Concept of infrastructure based environment perception for IN2Lab test field for automated driving. In: 2021 IEEE International Smart Cities Conference (ISC2), pp. 1–4. IEEE (2021)
3. Agrawal, S., et al.: Concept of smart infrastructure for connected vehicle assist and traffic flow optimization. In: VEHITS, pp. 360–367 (2022)
4. Chadwick, S., Maddern, W., Newman, P.: Distant vehicle detection using radar and vision. In: 2019 International Conference on Robotics and Automation (ICRA), pp. 8311–8317. IEEE (2019)
5. Chang, S., et al.: Spatial attention fusion for obstacle detection using mmwave radar and vision sensor. Sensors **20**(4), 956 (2020)
6. Creß, C., et al.: A9-dataset: multi-sensor infrastructure-based dataset for mobility research. In: 2022 IEEE Intelligent Vehicles Symposium (IV), pp. 965–970. IEEE (2022)
7. Fayad, F., Cherfaoui, V.: Object-level fusion and confidence management in a multi-sensor pedestrian tracking system. In: 2008 IEEE International Conference on Multisensor Fusion and Integration for Intelligent Systems, pp. 58–63. IEEE (2008)
8. Festag, A., Udupa, S., Garcia, L., Wellens, R., Hecht, M., Ulfig, P.: End-to-end performance measurements of drone communications in 5G cellular networks. In: 2021 IEEE 94th Vehicular Technology Conference (VTC2021-Fall), pp. 1–6 (2021). https://doi.org/10.1109/VTC2021-Fall52928.2021.9625429
9. Floudas, N., Polychronopoulos, A., Aycard, O., Burlet, J., Ahrholdt, M.: High level sensor data fusion approaches for object recognition in road environment. In: 2007 IEEE Intelligent Vehicles Symposium, pp. 136–141. IEEE (2007)
10. Frey, M.: Challenges in real traffic-test area autonomous driving baden-württemberg. In: Automated Mobility Conference-Changing the Game of Urban Mobility, Brüssel, Belgien (2019)
11. Gao, D., Duan, J., Yang, X., Zheng, B.: A method of spatial calibration for camera and radar. In: 2010 8th World Congress on Intelligent Control and Automation, pp. 6211–6215. IEEE (2010)
12. Gu, S., Chen, G., Zhang, L., Hou, J., Hu, Y., Knoll, A.: Constrained reinforcement learning for vehicle motion planning with topological reachability analysis. Robotics **11**(4), 81 (2022)
13. Gu, S., et al.: A review of safe reinforcement learning: Methods, theory and applications. arXiv preprint arXiv:2205.10330 (2022)
14. Hegde, A., Festag, A.: Artery-C: an OMNeT++ based discrete event simulation framework for cellular V2X. In: MSWiM 2020, pp. 47–51. Association for Computing Machinery (2020). https://doi.org/10.1145/3416010.3423240
15. Commsignia Inc.: Commsignia ITS-RS4 V2X enabled road side unit datasheet (2022). https://www.commsignia.com/wp-content/uploads/2020/11/Commsignia_ITS_RS4_ProductBrief_v.10.1_22052020_web.pdf
16. Ouster Inc.: Ouster OS1 lidar sensor datasheet (2022). https://data.ouster.io/downloads/datasheets/datasheet-rev06-v2p4-os1.pdf

17. John, V., Mita, S.: Deep feature-level sensor fusion using skip connections for real-time object detection in autonomous driving. Electronics **10**(4), 424 (2021)
18. Krämmer, A., Schöller, C., Gulati, D., Knoll, A.: Providentia-a large scale sensing system for the assistance of autonomous vehicles. In: Robotics: Science and Systems (RSS), Workshop on Scene and Situation Understanding for Autonomous Driving (2019)
19. Köhler, A.L., Koch, I., Ladwig, S.: Guiding drivers towards safer driving speed: exploiting visual dominance in speed adaptation. Transp. Res. Part F: Traffic Psychol. Behav. **90**, 438–450 (2022). https://doi.org/10.1016/j.trf.2022.09.011. https://www.sciencedirect.com/science/article/pii/S136984782200208X
20. Liu, X., Cai, Z.: Advanced obstacles detection and tracking by fusing millimeter wave radar and image sensor data. In: ICCAS 2010, pp. 1115–1120. IEEE (2010)
21. Maksimovski, D., Facchi, C., Festag, A.: Cooperative driving: research on generic decentralized maneuver coordination for connected and automated vehicles. In: Klein, C., Jarke, M., Helfert, M., Berns, K., Gusikhin, O. (eds.) Smart Cities, Green Technologies, and Intelligent Transport Systems. VEHITS SMARTGREENS 2021. CCIS, vol. 1612, pp. 348–370. Springer, Cham (2022). https://doi.org/10.1007/978-3-031-17098-0_18
22. Mazokha, S., Bao, F., Sklivanitis, G., Hallstrom, J.O.: Urban-scale testbed infrastructure for data-driven wireless research. In: 2021 IEEE 4th 5G World Forum (5GWF), pp. 517–522. IEEE (2021)
23. Nobis, F., Geisslinger, M., Weber, M., Betz, J., Lienkamp, M.: A deep learning-based radar and camera sensor fusion architecture for object detection. In: 2019 Sensor Data Fusion: Trends, Solutions, Applications (SDF), pp. 1–7. IEEE (2019)
24. von Schmidt, A., López Díaz, M., Schengen, A.: Creating a baseline scenario for simulating travel demand: a case study for preparing the region test bed lower Saxony, Germany. In: International Conference on Advances in System Simulation (SIMUL), pp. 51–57. ThinkMind (2021)
25. Continental Engineering Services: ARS548 RDI 3D/4D long range radar datasheet (2022). https://conti-engineering.com/wp-content/uploads/2020/02/RadarSensors_ARS548RDI.pdf
26. Song, R., Festag, A.: Analysis of existing approaches for information sharing in cooperative intelligent transport systems - V2X messaging and sensoris. In: 38th FISITA World Congress (2021). https://doi.org/10.46720/F2020-ACM-012
27. Song, R., Hegde, A., Senel, N., Knoll, A., Festag, A.: Edge-aided sensor data sharing in vehicular communication networks. In: 2022 IEEE 95th Vehicular Technology Conference: (VTC2022-Spring), pp. 1–7 (2022). https://doi.org/10.1109/VTC2022-Spring54318.2022.9860849
28. Song, R., et al.: Federated learning via decentralized dataset distillation in resource-constrained edge environments. arXiv preprint arXiv:2208.11311 (2022)
29. Song, R., Zhou, L., Lakshminarasimhan, V., Festag, A., Knoll, A.: Federated learning framework coping with hierarchical heterogeneity in cooperative its. In: 2022 IEEE 25th International Conference on Intelligent Transportation Systems (ITSC), pp. 3502–3508 (2022). https://doi.org/10.1109/ITSC55140.2022.9922064
30. IDS UI-5260CP-C-HQ rev.2 camera datasheet (2022). https://de.ids-imaging.com/IDS/datasheet_pdf.php?sku=AB00820
31. Tamron: Tamron M112FM08 lens datasheet (2022). https://www.tamron.vision/wp-content/uploads/2019/11/M112FM08_engl1.pdf
32. Tran, T.V., Sartipi, M.: Neuroevolution for transportation applications (2022)

33. Wei, Z., Zhang, F., Chang, S., Liu, Y., Wu, H., Feng, Z.: Mmwave radar and vision fusion for object detection in autonomous driving: a review. Sensors **22**(7), 2542 (2022)
34. Wiedemann, T., Vlaicu, C., Josifovski, J., Viseras, A.: Robotic information gathering with reinforcement learning assisted by domain knowledge: an application to gas source localization. IEEE Access **9**, 13159–13172 (2021). https://doi.org/10.1109/ACCESS.2021.3052024
35. Xu, R., Tu, Z., Xiang, H., Shao, W., Zhou, B., Ma, J.: Cobevt: cooperative bird's eye view semantic segmentation with sparse transformers. arXiv preprint arXiv:2207.02202 (2022)
36. Xu, R., Xiang, H., Tu, Z., Xia, X., Yang, M.H., Ma, J.: V2X-ViT: vehicle-to-everything cooperative perception with vision transformer. arXiv preprint arXiv:2203.10638 (2022)
37. Xu, R., Xiang, H., Xia, X., Han, X., Li, J., Ma, J.: OPV2V: an open benchmark dataset and fusion pipeline for perception with vehicle-to-vehicle communication. In: 2022 International Conference on Robotics and Automation (ICRA), pp. 2583–2589. IEEE (2022)
38. Zhou, Y., Dong, Y., Hou, F., Wu, J.: Review on millimeter-wave radar and camera fusion technology. Sustainability **14**(9), 5114 (2022)

Using Emotion Recognition and Temporary Mobile Social Network in On-Board Services for Car Passengers

Mario G. C. A. Cimino[1] (ID), Antonio Di Tecco[2,1] (ID), Pierfrancesco Foglia[1](✉) (ID), and Cosimo A. Prete[1] (ID)

[1] Department of Information Engineering, University of Pisa, Pisa, Italy
{mario.cimino,pierfrancesco.foglia}@unipi.it
[2] University of Florence, Florence, Italy
antonio.ditecco@unifi.it

Abstract. In next-generation cars, passengers will have more time for fun and relaxation, as well as the number of unknown passengers traveling together will increase. Thanks to the progress in Artificial Intelligence and Machine Learning techniques, new interaction models could be exploited to develop specialized applications that will be informed of the passengers' experience. The mood and the emotional state of driver and passengers can be detected, and utilized to improve safety and comfort by taking actions that improve driver and passengers' emotional state. Temporary Mobile Social Networking (TMSN) is a key functionality that can enhance passengers' user experience by allowing passengers to form a mobile social group with shared interests and activities for a time-limited period by utilizing their already existing social networking accounts. By minimizing isolation and promoting sociability, TMSN aims to redesign user profiles and interfaces automatically into a group-wise passengers' profile and a common interface. This work proposes and develops the generation of TMSN-inspired music selection through the Spotify music streaming service. The results obtained are promising and encourage further development toward the concept of in-car entertainment. Finally, we evaluate the performance of lightweight and heavy intelligent models that recognize the emotion of a person from its face, using Raspberry Pi 4 B devices. The results show that it is possible to realize a system with face detector and facial emotion recognition models on edge devices with sufficient performance (Frame per Second) to detect at least emotions expressed through macro-expressions.

Keywords: Autonomous car · In-car entertainment · Temporary mobile social networking · Music streaming service · Face detection · Emotion detection

1 Introduction

The automotive industry is witnessing a real revolution stemming from the dramatic increase of ICT usage for improving vehicle safety, while promoting new entertainment services and studying solutions for autonomous driving [1, 2].

C. Klein et al. (Eds.): SMARTGREENS 2022/VEHITS 2022, CCIS 1843, pp. 158–171, 2023.
https://doi.org/10.1007/978-3-031-37470-8_7

Nonetheless, the unstoppable and incremental advancement of autonomous cars, both owned or as shared commodities, will drive this innovation and consequently entertainment and personal assistance services will become essential for car passengers [3].

Thanks to the progress in Artificial Intelligence and Machine Learning techniques [4], new interaction models could be exploited to develop specialized applications that will be informed of the passengers' experience and situations, including personal interests and attractions, interactions within and outside the car environment, behavioral reactions to stimuli that change along the journey [3, 5]. Also, we will have the creating new model of temporary mobile social network, due to the increased time available to passengers as the level of car automation increases, and the presence of users sharing the same environment as in car sharing services [6].

In particular, the mood and the emotional state of driver and passengers can be detected [4], thanks to the enriched set of sensor available on-board. They can been utilized to improve safety and comfort by taking actions that improve the driver and passengers emotional state [4], and it can be exploited also to adapt the services offered by the applications to the user state via affective computing techniques [7, 8]. Preliminary examples are the BMW Emotional Browser [9] or the more recent Personal Assistant [10], that adapts the vehicle's interior to suit the drivers mood, but they utilize explicit driver inputs. The further innovation step is to realize a feedback tool, based on automatic user mood detection, that can be used to adapt the services offered to the needs of passengers [11, 12].

This paper is focused on the use of both Mobile Social Network (MSN) and Emotion Detection in the cart.

For what concern MSN, nowadays mobile technology ensures that car passengers have constant network connectivity and application functionality. As a result, they can easily obtain positive traveling experience by using mobile social networks, which offer a variety of entertainment options such as music and video streaming, feeds, stories, and so on [2, 13].

MSNs have already been introduced in cars through Android Auto or Apple CarPlay, the two major platforms for interoperability between smart phone and the car's dashboard information and entertainment unit. The number of MSN products can sensibly increase with the increasing level of car automation, in which the car controls a significant number of driving operations. Car sharing is also expected to gain popularity in this trend. As a result, next-generation cars will give passengers more time to have fun and relax, as well as increase the number of unknown passengers traveling together.

An important paradigm made possible by next generation cars is group-to-many interaction, which can further enrich an MSN user's interaction with the physical world by reducing his isolation. The user is alone in his physical world and is connected to the others via MSN in the traditional one-to-many interaction. With group-to-many interaction, a group of users temporarily lives in the same physical space (a car), interacts in person, and shares their MSN experience as a whole. The concept of Temporary MSN (TMSN) has received attention in the literature as a conceptual framework to be used at hotels, concerts, theme parks, and sports arenas, where people form a mobile social group for a limited time through common physical interaction [6]. People who are confined in a specific location (that can be a car) are allowed to join the TMSN and interact with others in a group-wise manner, improving mobile users' experiences with such temporal friends.

LobbyFriend was the first TMSN in the hotel industry, allowing establishments to maintain contact with guests throughout their stay, whether they were just staying at the same hotel or several in the area. All interactions in the TMSN are deleted when a guest leaves the establishment [6].

TMSN is more than just sharing a common space and a collaborative playlist [14, 15], it is about algorithms that exploit the user's profile and the current environmental context, allowing for augmented interaction through proactive services like automatic recommendation technology[16]. Today, powerful analytics and algorithms based on key techniques of modern sociology are successfully used to manage social media platforms. As such, in this study, TMSN is an additional intelligent layer on top of an existing ecosystem of services available on next-generation vehicles.

In this paper, a group-wise TMSN is proposed as a design paradigm for in-car entertainment. In particular, a functional design of an audio streaming automatic recommender protocol based on TMSN and Spotify analytics is illustrated in the context of social music. A prototype based on the Spotify API [17] has been developed and tested.

For what concern emotion detection, facial affect analysis is one of the less intrusive techniques that aims at estimating the emotions of a person [18], so its use can be exploited in the automotive environment [12]. According to the recent trend [18], a system for facial affect analysis is based on a Face Detector (FD), which find the location of a face (one or more faces) and extract it from an input image. The sub-image containing the face is then provided as input to a neural network (we call it FER – Face Emotion Recognition in the remaining of the paper) that finds facial landmarks estimates either categorical (happy, sad, etc.) or continuous dimensional measures of affective display, the most noteworthy of which are valence (how negative or positive the emotional display is) and arousal (how calming or exciting the emotional display looks like) [19].

FD and FER are generally realized by machine learning tools [12, 18], and their computational demand can be met by a cloud service, but this solution has limitations related to privacy, connectivity and the costs associated with building and maintaining the connected infrastructure [20]. An Edge solution, in which processing is performed locally, would greatly simplify the system architecture and solve the problems related to privacy an connectivity [20]. In this work, we identify also the level of performance achievable by running state-of-the-art Face Detection and Facial Emotion Recognition algorithms on devices typically used in the edge domain, and whether the achievable performance is compatible with real-time emotion detection, so that they can be executed on low cost in-vehicle hardware.

The paper extends [21], by performing new user experiments with a prototype TMSN system, and adds the evaluation of facial affect analysis on edge devices.

The paper is structured as follows. Section 2 illustrates the core concepts and functional design of a recommender protocol based on TMSN and Spotify analytics. Experimental results are given Sect. 3. Section 4 is devoted to the performance analysis of different FED and FER algorithms running on an edge device. Section 5 concludes the paper.

2 Functional Design of a TMSN Playlist Recommender

The TMSN-based playlist recommender uses the ambient (car) and MSN data, when dealing with audio streaming applications. In this context, it is better to base the design on a standard music ontology [22] to improve interoperability (an important issue when dealing with distributed systems [23]), as the ontology provides a common vocabulary for exchanging music-related data across various applications [24].

Figure 1 depicts an ontology diagram showing the fundamental concepts and static relationships for audio streaming recommendation. Each concept is enclosed in a rectangular shape in the figure. Relationships connect concepts, and are represented by labelled oriented edges. Properties, shown in lower case, may also characterize some concepts. A track recommendation based on the passengers' social profiles is the main outcome of the ontology. The passengers' social profiles include listened tracks, artists, and genres. From the top-middle, a Passenger is in a Mobile Social Net, is in a Car, listens a Track, which is made by an Artist, and belongs to a Genre. A Car plays a Track, and manages a Temporary Mobile Social Net. The Temporary Mobile Social Net generates a Passengers Profile. On the other side, a Mobile Social Net builds a Social Profile, which is merged in a Passengers Profile. As a final point, the Passengers Profile recommends a Track.

The protocol of an audio streaming recommender based on TMSN and Spotify analytics is described via the Business Process Model and Notation (BPMN). It is a graphical representation built on a solid mathematical foundation to enable consistency checking execution, simulation, and automation [25]. It is also appropriate for standardizing and facilitating communication among all parties involved. A rectangular area in BPMN represents a participant who, via exchange of messages, gets involved in a protocol. The protocol is handled in each rectangular area by events (circles), activities (rounded boxes), and decision/merge nodes (diamonds). Solid and dotted arrows represent sequence flows and data flows; cylindrical shapes are used to represent data storage.

Figure 2 depict an audio streaming recommender protocol based on TMSN and Spotify analytics, built on the ontology in described in Fig. 1 and represented via BPMN. For readability reasons, only the fundamental aspects of the proposed approach are covered. The protocol generates a playlist based on passengers' shared music interests (tracks, artists and genres), using Spotify Analytics.

The starting of the protocol is represented by a white envelope in a thin circle, while its ending by black envelopes in thick circles. When new passengers are detected by the TMSN, the protocol begins (on top left in Fig. 5). It ends when a playlist is determined. As a first step, the TMSN requests all passengers' social profiles from Spotify Analytics. The gear icon for the task indicates that it is a service task, which is supported by Spotify's web services. The collected social profiles include each passenger's listened tracks, artists, and genres (according to the defined ontology). Social profiles are stored for protocol's subsequent steps. In BPMN notation, script tasks represent internally developed task denoted by a sheet icon. The set of common tracks shared by all passengers is then identified by a script task. If any tracks are discovered, the recommended playlist is created. A script task, on the other hand, identifies the common artists. If common artists are found, the recommended play list is generated if some tracks are found by a service task that queries Spotify Analytics for the top tracks for them, or for their

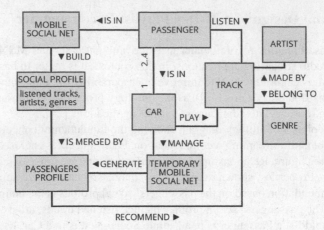

Fig. 1. TMSN Ontology in the context of audio streaming recommendation [21].

recommended tracks. If the last query produces no results, or there no common artist in the passengers' social profiles, the common genres in social profiles are identified and, if any are found, the recommended playlist is generated by asking Spotify Analytics for the recommended tracks for common genres. Finally, if the previous task generates no results, the playlist is generated by the recommended tracks for top artist asked to Spotify Analytics by a service task.

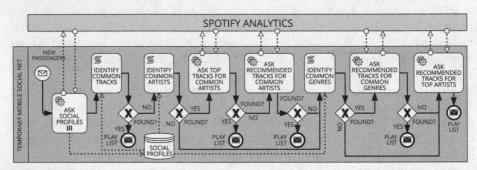

Fig. 2. BPMN protocol of an audio streaming recommender based on TMSN and Spotify analytics [21].

3   Experimental Analysis

The protocol is purposely designed to heavily exploit Spotify Analytics services. Indeed, it has been implemented and experimented on both a desktop computer and a Raspberry PI4b, a small CMP [26] single-board computer, equipped with WIFI. Detail on the implementation may be found in [21].

We performed user test on the liking of the generated playlist to assess the validity of the protocol described in the previous session. Six people took part in carrying out the following sessions: 8 two-passenger sessions, 5 three-passenger sessions and 5 four-passenger sessions.

Each passenger has given a rating of liking/disliking at the end of listening to a recommended track. Each passenger's approval rate was calculated at the end of listening to the recommended playlist as follows:

$$approval\ rate = \frac{number\ of\ liked\ tracks}{total\ number\ of\ tracks} \times 100 \qquad (1)$$

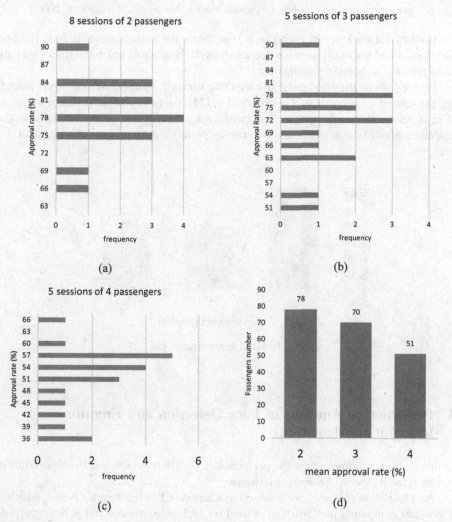

Fig. 3. Approval rate histograms for: 2 passengers (a), 3 passengers (b), 4 passengers (c) and mean approval rate vs passengers' number (d).

Results of the user test are given in Fig. 3. In particular, Fig. 3-a, -b, -c show the approval rate histograms for the 2, 3, and 4 passenger sessions, respectively. They show that the more the number of passengers increases, the more the approval rating decreases. This trend is due to the greater difficulty in finding common tracks, common artists and common genres as the number of passengers increases. Figure 3-d illustrates this trend based on the mean approval versus the number of passengers.

Finally, we evaluated the generalization ability of the recommended playlist generated by the protocol (the generalization ability of the protocol). The generalization is evaluated as follows:

$$generalization\ rate = No.\ of\ known\ tracks\ /No.\ of\ liked\ tracks \times 100 \qquad (2)$$

If all of the tracks in its own playlist are liked, the maximum value is 1. (i.e., no additional liked tracks). The value decreases as the number of unknown tracks that are liked grows (i.e., better generalization).

Figure 4 shows the mean generalization rate versus the number of passengers attending the session. In general, as also observed in [21], the ability of the protocol to generalize increases, due to the greater variety of tracks, authors and genres available in the passenger playlists, that represents the starting point for the recommender protocol.

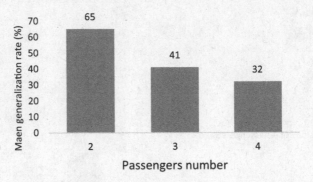

Fig. 4. Mean generalization rate

4 Performance Analysis of Face Detection and Emotion Recognition Algorithms

In this section, we characterize the performance of different FER and FD algorithms as run on Edge (low cost) hardware platforms.

As a hardware platform, we choose the Raspberry PI4-b computer board, which is a low-cost computing platform that is used for embedded system and general-purpose computing applications [27], equipped with WIFI interface. Thanks to its computing power that can be extended via accelerator, has been successfully utilized for realizing systems that run machine learning and deep neural network algorithm [28, 29].

4.1 Hardware Systems

We utilized a Raspberry Pi 4 B as a base system to run the FD and FER algorithms by using the accelerator Neural compute stick 2 (NCS2).

The Raspberry Pi 4 B has 2 GB RAM, quad core Cortex-A72 64-bit 1.5 GHz CPU [30], 128 GB class 10 micro sd card, and we installed Raspbian Bullseye 11 64-bit OS thought Raspberry Pi Imager on Raspberry [31].

We used the accelerator Neural Compute Stick 2 (NCS2) to improve computing performance on Raspberries [32]. It has Intel Movidius Myriad X Vision Processing Unit processor, and an USB 3.0 Type-A to communicate with host devices. OpenVINO toolkit must be installed on host device for optimizing and deploying AI inference models in NCS2 device [33].

4.2 Selected Face Detection Algorithms

FD finds the location of a face (one or more faces) and extract it from an input image.

We studied and tested performance (mean execution time) by using algorithms present in the frameworks OpenCV and Darknet.

OpenCV is an open-source real-time optimized Computer Vision library used for different scopes [34–36]. OpenCV has many face detections algorithms, but after an explorative analysis based on the execution time, we selected Haar cascade [37] and Improved Local Binary Patterns (ILBP) [38] for further analysis.

Darknet is an open-source neural network framework available for different hardware architectures [39]. In Darknet, we considered the Yoloface-500k v2 lightweight machine learning algorithms for face detection [40]. This model is seen as an improvement based on YOLOv3 [41].

4.3 Selected Face Emotion Recognition Algorithms

FER algorithms find facial landmarks and estimates either categorical emotion or continuous dimensional measures of affective display, the most noteworthy of which are valence and arousal [18].

We studied and tested performance in term of accuracy by using two algorithms available in scientific literature. One algorithm is into Deepface framework, a lightweight deep face recognition library for Python [42], and the other one is Emonet [18].

Deepface FER neural network classifier that can distinguish among seven kinds of emotions as angry, disgust, fear, happy, sad, surprise, neutral. Author reports an accuracy of 59% on the FER dataset. Emonet is a more complex neural classifier that distinguish among eight kinds of emotions like contempt, etc., and generates as output also valence and arousal values, and other data. It has been specifically designed for the analysis of images of facial display recorded in naturalistic conditions. Authors report an accuracy of 75% on the AffectNet dataset.

We chose these two algorithms because they have different complexity, and therefore different computational requirements.

4.4 Analysis of Face Detection Algorithm

Methodology. We recorded an experimental video to study the FD algorithms and compute the performance indexes to find the optimal FD.

The video was gathered through a webcam at 17 frame per second (FPS) in HD resolution by a volunteer that watched a movie of 01:15 min. The video contained 1275 frames with the participant's face. Then, the video has been converted in different resolutions by using the OpenCV bicubic interpolation method: $256 \times 144, 426 \times 240, 640 \times 360, 854 \times 480, 1280 \times 720$, and 1920×1080, to evaluate the effects of resolution on performance. The FD elaborated all frames for each resolution 30 times to compute the performances indexes.

We defined two main performance indexes: the execution time and the number of faces. The former is related to performance, the latter to detection quality.

Performance Analysis. We compared the performance of the 3 chosen FD algorithms (HAAR, ILBP and Yoloface-500k v2) to select an FD for use in the subsequent analysis with RES systems. Our aims is to find a fast enough algorithm, with an acceptable quality of detection.

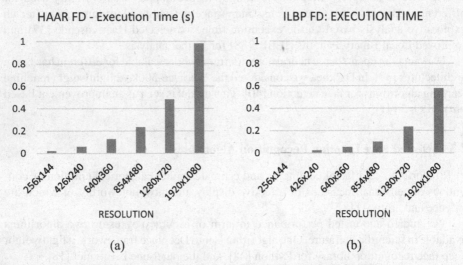

(a)   (b)

Fig. 5. Execution Time of: (a) HAAR FD and (b) ILBP FD.

Figure 5 (a) and (b) and Fig. 6 show the execution time as the resolution varies for the HAAR, ILPB and Yoloface-500k v2, respectively. Execution time increases as resolution increases for both HAAR and BLP, and is less in BLP (about half). It is almost unchanged for Yoloface-500k v2 as the resolution varies, and is significantly lower than the other FDs (except for the two lowest resolutions). This is because Yoloface-500k v2 works on a constant frame size (352×288), and acquired frames are resized with a time on the order of a few msec. From the perspective of the number of faces not detected, Yoloface-500k v2 detects all faces in our experiments (figure not shown), HAAR (Fig. 7-a) has a small number of undetected faces, while ILPB (Fig. 7-b) has a large number of undetected faces at the lowest resolution. This value decreases significantly and then settles down to zero. Given the performance measured in our experiments, FD Yoloface-500k v2 will be used in subsequent analyses.

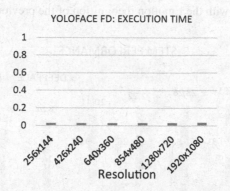

Fig. 6. Execution Time of the YOLOFACE FD.

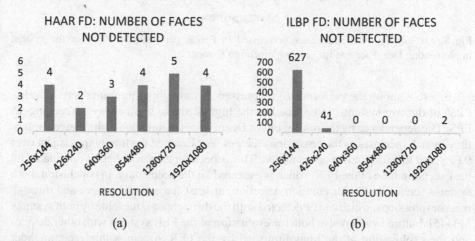

Fig. 7. Number of Faces not detected for: (a) HAAR FD and (b) ILBP FD.

4.5 Overall System Performance

After the selection of the Face Detector, two versions of the overall systems were built utilizing the DeepFace and Emonet FER models, and their performance were compared. How did in the previous cases, to collect performance data, we run the experiments 30 times for each of the different resolution videos-considered.

The overall system with Deepface was deployed with both the FD and the FER running on the Raspberry Pi 4 B. The system implementing the Emonet FER was deployed with the FD running on the Raspberry and the FER running on the NCS2 accelerator. We used the accelerator because Emonet takes more than 10 s to process a frame when run on the raspberry, and this value is not compatible with a real-time detection. Moreover, we improved the execution time of the system deploying Emonet by configuring the accelerator to run in asynchronous (pipelined) mode [33], so that the face detection of a frame was overlapped with the Emotion recognition of the previous frame.

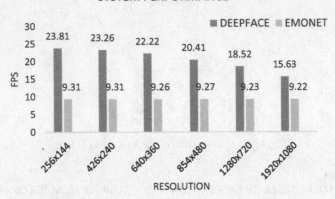

Fig. 8. Overall System Performance (expressed in Frame per Seconds, FPS) for the system implementing DeepFace and the one implementing Emonet..

Figure 8 shows the performance (expressed as throughput, in frame per seconds - FPS) of the two systems. DeepFace has the highest throughput, always exceeding 15 FPS. The dependence by the resolution for DeepFace is mainly due to the image capture time, which increases as the resolution changes. For Emonet, the throughput is just over 9 FPS, and little dependent on resolution. This is because the throughput is dominated by the execution time of the FER, which is executed on the accelerator. In conclusion, both systems seem suitable for emotion detection, at least for emotions expressed through macroexpressions, which can be detected with the throughput achievable by both systems [43–45]. Future work involve both the evaluation of the FER systems with other devices and the exploitation of the hints furnished by the FER system within recommender systems.

5   Conclusions

In next-generation cars, passengers will have more time for fun and relaxation, as well as will increase the number of unknown passengers traveling together. Thanks to technological advances, new class of services can be introduced to improve drive and passenger's user experience and state.

In this work, we propose group-wise Temporary Mobile Social Networking recommender as a design paradigm for in-car entertainment. A functional design is illustrated in the context of social music and a prototype has been implemented, based on Spotify

Analytics and running on Raspberry device. User test have been conducted by involving six people in various sessions attended by a different number of participants.

The approval and generalization rates obtained from the experiments show that as the number of passengers increases, the approval rate decreases for the lower number of common tracks, artists, and genres among passengers. Nevertheless, as the number of passengers increases, the generalization capacity of the system increases, providing a growing number of liked tracks that are not already known. The results of user tests are encouraging, and in particular the system's ability to generalize demonstrates the potential of the proposed approach in improving user experience. We plan to investigate the method further, enhancing the analytics of the system that creates the playlists and focusing more on the user experience while expanding our experimentation.

Finally, we evaluate the performance of lightweight and heavy intelligent models that recognize the emotion of a person from its face, using Raspberry Pi 4 B devices, to investigate the feasibility of implementing basic emotion detection services on board on low performance device without the support of external services. The results show that is possible to realize a system with Face detector and Facial emotion recognition models on edge devices with sufficient performance (Frame per Second) to detect at least emotion expressed through macro-expressions.

Future work involves both the evaluation of the intelligent model on other devices and the exploitation of the hints furnished by the FER system within recommender systems.

Acknowledgements. Work partially supported by the Italian Ministry of Education and Research (MIUR) in the framework of: (i) the CrossLab project (Departments of Excellence); (ii) the FoRe-Lab project (Departments of Excellence); (iii) the National Recovery and Resilience Plan in the National Center for Sustainable Mobility MOST/Spoke10. Work partially carried out by the University of Pisa in the framework of the PRA_2022_101 project "Decision Support Systems for territorial networks for managing ecosystem services". Research partially funded by PNRR - M4C2 - Investimento 1.3, Partenariato Esteso PE00000013 - "FAIR - Future Artificial Intelligence Research" - Spoke 1 "Human-centered AI", funded by the European Commission under the NextGeneration EU programme.

References

1. Athanasopoulou, A., de Reuver, M., Nikou, S., Bouwman, H.: What technology enabled services impact business models in the automotive industry? An explanatory study? Futures **109**, 73–83 (2019)
2. Bilius, L.B., Vatavu, R.D.: A multistudy investigation of drivers and passengers' gesture and voice input preferences for in-vehicle interactions. J. Intell. Transp. Syst. **25**(2), 197–220 (2020)
3. Connected car report : Opportunities, risk, and turmoil on the road to autonomous vehicles. Strategy (2016). https://www.strategyand.pwc.com/reports/connected-car-2016-study
4. Rong, Y., Han, C., et al.: Artificial Intelligence Methods in In-Cabin Use Cases: A Survey. IEEE Intelligent Transportation Systems Magazine (2021)
5. Arena, F., Pau, G., Severino, A.: An overview on the current status and future perspectives of smart cars. Infrastructures. **5**, 53 (2020)
6. Yin, Y., Xia, J., Li, Y., Xu, W., Yu, L.: Group-wise itinerary planning in temporary mobile social network. IEEE Access **7**, 83682–83693 (2019)

7. Aranha, R.V., Corrêa, C.G., Nunes, F.L.: Adapting software with affective computing: a systematic review. IEEE Trans. Affect. Comput. **12**(4), 883–899 (2019)
8. Foglia, P., Zanda, M., Prete, C.A.: Towards relating physiological signals to usability metrics: a case study with a web avatar. WSEAS Trans. Comput. **13**, 624 (2014)
9. Meixner, G.: Retrospective and future automotive infotainment systems—100 years of user interface evolution. In: Meixner, G., Müller, C. (eds.) Automotive User Interfaces, pp. 3–53. Springer International Publishing, Cham (2017). https://doi.org/10.1007/978-3-319-494 48-7_1
10. Yvkoff, L.: BMW Rolls-Out Its Intelligent Personal Assistant Feature Via Over-The-Air Update. https://www.forbes.com/sites/lianeyvkoff/2019/05/30/bmw-rolls-out-its-intelligent-personal-assistant-feature-via-over-the-air-update/. Accessed Dec 2022
11. Trends that Will Shape the Future of the Car Industry by 2030. https://www.hyundai.news/eu/stories/12-trends-that-will-shape-the-future-of-the-car-industry-by-2030/. Accessed Dec 2020
12. Zepf, S., Hernandez, J., et al.: Driver emotion recognition for intelligent vehicles: a survey. ACM Comput. Surv. **53**, 1–30 (2020). https://doi.org/10.1145/3388790
13. Coppola, R., Morisio, M.: Connected car: technologies, issues, future trends. ACM Comput. Surv. (CSUR) **49**(3), 1–36 (2016)
14. Spotify, C.L.: Collaborative Playlist, support.spotify.com/us/ article/collaborative-playlists/. Accessed Dec 2022
15. Spotify FM, Family Mix, support.spotify.com/us/article/ family-mix/. Accessed Dec 2022
16. Cimino M.G.C.A., Lazzerini B., Marcelloni F., Castellano G., Fanelli A.M., Torsello M.A.: A collaborative situation-aware scheme for mobile service recommendation. In: Proceedings of the 11th International Conference on Intelligent Systems Design and Applications, pp. 130–135 (2011)
17. Spotify API, support.spotify.com/us/article/spotify-in-the-car/, accessed Dec 2022
18. Toisoul, A., Kossaifi, J., Bulat, A., Tzimiropoulos, G., Pantic, M.: Estimation of continuous valence and arousal levels from faces in naturalistic conditions. Nat. Mach. Intell. **3**(1), 42–50 (2021)
19. Kuppens, P., Tuerlinckx, F., Russell, J.A., Barrett, L.F.: The relation between valence and arousal in subjective experience. Psychol. Bull. **139**(4), 917 (2013)
20. Lee, Y.-L., Tsung, P.-K., Wu, M.: Technology trend of edge AI. In: 2018 International Symposium on VLSI Design, Automation and Test (VLSI-DAT), pp. 1–2 (2018)
21. Cimino M.G.C.A., Di Tecco A., Foglia P., et al.: In-car entertainment via group-wise temporary mobile social networking. In: International Conference on Vehicle Technology and Intelligent Transport Systems, VEHITS - Proceedings, pp. 432 – 437 (2022). https://doi.org/10.5220/0011096000003191
22. MO, Music Ontology, musicontology.com, accessed Dec. 2022
23. Campanelli, S., Foglia, P., Prete, C.A.: An architecture to integrate IEC 61131–3 systems in an IEC 61499 distributed solution. Comput. Ind. **72**, 47–67 (2015)
24. Ciaramella, A., Cimino, M.G.C.A., Marcelloni, F., Straccia, U.: Combining fuzzy logic and semantic web to enable situation-awareness in service recommendation. In: Bringas, P.G., Hameurlain, A., Quirchmayr, G. (eds.) Database and Expert Systems Applications, pp. 31–45. Springer, Heidelberg (2010). https://doi.org/10.1007/978-3-642-15364-8_3
25. Cimino, M.G.C.A., Palumbo, F., Vaglini, G., Ferro, E., Celandroni, N., La Rosa, D.: Evaluating the impact of smart technologies on harbor's logistics via BPMN modeling and simulation. Inf. Technol. Manage. **18**(3), 223–239 (2016). https://doi.org/10.1007/s10799-016-0266-4
26. Foglia, P., Solinas, M.: Exploiting replication to improve performances of NUCA-based CMP systems. ACM Trans. Embed. Comput. Syst. **13**(3s), 1–23 (2014). https://doi.org/10.1145/2566568

27. Daher, A.W., Rizik, A., Muselli, M., Chible, H., Caviglia, D.D.: Porting rulex machine learning software to the raspberry pi as an edge computing device. In: Saponara, S., DeGloria, A. (eds.) Applications in Electronics Pervading Industry, Environment and Society. LNEE, vol. 738, pp. 273–279. Springer, Cham (2021). https://doi.org/10.1007/978-3-030-66729-0_33
28. Zamir, M., Ali, N., Naseem, A., et al.: A. Face Detection & Recognition from Images & Videos Based on CNN & Raspberry Pi. Computation. **10**, 148 (2022)
29. Süzen, A.A., Duman, B., Şen, B.: Benchmark analysis of Jetson TX2, Jetson Nano and Raspberry PI using Deep-CNN. In: 2020 International Congress on Human-Computer Interaction, Optimization and Robotic Applications (HORA), pp. 1–5 (2020)
30. Raspberry Pi 4 B. https://www.raspberrypi.com/products/raspberry-pi-4-model-b/. Accessed Dec 2022
31. Raspberry Pi Imager. https://www.raspberrypi.com/software. Accessed Dec 2022
32. Neural Compute Stick 2. www.intel.com/content/www/us/en/developer/articles/tool/neural computestick.html. Accessed Dec 2022
33. Intel Distribution of OpenVINO Toolkit. www.intel.com/content/www/us/en/developer/tools/openvinotoolkit/overview.html. Accessed Dec 2022
34. OpenCV. https://opencv.org/. Accessed Dec 2022
35. Bradski, G., Kaehler, A.: Learning OpenCV: Computer Vision with the OpenCV Library. O'Reilly Media Inc., Sebastopol (2008)
36. De Vitis, G.A., Foglia, P., Prete, C.A.: Row-level algorithm to improve real-time performance of glass tube defect detection in the production phase. IET Image Process. **14**, 2911–2921 (2020). https://doi.org/10.1049/iet-ipr.2019.1506
37. Viola, P., Jones, M.J.: Robust real-time face detection. Int. J. Comput. Vision **57**(2), 137–154 (2004)
38. Jin, H., Liu, Q., et al.: Face detection using improved LBP under Bayesian framework. In: Third International Conference on Image and Graphics (ICIG 2004), pp. 306–309. IEEE (2004)
39. Joseph Redmon, Darknet: Open-Source Neural Networks in C, Darknet, https://pjreddie.com/darknet/. Accessed Dec 2022
40. Ma, X.: https://github.com/dog-qiuqiu/MobileNet-Yolo. Accessed Dec 2022
41. Redmon, J., Farhadi, A.: Yolov3: An incremental improvement. arXiv preprint arXiv:1804. 02767 (2018)
42. Serengil, S.I., Ozpinar, A.: Hyperextended lightface: a facial attribute analysis framework. In: 2021 International Conference on Engineering and Emerging Technologies (ICEET), pp. 1–4. IEEE, October 2021
43. Bhatti, Y.K., Jamil, A., Nida, N., Yousaf, M.H., Viriri, S., Velastin, S.A.: Facial expression recognition of instructor using deep features and extreme learning machine. Comput. Intell. Neurosci. **2021**, 1–17 (2021). https://doi.org/10.1155/2021/5570870
44. Matsumoto, D., Hwang, H.S.: Reading facial expressions of emotion. Psychol. Sci. Agenda. 25 (2011)
45. Ekman, P.: Emotions Revealed, 2nd edn. Times Books, New York (2003)

Author Index

C. Klein et al. (Eds.): SMARTGREENS 2022/VEHITS 2022, CCIS 1843, p. 173, 2023.
https://doi.org/10.1007/978-3-031-37470-8

Printed in the United States
by Baker & Taylor Publisher Services